# THE STRUCTURAL BASIS
# OF ARCHITECTURE

# THE STRUCTURAL BASIS
# OF ARCHITECTURE

BJØRN NORMANN SANDAKER AND ARNE PETTER EGGEN

TRANSLATION BY STEVEN KIRWIN

WHITNEY LIBRARY OF DESIGN

an imprint of Watson-Guptill Publications/New York

This book was made possible with a grant from
the Oslo Architecture School, Oslo, Norway.


Senior Editor: Roberto de Alba
Associate Editor: Carl D. Rosen
Designer: Bob Fillie, Graphiti Graphics
Production Manager: Ellen Greene

First published in the United States in 1992 by Whitney Library of Design,
an imprint of Watson-Guptill Publications, a division of BPI
Communications, Inc., 1515 Broadway, New York, NY 10036

**Library of Congress Cataloging-in-Publication Data**

Sandaker, Bjørn Normann, 1954-
   [Arkitekturens konstruktive grunnlag. English]
   The Structural basis of architecture / by Bjørn Normann Sandaker
and Arne Petter Eggen : translation by Steven Kirwin.
      p.   cm.
   Includes bibliographical references and index.
   ISBN 0-8230-4936-1
   1. Architectural design.  2. Structural design.  I. Eggen, Arne
Petter.  II. Title.
   NA2750.S2313  1992
721—dc20                                        92-19153
                                                   CIP

Manufactured in the United States of America

First printing, 1992

1 2 3 4 5 6 7 8 9 10/97 96 95 94 93 92

Our traveling globe in galactic endlessness is divided into latitude and longitude.

With help of this grid, every point on the earth's surface has its number.

At the grid's intersections each receives nourishment, each creature receives its individual technology, its structure formed and created by the clouds' movements, the wind's strength, and the shifting positions of the sun.

On this organic mat, the acrobat (builder) attempts, with the help of instruments, to deceive gravity and challenge death with every leap.

And when the perplexities of thought within your soul should create space on earth, arises a duel with substance. Midst brutality's heat, beauty is born...

SVERRE FEHN

# Foreword

The idea for this book grew from our teaching of building technology at the Oslo School of Architecture, Oslo, Norway.

Our intention is to give the reader a basic knowledge of structural theory in order to understand how structures work. Structural theory is described and illustrated with the help of architectural examples. In this way, we attempt to bridge the gap between the differing expertise of the architect and the engineer.

Architecture is used to give theory meaning, and the architectural examples are chosen to inspire and stimulate interest.

Structures are subject to a variety of conditions that they must endure; winds and snow loads, the weight of components, inhabitants, and equipment.

To be sure that the building can withstand such loads without severe deformation or collapse, theoretical and practical analysis must be performed beforehand. Statics is part of the theory applied for this purpose.

Statics gives us a theoretical and scientific background for understanding why architectural structures look as they do, both in form and dimension. Our knowledge of structures can also influence such architectural concepts as visual appearance, function, weight, texture, light, shade, and shadow. Good architecture can result if the structure's own logic is founded on these concepts.

Though structural theory is universal, architecture varies according to time and place. The forces that are transferred from the beam to the column are the same,

whether at the limestone Doric Aphaian temple at Aegina outside Pireus from the 5th century B.C. or at Mies van der Rohe's steel Crown Hall in Chicago from 1952.

During the three-year process of writing this book, with many new projects continually appearing, we understandably had to draw the line for our material at the new monuments in Paris, the pyramid at the Louvre and the Triumphal Arch at la Defense. Thereafter the reader can supplement this text with his or her own examples.

We would like to use the occasion to thank the persons who have helped make this book possible. The most valuable contribution came from Tryggve Mjøset, civil engineer at Multiconsult, Consulting Engineers, and his work with the text and drawing of illustrations. Without Tryggve Mjøset, the realization of the original version of this book would have been most uncertain.

We would also like to thank the Oslo School of Architecture and its former dean Professor Sverre Fehn for their interest and support. Involvement and interest of others is vital in the realization of both small- and large-scale projects.

Last but not least, the students at the Oslo School of Architecture, with their youthful presence and high expectations, were a great inspiration for completing the book. At the same time, the high-quality structural models made by the students were an integral facet in illustrating architectural and structural principles.

—Oslo, Norway, May 1992
BJØRN NORMANN SANDAKER
ARNE PETTER EGGEN

# Contents

# Chapter 1

# ABOUT BUILDING STRUCTURES

*Piazza duomo with cathedral and baptistery. Parma, Italy. 11th-12th century.*

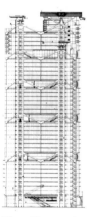

*Hong Kong and
Shanghai Bank.
1985.
Architect:
Norman Foster
Associates.*

## 1.1 STRUCTURAL DUALISM

A building structure can be said to have at least two aims of equal importance: the technical and the aesthetic. The first aim, the technical function, is to stand upright, secure from collapse or excessive deformation. The structure accomplishes this by withstanding loads and transferring them, through the building components, to the ground.

The second aim, the aesthetic function, is to act as a potent and meaningful visual vehicle that, through the process of refinement, can become a convincing and recognizable medium of architectural expression.

Both the technical and the aesthetic function of a building structure must be satisfied simultaneously if the structure is to be more than just an assemblage of answers to various technical problems.

There is little disagreement with regard to the theory of statics that is presented in this book. It is mathematically and scientifically founded and logical in its composition. At present, however, there are many opinions about the world of structural design to which this theory can be applied, especially in an architectural context.

Our choice of architectural works that illustrate the general theory of statics, and the means by which the works are presented,

says something about our viewpoint. We do not believe it is wrong to take a position, albeit subjective, in the architectural debate, even in a book with the objective of accounting for the "indisputable" structural theory of statics. This theory is actually more interesting if it can be applied to an understanding of structural form and the architectural potential that lies in structures.

To better illustrate our viewpoint in the study of statics, we compare the architect

*Les Espaces
d'Abraxas
housing complex.
Marne-la-Vallée,
France.
1983.
Architect:
Ricardo Bofill.*

Norman Foster's Hong Kong and Shanghai Bank and the architect Ricardo Bofill's housing complex at Marne-la-Vallée outside Paris.

The Hong Kong and Shanghai Bank preserves the economic policies of the British crown colonies and runs a worldwide financial institution. A new office headquarters is meant to stand as a guarantee for the colony's existence, both now and after 1996, when China resumes control of Hong Kong.

The bank chose Foster in a closed competition for a landmark in an area nearly as densely built as Manhattan, giving him the unique opportunity to address the problem of the skyscraper and its architectural meaning.

By incorporating gigantic suspended structures, Foster was successful in creating floor areas with a free span of up to 30 meters (98 feet) and a great variety of room heights. The main bearing structure consists of a frame with dual columns and gigantic bracket-shaped steel beams. This theme is repeated at different levels of the building. A number of floors are suspended from the lateral structural members by stays. This makes for free floor area in the floor stacks, which are uninterrupted by bearing structures. Floor loads go, in part, directly to the main beams, which are directly carried by the double columns, and, in part, to beams suspended from the stays. Tension forces in the stays are harnessed by the brackets, which transfer the loads to the double columns. The total structural system is fully exposed in the facades.

We could imagine a similar principle designed in a more conventional manner with a stack of floors carried by columns and simply resting on brackets at various levels. However, it is exactly these suspension structures that create the excitement and interest in this 47-floor-high work of architecture.

The Spanish architect Ricardo Bofill, born in 1939, has pointed out that French architecture is traditionally characterized by large public spaces marked by monuments: the palace, the temple, or the triumphal arch are incorporated in the disposition of space.

Bofill's housing complex, les Espaces d'Abraxas at Marne-la-Vallée, built in 1983, is composed of three monumental structures and an open space. The buildings, solely comprised of simple apartments, appear externally as an accumulation of classical elements.

The columns in particular have been subject to a number of interpretations beyond the simple bearing function. A column may be used as fire stairs or a room. The figure on page 13 depicts the column as both a positive and a negative form. In the negative form, the column is completely removed, but the building still stands owing to the fact that it is built as an ordinary wall/slab construction.

The complex is grand and open to many interpretations, but one can raise the question as to whether it is a "correct" method of building.

The Hong Kong and Shanghai Bank represents a building where the structure, that is, the "process of building," constitutes the architectural expression. Bofill's complex, however, is an example of buildings where the facade and the structural backbone exist in two different worlds with little interaction. The facade seems to be staged as if the architect were preoccupied with urban space and had orchestrated it with classical architectural motifs to express his idea. Behind the facade, the structure and the cramped apartments live their own trivial lives, more or less independent of the building's outer appearance.

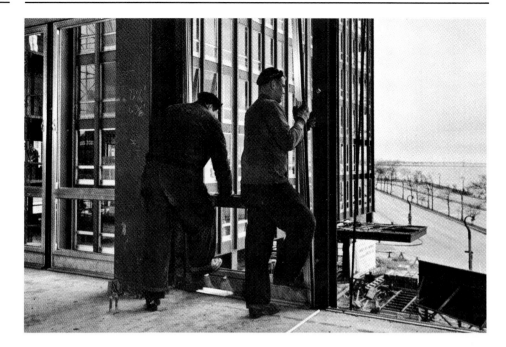

*Lake Shore Drive apartments. Chicago. 1953-1956. Architect: Ludwig Mies van der Rohe.*

## 1.2 STRUCTURAL LOADS

*Lake Shore Drive apartments. Chicago. Architect: Ludwig Mies van der Rohe.*

In this book we have chosen to divide the building into such structural elements as the column, the beam, the frame, and the arch. This has proven a valuable means of presenting the definition of terms for statics, because each of these building components represents structural form with clear yet varied effects. The building as a structure and as an architectural object clearly represents a whole. Each individual element of a building has a form and a message, but only the combined harmony of elements is conclusive. Breaking down the building into simple elements, therefore, is of particular value for theoretical analysis.

We first examine the whole building for the types of strains it can experience. Historically, structural elements and systems are developed and improved over a very long period of time. Experience from one building project has always been the basis for the erection of the next. With each new building, the builders may have slightly changed the radius of the columns, shortened the column spacing, and built slightly higher or longer. They knew the material and understood the natural forces present at

the site of each new project, conclusive assumptions for the structural and formal decisions made in the planning process. Thus, building was based on classical methods, where knowledge was passed from person to person from one generation to another.

Things changed after the Industrial Revolution. The development of new materials took root in the building industry and grew rapidly. New businesses required new building types. Buildings became more complex, had longer spans, were taller, and the materials were put to even greater use. Simultaneously, a scientific revolution was under way with the development of theoretical models for comprehending the effects of nature. This activity also gave rise to research into the structural properties of materials.

The employment of wrought iron, cast iron, and, with time, steel and reinforced concrete brought about a gradual transition to the use of theoretical assistance in analyzing building structures at the planning stage. The absence of experience with related building types using new materials, which could have been used as case models, and the demand for economy and rationality in the building process, gave birth to a new methodology in project planning. Today, it is required to show theoretically that a building is designed to withstand all possible forces before a building permit can be issued. Structural calculations must be sent to the proper building authorities.

A *load*, in this context, is defined as any influence that causes forces or deformations in a structure. It can take the form of compression forces in a column or stretching forces acting on a steel cable. A load can be the weight of a grand piano or a temperature change from 10 to 20°C (50 to 68°F), which, for example, can cause stress in a beam fastened at both ends that has no room for expansion with increases in temperature.

For simplicity's sake, loads can be divided into separate categories. The two major types are *dead loads* and *live loads*. Dead loads are loads that are considered constant through time. The most important dead load is the weight of the structural elements and building materials themselves. This load has a vertical orientation and, owing to gravity, is directed downward. It can be

determined by tedious calculation of each element's volume multiplied by the material's own density. Initially, then, one must make a calculated estimate of a building element's size and volume before calculating actual dimensions. If, for example, the depth of the beams must increase over the initial estimate, then recalculating the structure's dead load is necessary before making any further calculations.

Another type of dead load is soil pressure. Soil pressure is the load from earthen or gravel fill against, for example, a foundation wall. The magnitude of the load varies with the height and weight of the earthen mass.

Live loads are loads that vary over time. The most important types of live loads are snow loads, wind loads, and occupant/user loads.

Snow loads can be considerable and vary with topography and local climate. Calculations begin with the amount of snow that falls to the ground. Assume a certain amount of snow as the load for different roof forms. For example, a pitched roof with a pitch steeper than 60° has no snow load. Snow loads can range from 1.5 kN/m² to 4.5 kN/m².

The primary wind load value $q(N/m^2)$ in relation to the maximum wind speed $v(m/s)$ can be expressed as:

$$q \sim v^2/1.6$$

Thus a powerful storm with a wind speed of $v = 30$ m/s results in a wind pressure of:

$$q = 30^2/1.6 = 563 \text{ N/m}^2 = 56.3 \text{ hp/m}^2$$

As with snow loads, wind load values vary on the building surface depending on wind direction and the building's form and height. On the wall and roof surfaces, wind loads result in both wind pressure and wind suction. There are also both external and internal wind loads. The internal wind load results from positive or negative air pressure within the structure. The magnitude of

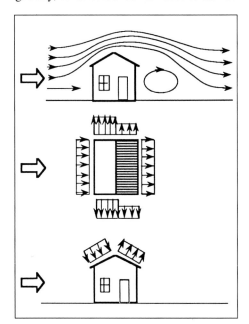

*Wind loads on a pitched roof. The air stream rushes over one plane of the roof and has a suction effect on the opposite roof plane and leeward wall. The gable walls will also experience suction forces while the windward wall is under compression forces.*

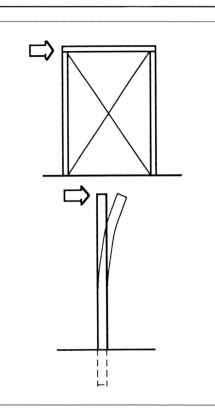

*An example of rigid wind bracing (top) and flexible wind bracing.*

*Wind loads are transferred through the building elements to the wind bracing where the wind forces can be transferred into the ground.*

*From the top:*

*Flexible frame bracing.*

*Rigid cross bracing.*

*Rigid diagonal bracing.*

*Flexible bracing with fixed columns.*

*Rigid bracing with guys or stays.*

*Rigid wall bracing.*

the load is a direct result of the wind speed outside.

Occupant/user loads are loads from people, inventory, and equipment in a building, that is, all loads that cannot be considered constant. Occupant/user loads are normally vertical and directed downward, but in some cases the loads can be horizontal. Examples of this include people leaning against a railing or the load resulting from an automobile braking on a bridge.

Uniformly distributed vertical occupant/user loads vary in magnitude with building type and function. The lowest occupant/user load is for an attic with no head room where the only entrance is a trapdoor (0.5 $kN/m^2$). The largest occupant/user loads are calculated for industrial buildings, factories, workshops, etc. (5.0 $kN/m^2$ or higher).

In addition to live and dead loads, there are several others that we will describe later. Structural building elements must absorb all these loads, which may act simultaneously, and transfer them through the build-

ing and to the earth without any damage. To accomplish this, it is not enough that every building element has sufficient strength and stiffness to withstand loading.

The building elements together must comprise a stable structural system that prevents the building from collapsing. The structure, as a whole, must be braced. Let's examine some principles for lateral bracing of a building. Wind loads are the most important load for which lateral bracing is essential. For a building of column and beam construction, there are two main types of lateral bracing methods to hinder the columns from leaning or falling when the wind blows. They are a more or less *fixed lateral bracing* and a *flexible lateral bracing*.

Fixed lateral bracing incorporates a rigid bracing element that, when stress is experienced, must expand or contract if the column is to react correctly under loading. Flexible lateral bracing has an element that will bend under loading. Although bending in structural elements occurs more often than expansion or contraction, both the rigid and the flexible systems can be used as principles in developing structural unity in a building.

Rigid systems do not necessarily include the whole building. From one rigid compo-

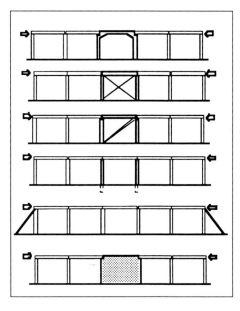

*Bracing principles
illustrated with rigid
walls.
Three rigid walls are
generally required,
with one placed in
each of the structure's
major directions.*

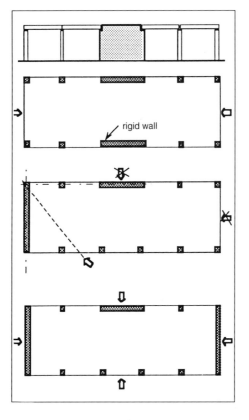

rigid wall

*Johnson Wax
Building.
Wisconsin.
1939.
Architect: Frank
Lloyd Wright.
This is a tall structure
with a rigid core
bracing that acts
as a cantilever.*

nent, elements can be built that are not rigid but get their rigidity from the first rigid component—this is assuming that the wind load can be transferred through the non-rigid elements to the one rigid component. The load must be transferable through beams that are designed for compression and tension, through a rigid floor deck or rigid roof.

A building plan will tell us something about the principles of rigidity. In a situation where there are rooms with wind loads from all possible directions, rigid components can be provided for in two directions, but if we use only one component in each direction, the building is not properly secure. Two rigid components have lines of action that will meet at one point, and as long as the wind stays constantly directed toward that point, the structure is secure. But with different wind directions, the building will have a tendency to twist around that point without hindrance from the wind bracing. The conclusion is that we must plan for three rigid structural components with a minimum of one in each of a building's two main structural directions.

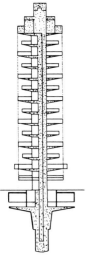

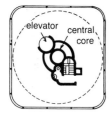

elevator  central
core

## 1.3 MATERIALS AND FORCES

A structure is the material's answer to an architectural problem.

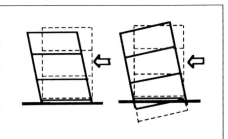

It is meaningless to design a structure without respect for and understanding of the materials to be used. The structural design, as a whole and in detail, must be in accordance with the inherent properties of the structural material. For this reason a brick building manifests itself in a considerably different fashion from a steel building. Later we will look at the most important structural materials.

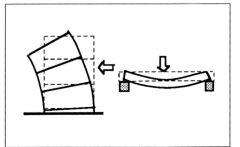

First, however, we must ascertain various relationships. In the previous section we discussed the most important types of loads a building can be subject to. We emphasized that the most important task for a structure is that it be able to withstand these loads and to transfer them down to the ground. There are many other things that can happen to a structure:

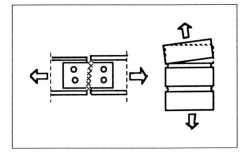

• The whole building can tilt because it is not properly braced or its foundations are inadequate.

• The building can suffer costly excessive deformation and/or fractures so that functional and architectural requirements cannot be fulfilled. This can occur with the building as a whole or in portions and result from inadequate bracing.

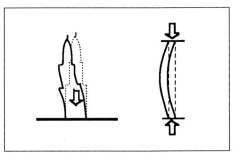

• Portions of the building can pull away from each other owing to failure at the joints. This can occur, for example, in a bolted connection between two beams or between bricks and mortar.

• The structure, or any of its parts, can deform. A slender column under compression can bend to the extent that, unless the load is not removed, it collapses.

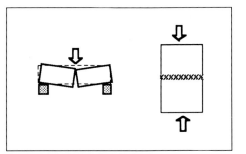

• The material comprising the structural components can be overloaded. This means that a concrete beam can crack, a

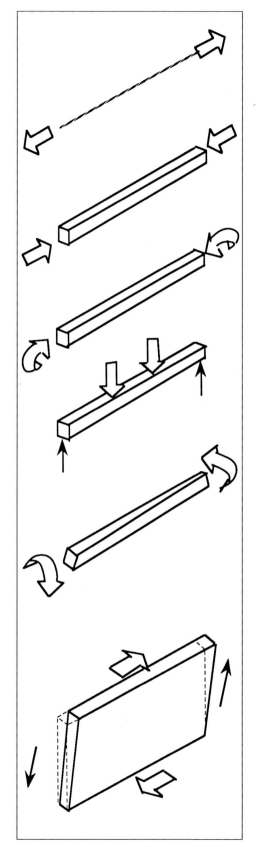

brick can crumble, or a steel rod snap.

• Over a period of time, structural components can corrode or decompose due to pollution. <u>Pollution can thus cause structural failure.</u>

The overloading of materials, however, is most often the deciding factor in the failure of the structure. Building components are subject to forces from loading. The material must respond to and tolerate these forces in the various portions of the building.

There is a great difference in the types of forces and abilities of various materials to withstand these forces. Depending on the direction of the load with respect to the portion of the building under stress and a host of other conditions, the load can result in:

• tension, which is the effect of two forces pulling in opposite directions

• compression, which is the effect of two forces pushing against each other

• bending, or the bending of the component, which usually occurs when the component is subjected to transverse loading between two supports

• torsion, which is the twisting of the ends of a component in opposite directions

• shear, which causes two contiguous parts of a structural element to slide relative to each other in a direction parallel to their plane of contact.

Many of these forces can be present simultaneously in a structural element. With regard to the various materials, it is important to find out which kind of forces the load will result in. A material that withstands compression well, such as masonry, will not necessarily tolerate a great amount of tension. When we build in masonry, the structure is designed for as much compression as possible, rather than for bending or tension.

Similarly, for other structural materials,

such as steel, concrete, wood, and artificial textiles, we can compile strong and weak constructive qualities.

*Steel* is an alloy comprised of iron and carbon. With few additives, it can have very special characteristics. For example, nickel can be added to make stainless steel. The carbon content of soft commercial steel is about 0.2%. If the amount of carbon exceeds 1.7%, cast iron is produced. Cast iron is easy to melt but is hard and brittle in its solid state. A carbon content under 0.1% produces a soft, malleable iron called wrought iron.

Steel characteristically oxidizes, or rusts, when it comes in contact with air and moisture. It therefore requires protection in the form of special paints or galvanizing. A type of steel has been developed that cannot be called stainless steel because it rusts, but oxidation occurs only for a limited period of time and then theoretically does not corrode deeper into the steel. The commercial name of this steel is CORE-TEN, and it has a thin layer of rust on the surface with good color and texture characteristics.

Modern structural steel handles compression and tension stresses equally well. This means that steel withstands bending well, and the cross sections of the members are designed to absorb both compression and tension stresses. Rolled steel is most commonly used, and under compression it is quite vulnerable to the type of deformation called buckling. Small cross sections under bending stress can cause considerable deformation, a condition that shows that the strength of the steel is being utilized in a limited fashion.

Steel remains the structural material with the greatest strength per total area. Under the stress of fire, however, the strength of steel is dramatically reduced. Steel is therefore thermally protected in buildings where fire protection of the bearing structure is required. This is accomplished by sheathing the steel profiles with fire resistant insulation (gypsum board) or by spraying the steel with flame retardant paint.

*Concrete* is a blending of cement, sand, aggregate, and water. Concrete, in its hardened form, is solid and has great compression strength. The tensile strength of unreinforced concrete is just about 10% of its compression strength and therefore has no structural value. To overcome this, steel reinforcing rods are placed in wet concrete so that steel's superb tensile qualities are combined with concrete's excellent compression qualities. The result is reinforced concrete, which responds superbly under bending stresses. Pure tension is not an intrinsic strength of reinforced concrete.

Concrete's weakness is its tendency to contract and crack while drying. To prevent this, reinforcing is used to hinder excessive contraction. Further, freshly poured concrete should be wetted to retard the drying process.

In the last few years, a new problem with concrete has appeared, namely, the so-called carbonization of concrete. This concerns a shift in concrete's natural alkaline character to acidic. As long as the pH value is over 7, concrete is basic and will hinder the rusting of reinforcing steel. Pollution and acid rain cause concrete to gradually turn acidic, cancelling concrete's natural rust-protective quality. When moisture gains access to the steel reinforcing, rust develops, the concrete breaks up, and the material is consequently destroyed. To counteract this, it is important that reinforcing is adequately covered by concrete and that the concrete dries without air pockets.

Concrete's compression strength is one-fifth that of steel, but the strength can vary greatly depending on the mixing ratio between cement, sand, and water. Structurally, this means that concrete is naturally "hefty" in proportion to steel. The natural plasticity of concrete is well suited in wall and slab constructions, as well as in structures of a highly sculptural expression.

*Wood* is a natural product with a long tradition as a building material. Spruce and pine are the most important structural wood types. The direction of the fiber grain in a structural element is the deciding factor in determining the material's structural strength. With the grain running parallel to the length of the structural member, wood has relatively equal compression and tension properties. The compression strength of wood is comparable to that of weak concrete when the grain runs parallel to the member's length, and only one-sixth of that when the grain runs perpendicular to the member's length. Wood is used as beams and columns in small to medium-size buildings and as roof trusses. In structures under tension, the joint between wood elements is the weakest point. It is desirable to use a steel bolt and plate joint, which can be more expensive than the wood itself. Knots in wood will greatly reduce structural strength. Laminated wood beams use glued plies to eliminate the occurrence of knots in the beam; therefore, the strength of a laminated wood beam is greater than a standard wood beam.

*Masonry* is a group of materials consisting of stone, brick, concrete brick or block, lightweight concrete block, and mortar. Mortar is the binding material between the masonry units and consists of cement and/or lime mixed with sand and water. Masonry, as a structural material, is normally not reinforced and is first and foremost a material designed for structural compression. The compression strength is directly dependent on the material composition of the brick or block. Traditionally, masonry is an unsuitable material in tension, but in recent years reinforced masonry has become of interest as a structural material.

Masonry, as a building material, is most often used for vertical bearing structures, such as pillars, columns, or walls. The masonry wall is, of course, well suited as a wind-bracing element. The arch is an excellent masonry-bearing structure because it primarily handles compression stresses.

Textiles are of no value in compression but can withstand great amounts of tensile stress. These man-made materials are used in soft tensile structures with a doubly crowned form.

Keeping in mind the structural merits of materials, we will examine the most common structures and types of stresses that occur under varying loads, but first, some general observations regarding proportions and dimensions of structural materials.

*Louis I. Kahn.*
*The Assembly*
*Building*
*Ahmemabad, India.*
*1972.*

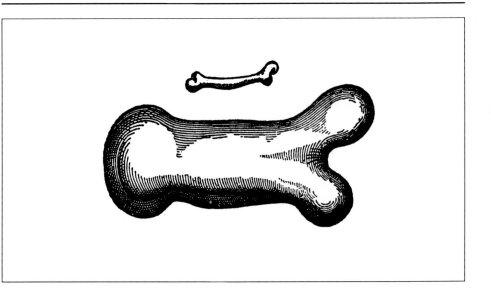

*Galileo Galilei.*
*Bone comparison*
*sketches.*
*1638.*

# 1.4 STRUCTURAL SIZE

In his discussion of different types of bridges, Palladio wrote that all bridges could have an unlimited span, as long as their internal proportions remained constant. Palladio was actually wrong. Over a certain span, his bridges, and for that matter all bridges, would collapse.

If we imagine a freely supported beam with a cross section of 1 x 1 m (3'-3" x 3'-3") and a length of 10 m (33'), then double the dimensions so that the cross section becomes 2 x 2 m (6'-6"x 6'-6") and the length 20 m (66'), we will see that the actual weight increases by the factor of 8. The strength of the beam is proportional to the increase in the cross section and thus increases 4 times, but the weight is proportional to the volume and is multiplied 8 times. If we continue to proportionally increase the dimensions of the beam, it will eventually fail owing to its own weight.

The first to discover that maximum span widths do exist was Galileo Galilei, as demonstrated in "Dialogues Concerning Two New Sciences" from 1638. The work is written as a dialogue between Galileo and a pupil. They discuss a number of examples that show that the size of an object or a building has an important influence on the economic use of construction materials. Certain types of constructions are only feasible within a certain range of sizes.

One of Galileo's examples shows how a bone in a small animal would look if it were to fulfill the same function in an animal three times as large. The bone would be three times larger. But the increase in the load would be greater than the increase in the cross section of the bone. The bone, therefore, would need to be enlarged further to withstand the actual load. As a result of this, the proportions of the bone would be changed. Similar changes would occur with all of the joints in the animal, and we can, in a way, imagine a new type of animal considerably sturdier and heavier than it was originally.

In the animal world, we can see exactly how the phenomenon has manifested itself. Large animals such as the elephant and the buffalo have massive bone structures and move slowly in relation to their weight, while an antelope with it's spindly bone structure can move quickly. Dinosaurs with their colossal bones are long since extinct, perhaps because they became too heavy, too slow, and lost the battle for survival against smaller and quicker species.

Many buildings of the past were planned with the help of small-scale models with which load tests and evaluations were conducted. From the experience we have today, we know that the principles that apply for a model do not necessarily apply for a completed building, which could be 100 times larger. In Hagia Sophia in Istanbul, where we can be almost certain that a model was used in planning, the latest investigations and calculations conclude that the existing foundations are on the verge of collapse.

To summarize, one can conclude that the size of every structure has its upper and lower limits. Let's look closer at how this applies to tall buildings and how the height and number of floors are related to the choice of materials and type of structure.

An example of limits is the world's tallest brick building, Chicago's Monadnock Building, completed in 1891 by the architects Burnham and Root. To bear the building's 16 floors, there are massive brick load-bearing walls that are 1.8 meters (6 feet) wide at their base and that gradually taper with each ensuing floor. In spite of recent brick technology with vertically reinforced columns, the structural limit of brick is still between 16 and 20 floors. Beyond this, the structure would consume unreasonably large amounts of ground floor area.

Similarly, a concrete skeleton consisting of columns and slabs has a practical height restriction of 30 to 35 floors. Otherwise, the dimensions of the ground floor columns would take up too much floor area.

After World War II, the development of structural forms enabling us to tremendously increase the number of floors took place around the campus of the Illinois Institute of Technology (IIT) and the architectural firm of Skidmore, Owings, and Merrill (SOM). In 1948, Myron Goldsmith, senior partner at SOM and professor at IIT, in collaboration with Jim Ferris, made a sketch of ideas for a tall building exposing on the facade the diagonal wind bracing. These new structural ideas, based on steel, were later realized in such buildings as the John Hancock Building in 1969 with its 100 floors and the Sears Tower in 1974 with 110 floors.

A large building cannot be built in the same manner as a small building.

The challenge for architects and engineers lies in finding the structural method that is best suited to the scope of the project. New structural systems create the possibilities for new architectural expressions.

*Skeleton of a Camarosaurus from the Jurassic period.*

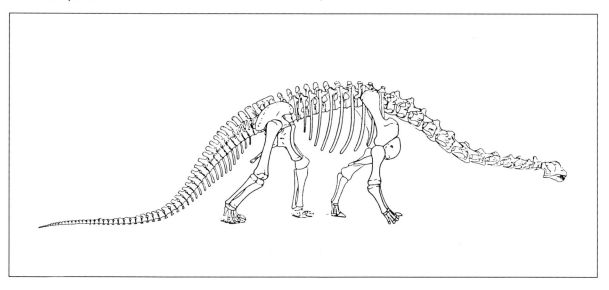

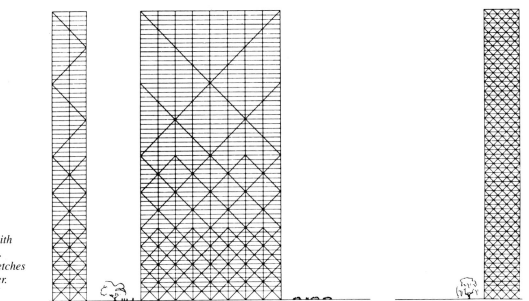

*Myron Goldsmith and Jim Ferris. Conceptual sketches for a skyscraper. 1948.*

*John Hancock Center. 1969. Architect: SOM. Engineer: Fazlur Khan. Model by architectural students: Ruth Damman Holme, Dorota Jarochowska, and Hanna Rîgnvaldsdôttir.*

*Sears Tower. 1974. Architect: SOM. Engineer: Fazlur Khan.*

# Chapter 2

# STATICS: THE BASIS FOR UNDERSTANDING STRUCTURES

*Gare d' Austerlitz,
Paris.
1886.
Architect:
Louis Renaud
Engineer: Sévène.*

## 2.1 STATICS AND ARCHITECTURE

Throughout history, buildings have been built with traditional materials and traditional methods, based on historical experience: Builders learned from past failures and tried to correct them by further developing the construction methods and systems for each building type. Development in the art of building was continually colored by this process for centuries.

The master builders of the Gothic period were skilled craftsmen in architecture, engineering, and detailed handiwork. They were equally qualified as designers and technicians. Sketchbooks and notes from that period show that they were well traveled, and we can be sure that they kept an attentive eye open for new solutions.

The cathedral at Beauvais (begun 1247) stands as a symbol of the Gothic period's heaven-defying world view. However, the tension between heaven and earth was too great for the 60 meter-high (198 feet) chancellory: A few columns failed and the chancellory collapsed like an avalanche, as described in Erik Lundberg's book *The Visual Language of Architecture*. After thorough examination of the ruins, it was concluded that the columns had to be strengthened. The builders made a fresh start, and after a few years the cathedral was reconstructed.

*Cathedral. Beauvais, France.*
*Begun in 1247.*
*Flying buttresses and arches.*

The science of engineering, in our time, has developed methods for calculating the correlation between forces and design of bearing structures. The direction of forces in materials can be analytically derived and structural dimensions calculated to prevent deformation or, even worse, collapse. A line of newer structural designs—for example, shells, membranes, and cables—in practice today will often be visualized with advanced computer-assisted calculations. For the time being, it is important that this attitude toward structural understanding isn't an isolated means in evaluating such quantities as numbers, arrows, and triangles, but must be seen in relation to the total building project. We must take heed of the Gothic masters' versatility and all-around vision.

*Le Corbusier.*
*Interior of the Parliament Building.*
*Chandigarh, India.*
*1956-1959.*

Le Corbusier, Kahn, and Mies van der Rohe had an underlying structural insight, even though they were preoccupied with other ingredients of building design, such as light, volume, and materials.

There is a strong correspondence between classical Greek architecture and the iron and steel architecture of the nineteenth century. They are both noted for discovering and developing structural bearing systems. The structural idea must find its correct structural expression.

In the Baroque period, architects were pre-occupied with such aspects of building design as the plastic forming of space. Vaulting was masked as though it didn't exist. Paradoxically, building technology was just as advanced and demanding during this time as in more structurally concerned periods; for example, Saint Peter's Cathedral in Rome, where the enormous cuppola, 60 meters (160 feet) in diameter, rests on a cylinder 80 meters (265 feet) over Saint Peter's Square, is from this era.

Builders possessed the necessary structural insight even though the structure was not exposed.

*Louis I. Kahn.*
*Library.*
*Exeter, New*
*Hampshire. 1972.*

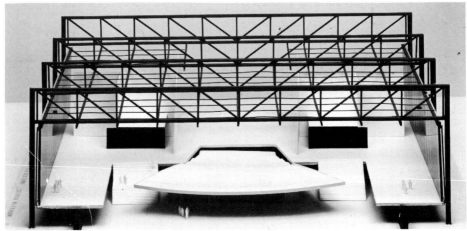

*Mies van der Rohe.*
*Theater project for*
*Mannheim.*
*1953.*
*Model by*
*architectural students:*
*Niels Marius Askim,*
*Alma Elisabeth*
*Oftedal, and*
*Helle Kristiansen.*

*Nature and
nature's law
lay hid in the night:
God said: "Let
Newton be!"
and all was light.*

—ALEXANDER POPE*

*This could not last,
the devil howling,
"Ho!
let Einstein be!"
restored the status
quo.*

—ANONYMOUS*

*But light it is,
as light it was!
Old Isaac's
perfectly
right for us.*

—BNS

*From Henry Cowan,
Architectural
Structures.

## 2.2 NEWTON'S LAWS: THE MEANING OF FORCE

The word *static* comes from the Greek word *statikos*, meaning "to make something stand still." The idea of statics is based on the principle that buildings and building elements "shall stand still." This is the foundation for our understanding of structures. If beams, columns, and arches cannot be held in place when loaded, they are of little value.

Sir Isaac Newton (1642-1727) discovered the link between the principles of a body in a state of rest and the notion of force. In what has come to be called Newton's first law, or the law of inertia, Newton stated that a body will move at a constant rate or be at rest as long as no resultant force acts on it. The abstract body described by Newton can, for our purposes, be considered a beam, a column, a support, or any building component. Thus, a structural body will not "stand still" as long as a resultant force is acting on it.

In classical physics, a force can change or attempt to change a body in a state of rest. A force acting on a body can cause deformation. The only way to measure a force is to register its effects, such as the amount of deformation resulting from a tension force.

Without a resultant force, a body is in constant motion in a straight line or it is at rest. When a resultant force acts on a body at rest, it will cause the body to accelerate. This acceleration is proportional to the acting resultant force, which means that if a given force doubles, acceleration will also double. Thus, force and acceleration increase or decrease in the same fashion. The relationship between force and acceleration is described in Newton's second law, or the law of dynamics, which states that force is an action that changes the state of motion or rest of the body on which it acts. Mathematically this law is represented as follows:

$$F = m \cdot a$$

where F is the force, m, the mass, and a, acceleration. Newton's second law can therefore be defined as: The sum of forces or the resultant force that acts on a body is equal to the body's mass multiplied by the acceleration that the force has induced in the body.

Since acceleration is a measure of how quickly speed changes, Newton's first law is considered to be a special case derived from his second law. If in the formula for Newton's second law we write zero for acceleration (a), because "constant motion" means that acceleration is zero, we see that the force (F) is also equal to zero. Also, constant speed implies that there are no resultant forces. If we use Newton's second

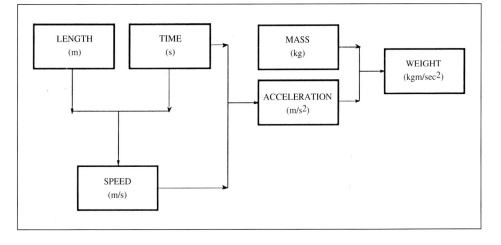

*The basic physical notions: length, time, and mass combine into the terms speed, acceleration, and weight.*

law, we have the force in terms of the unit $kgm/s^2$. This unit of force, called a Newton (N), is of such magnitude that under its influence a mass of one kilogram would experience an acceleration of one meter per second per second.

The notion of mass is difficult to define. Mass is directly related to what we call inertia of a body and the weight of a body. While a body's weight differs, for example, on the earth and the moon, its mass will remain constant.

The notion of a body's weight is represented by the force (inertia) of a mass acting within a gravitational field. The mass (m) is multiplied by the acceleration owed to gravity (g). A body therefore has a weight (G), which is equal to its own mass times the force of the earth pulling on the body. This force is the force of gravity operating downward on the base. Weight (G), in Newton's third law, is written as:

$$G = m \cdot g$$

where m is the mass and g is acceleration

owed to gravity ($g = 9.81$ m/s$^2$).

According to Newton's second law, a body laying on a base will accelerate downward if G is the force acting on it. If the body doesn't move downward, then obviously another force is acting on the body, holding G in balance so that the resultant force is equal to zero and the body is at rest. That other force is the reaction of the base, which is as large as the gravitational force but in the opposite direction. This hinders the body from falling as the two forces hold each other in equilibrium. This is Newton's third law, the law pertaining to force and equilibrium: To every action there is an equal and opposite reaction.

The weight of a body laying on a base has a downward action that is opposed by the resistance from the base-upward reaction on the body. The resistance is equal in magnitude to the weight. A force has direction and magnitude and is symbolized by a straight line or vector. The length of the vector represents the force's magnitude, and the direction of the vector represents the force's direction.

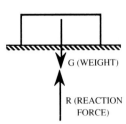

*The weight of the body held in equilibrium by a reaction from the base.*

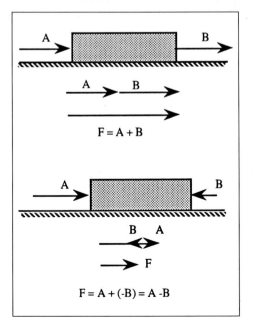

## 2.3 COMPOSITION OF INTERSECTING FORCES

Forces acting in the same direction or in opposite directions from each other and along the same line of action can be added using simple arithmetic. The sum of the figures is called the resultant force. The resultant force is a simple force with an effect equal to the sum of two or more forces.

Forces passing through the same point, but with different lines of action, can be combined by adding force triangles or force polygons.

*Summation of the forces along the same line of action. The force resultant will be the arithmetic sum (with its sign) of the forces.*

Forces can be added by setting the vectors together, one after the other, while maintaining the force direction and magnitude. The succession of vectors is unimportant, and their sum, the resultant force, is the vector force that moves from the tail of the

$$F = A + B$$

$$F = A + (-B) = A - B$$

first to the point of the last vector. This sum is called the vector sum and can be written as a simple arithmetic sum as long as the numbers are marked with a line over each coefficient. A force is also a vector, that is to say, a physical magnitude with direction.

The method for the adding of forces was first used by Leonardo da Vinci (1452-1519) in the fifteenth century, but Stevinius from Brügge (1548-1620) was the first to publicize Leonardo's method formally in 1586.

*Pulling of the Condeep platform in the North Sea. The tugboats' lines of force will together comprise the speed and direction of the platform.*

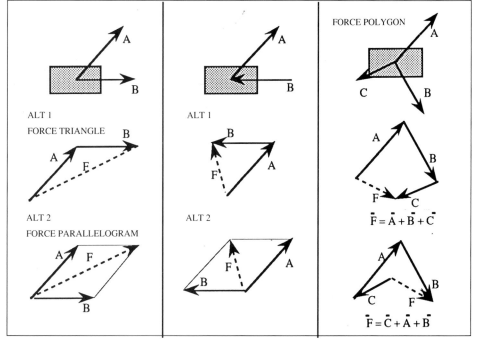

*Addition of two or more forces that intersect with each other. The sum of the forces, the resultant, is the vector that can be drawn from the tail of the first to the point of the last force vector.*

## 2.4 EXAMPLES USING NEWTOW'S LAWS

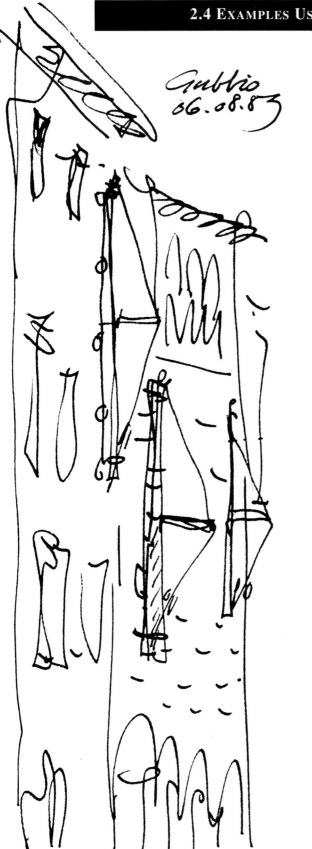

A couple of examples in the Italian city of Gubbio can help shed some light on Newton's laws.

Along the street leading to Piazza della Signoria stands a masonry dwelling of four or five floors. For several reasons and over the course of many years, the facade has had the tendency to lean farther and farther out to the point that it has been necessary to prevent it from toppling into the street.

The solution was a vertical, two-story-high suspension system mounted to the facade with a few bolts. With the help of a turn-buckle in a steel rod, the suspension system can put the facade into tension and there-fore keep the original forces responsible for deformation under control. The situation is now stable, achieving equilibrium between the facade and suspension system (Newton's first law). The result of these emergency arrangements, as we must call them, has enriched the character of the streetscape.

In the same street, a bit closer to the piazza, a crossbow is for sale in an antique store. The tension system of the crossbow pre-sents a situation similar to that of the sus-pension system bolted to the sagging facade. When the crossbow is cocked, the system is in equilibrium—in accordance with Newton's first law. The moment we place our finger on the trigger and fire, the tension is unleashed and the arrow flies, fulfilling Newton's second law.

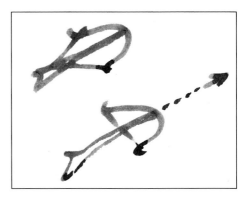

## 2.5 RESOLUTION OF FORCES

*Decomposition of the force F into the components $A_1$, $B_1$, and $A_1$, $B_1$.*

Since we can combine two or more forces into one resultant force that has the same combined effect as all of the others, we can do the opposite and split a force into new subforces as long as the resultant forces equal the original. These subforces are called component forces, and the action of splitting a force is called decomposition. For example, a force can be decomposed into component forces in innumerable ways, as long as the principle of closed force triangles or force parallelograms is followed. The force F has the components $A_1$, $B_1$, $A_2$, and $B_2$ along with countless others. The number of components (subforces with "new" magnitudes and directions) we wish to decompose a force into will be dependent on the geometry that fits this situation best and what function we want the components to accomplish. Often we decompose forces into their horizontal and vertical components.

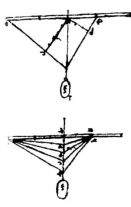

*Leonardo da Vinci's decomposition illustration.*

When we orient subforces in a coordinate system, we call the horizontal forces x-forces, which act along the x-axis, and the vertical forces y-forces, which act along the y-axis.

*$F_y$, component for the force F in the y direction, $F_x$, component for the force F in the x direction.*

If the force F rises at the angle $\alpha$ from the horizontal, we can easily derive the magnitude of the components in the x and y axes. This is accomplished graphically by drawing to scale the force F. Then, by drawing parallel lines to the x and y axes through the force's end points, we can find the magnitude of the x and y components.

It is, however, more common to find the components with the use of trigonometry. When the force F's magnitude and direction are given, we know one side and two angles ($\alpha$ and $90°$) of the triangle and that the other two sides can be calculated. If the angle is $\alpha$, we find:

*Definition for trigonometric relations.*

$$\sin \alpha = F_y/F \quad F_y = F \cdot \sin \alpha$$
and
$$\cos \alpha = F_x/F \quad F_x = F \cdot \cos \alpha$$

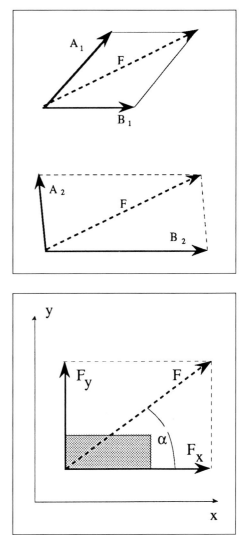

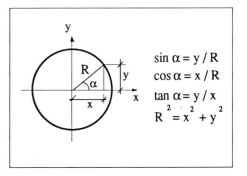

$$\sin \alpha = y / R$$
$$\cos \alpha = x / R$$
$$\tan \alpha = y / x$$
$$R^2 = x^2 + y^2$$

*A state of equilibrium is only attractive when we walk a tightrope; sitting on the ground it is not as marvelous.*

—ANDRE GIDE

*The body acted on by the forces A and B is held in equilibrium by the force R.*

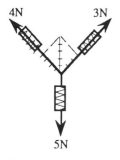

*Experimental control of the equilibrium of forces with scales.*

*The load R acting on the joint, a structural joint. The forces A, B, and C in the members hold the joint in equilibrium. The force polygon is closed.*

In the previous examples bodies were acted on by the forces A and B. The resultant was the force F, which caused a body to accelerate. In a building, we cannot allow the elements to move, and therefore we must be certain that the resultant of these forces is met by an equally large but directly opposite force. The sum of all the forces must be zero so that building components are held at rest (Newton's first law). This is the force that "closes" the force triangle or force polygon. It is called R and is equal in magnitude to F but acts in the opposite direction. If a structural joint is to remain at rest, and in static balance, the sum of all the forces acting on the joint must yield a closed triangle of forces or polygon of forces.

Empirically, this can easily be observed with three spring scales. Connect the scales together with a string so that two scales pull in different directions with the third scale held stationary, creating static equilibrium. When the direction is decided, the magnitude of the forces can be read from the spring scales.

A diagram will show the magnitude and direction of the force needed to set the first two forces to rest, the equilibrium of the forces. The force's magnitude can then be checked by using the scales.

With the help of Newton's first law, we have seen that a body will be at rest as long as no resultant forces act on it. This doesn't mean that forces are not present but that the sum of the acting forces, the resultant, must be equal to zero. For forces with the same line of action, it is best depicted by thinking of a "tug-of-war," which is two teams, comprised of several people, pulling at either end of a rope with different forces. The rope will be at rest if the sum of tension forces that form one team is the sum of the tension forces of the other. This is to say that the rope is acted on by two equal forces but in opposite directions. The resul-

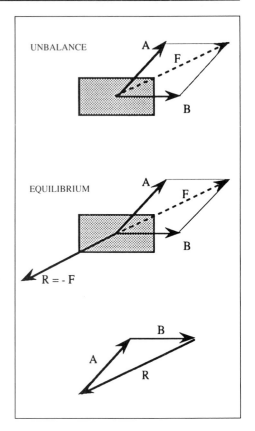

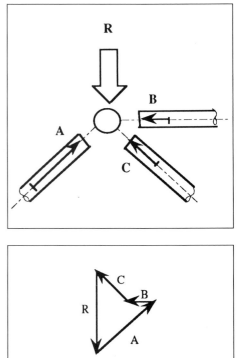

*Claude Monet. Gare St. Lazare. 1877. Practical application of the theory of equilibrium. The so-called Polonceau roof truss makes long spans possible over the platforms. With its spider web's lightness, the structure allows for rich natural lighting. In Monet's oil painting, direct sunlight is blended with the locomotive's smoke and steam and erases the contours in our field of vision.*

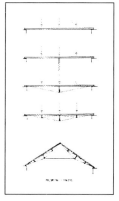

*The principle for the Polonceau roof truss, named after the engineer Camille Polonceau (1813-1859). The beam's span is divided by point supports. In order to eliminate columns, the supports are suspended from tension rods that are connected to the beams*

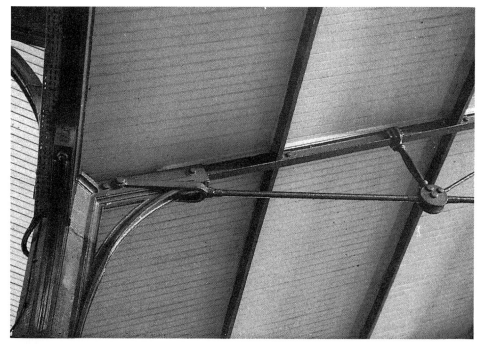

*Gare St. Lazare. Paris 1852. Engineer: Flachat. Architect: Lamand.*

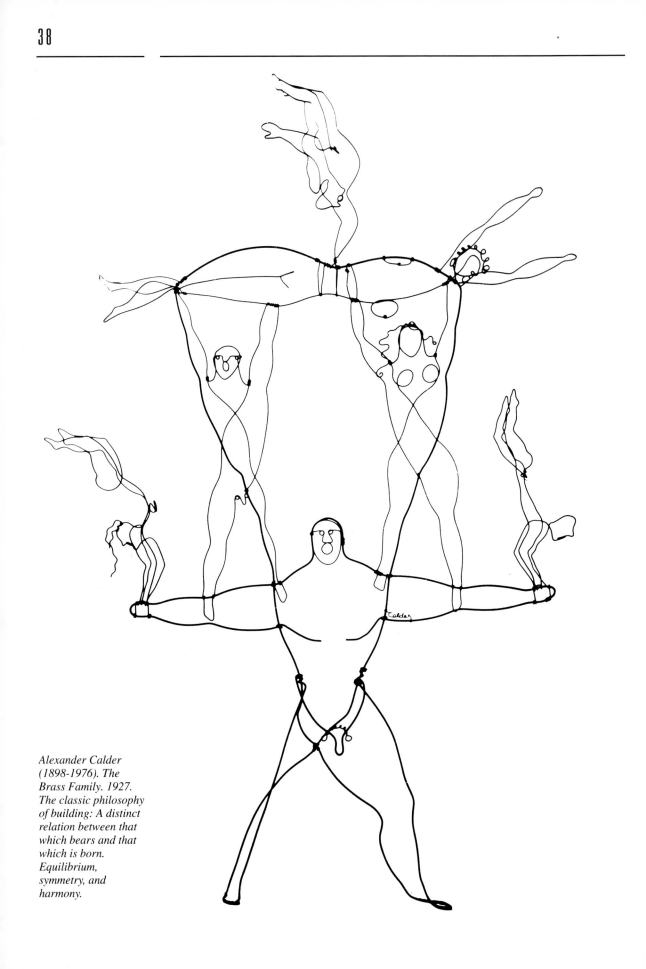

*Alexander Calder
(1898-1976). The
Brass Family. 1927.
The classic philosophy
of building: A distinct
relation between that
which bears and that
which is born.
Equilibrium,
symmetry, and
harmony.*

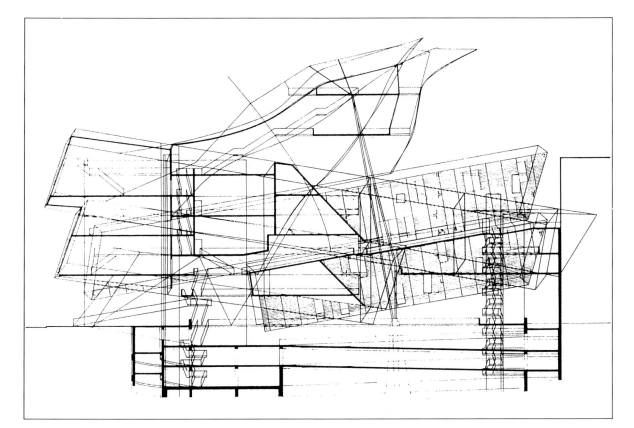

*Housing project
in Vienna. 1986.
Architects:
Coop Himmelblau.
Long section.
Deconstruction, where
the components form
a new composition.
Visual, but no actual
physical unbalance.*

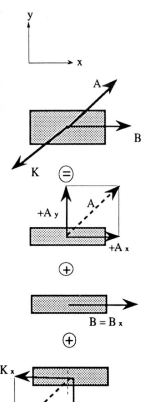

*Force equilibrium is sought by the addition of the force components in the x and y directions.*

tant is equal to zero, and the rope will be at rest.

The forces acting in the horizontal direction are normally along the x axis. The forces acting in the vertical direction are along the y axis. Therefore, we can formulate the conditions for equilibrium in this way: The sum of all of the forces acting parallel to the x axis must be equal to zero and the sum of all of the forces acting along the y axis must be equal to zero for the structure to be at rest, in static equilibrium.

Mathematically, this condition for equilibrium is written:

$$\sum F_x = 0 \quad \sum F_y = 0$$

where the letter $\sum$ means "the sum of" and indices x and y describe the direction. In both the x and y directions, the forces must be added with their sign, + or -, depending on the direction it is acting in, relative to the coordinate system.

To understand the equilibrium of forces that do not act along the same straight line, but cross each other at a common intersecting point, it is useful to draw force polygons or to derive the forces arithmetically after having decomposed them into components with the same line of action.

The condition of equilibrium gives us:

$$\sum F_x = 0$$

$$A_x + B_x - K_x = 0$$

$$\sum F_y = 0$$

$$A_y + 0 - K_y = 0$$

As we have seen, it is common to assign forces a name using capital letters. Often F is used, but also N, K, W, S or C. The choice of a letter is arbitrary, but it can be used to indicate the type of force, for example, C can be used for the force of compression or W for weight.

## 2.7 THE STATIC EQUILIBRIUM OF PARALLEL FORCES: THE LEVER PRINCIPLE

We have looked at forces acting along the same straight line or having common points of intersection, which can be added or subtracted with simple arithmetic or with force polygons. The effect of simple forces combined is the same as that of the resultant force. In instances where parallel forces act on a body, the distance between the forces also must be calculated to find their full effect.

Let's consider a beam having one point of support. From the beam, hang two weights with different loads, F and K, one on each side of the support. The loads hang different distances from the support, $a_1$ and $a_2$, so that the beam doesn't tilt. In this case it is not just the loads' magnitude that is of importance but also their distance from the support point. Archimedes of Syracuse first used the principle of the lever in about 250

B.C., when he built catapults as weapons of defense against Roman invaders.

To maintain the beam in equilibrium, the smaller force K must be farther away from the point of support than the larger load F. There are many combinations of loading magnitudes and distances from the point of support that are decisive. We call *moment* the product of a force multiplied by its distance from the point of support.

Force · distance = moment

The force's distance from the support is called the *moment arm*. To assure that the beam does not tip, therefore, the smaller force K must have a moment around the point of support equal to that of the larger load F. We have the following condition of equilibrium:

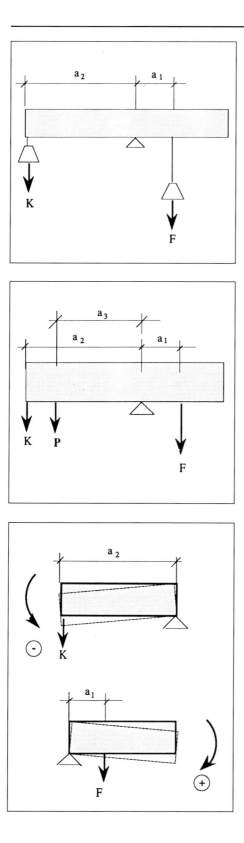

*Lever: Beam on a balancing point. The beam is loaded with two weights that hold the beam in equilibrium.*

*Beam with three concentrated loads: K and P attempt to turn the beam counterclockwise; the force F must counteract the turning.*

*The sign rules for moments: Forces that turn the element clockwise result in positive moments. The forces that turn the element counterclockwise result in negative moments.*

$$F \cdot a_1 = K \cdot a_2$$

In this expression lies also an indication that the moment has direction, that is to say, a vector. The moment must also have a clear indication of its sign. Moments that attempt to rotate the beam counterclockwise are negative moments.

Moment $F \cdot a_1$ is positive, and the moment $K \cdot a_2$ is negative.

Moments that are acting around the same point of support, since they have signs, are either added or subtracted. An extra load, P, to the left of the support will increase the moment K such that the negative moments combined will be:

$$-K \cdot a_2 - P \cdot a_3$$

If the beam is to be at rest, in equilibrium, the negative moments on the left side must nullify the positive moments on the right side. The sum of all of the moments, with their sign, must be equal to zero.

$$-K \cdot a_2 - P_3 \cdot a_3 + F \cdot a_1 = 0$$

or

$$F \cdot a_1 = K \cdot a_2 + P \cdot a_3$$

We have formulated a third equilibrium equation for systems with parallel forces. We can generally state: The sum of the moments around any point in a structure must be equal to zero if the structure is to be at rest and not rotate around the point.

Mathematically this is written:

$$\sum M_i = 0$$

M stands for the moments and the index "i" symbolizes that the sum of the moments can be taken around any point. Moments are products of force and distance and therefore the unit $[N] \cdot [m] = [Nm]$ (Newtonmeter).

*Equilibrium studies by Leonardo da Vinci.*

*Galileo investigated the effects of moments in a cantilevered wood beam loaded with a weight hanging from its end.*

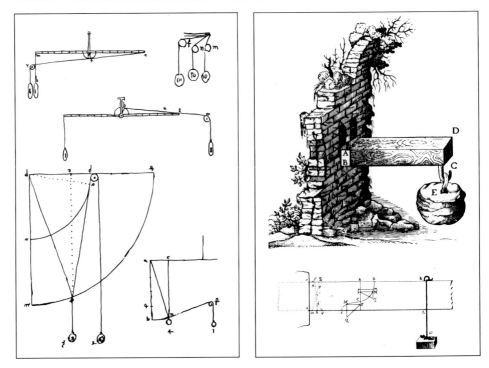

# 2.8 MOMENTS OF FORCES

Galileo Galilei (1564-1642) analyzed the effects of moments in a wood beam built into a stone wall and loaded with a weight. We shall do the same.

Let's imagine we have a 2-meter-long (6'-6") beam with one end solidly fastened in a wall. This type of beam is called a cantilevered beam. The beam is loaded in the middle with a concentrated load of 10 kN (22 Kips) = 10,000N (22,000 lb.). We will first ignore the beam's own weight. Since the distance from the load to the wall is 1 meter (3'-3"), the load must cause a moment in the wall of:

$$+10\,kN \cdot 1m = +10\,kNm.$$

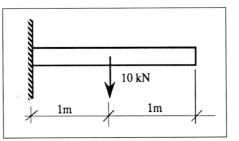

*Cantilevered beam loaded at its middle.*

But how is the beam staying in equilibrium? Which moment hinders the rotation of the beam?

If we examine the intersection of beam and wall, we will see that the attempt to rotate the beam clockwise creates a force that pushes against the wall from the lower half of the beam and pulls outward from the wall at the upper half of the beam. The reactions to those forces acting on the beam result in tension in the upper half of the beam and compression in the lower half. The forces appear in pairs and are equal in magnitude but act in opposite directions. They are called force pairs and have a resultant force equal to zero, but the resultant moment is equal to the forces' magnitude multiplied by the distance between them. A force pair is also the same as a moment:

$$M_{kp} = S \cdot a = T \cdot a$$

A moment can always be decomposed and replaced by two equally large forces that

*The force pair S and T acts on the wall and on the end of the beam with forces in opposing directions.*

*Top: Forces on the wall.*

*Bottom: Forces on the beam.*

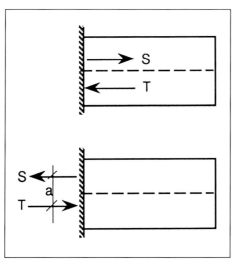

act in opposing directions and work a certain distance from each other.

The force pair, in this example, attempts to rotate the end of the beam counterclockwise, therefore creating a negative moment that must be equal in magnitude to the positive moment in order to keep the beam at rest.

$\sum M_i = 0$, resulting in $+10kNm - M_{kp} = 0$

$M_{kp} = 10kNm$ and

$M_{kp} = S \cdot a = T \cdot a = 10kNm$.

Where $a = 0.3m$ we find:

$S = T = 10kNm/0.3m = 33.3kN$

With that, we have found the horizontal forces that work in the fixed end, and the forces causing tension in the upper half of the beam and compression in the lower half. The requirement on moment equilibrium has been fulfilled, and we can be assured that the beam will remain at rest. The beam should be at rest both vertically and horizontally for the requirements on force equilibrium to be satisfied. In the horizontal direction:

$\sum K_x = 0$

The requirements are fulfilled since there isn't any outer load that acts in the horizon-

*Force and moment equilibrium for the cantilevered beam: Three conditions for equilibrium must be fulfilled.*

tal direction. The force pair, as we have seen, is a group in equilibrium. In the vertical direction:

$\sum K_y = 0$

The outer load of 10kN must be balanced with an equally large but directionally opposed force acting on the beam to maintain equilibrium. This means that the wall reacts with a force V that acts upward on the beam.

$V - 10kN = 0 \quad V = 10kN$.

Let's look at the same beam with another load, for example, the beam's own weight (the weight of the beam is also a force). Since the beam is uniformly thick, the load of itself has an uniform magnitude along its entire length. Every portion of the beam represents the load of itself with a magnitude equal to the element's own weight. The load is symbolized by a series of force vectors of the same magnitude. This type of uniform loading is called a uniformly distributed load.

Each vector represents the load's intensity, that is, load per unit length along the beam. The intensity of the load is represented by small letters, for example, q or p. The unit is in Newton's per meter (N/m) (lb./ft.) or kiloNewtons per meter (kN/m) (Kips/ft.). When we look at the intensity of loading of a two-dimensional structure, such as a slab, we have loading over an area. The unit is therefore Newtons per square meter (N/m$^2$) (lb./ft.$^2$) or kiloNewtons per square meter (kN/m$^2$) (Kips/ft.$^2$).

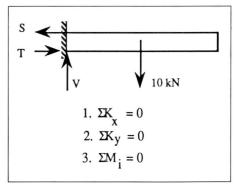

1. $\sum K_x = 0$
2. $\sum K_y = 0$
3. $\sum M_i = 0$

*The resultant load represents the sum of each load vector and acts at their center of gravity. The magnitude of the resultant load is equal to the area of the load diagram.*

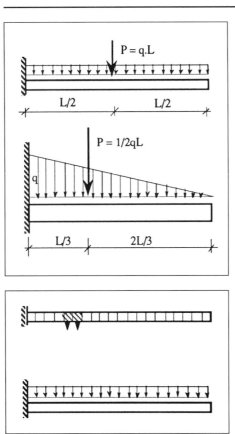

To discover the moment action of "simple loads" on a cantilevered beam, we could take the load from a unit length multiplied by the unit length's distance from the fixed end. Instead, we let the last resultant P represent the sum of all "simple loads." The moment arm therefore would be the distance from the resultant load to the fixed end. The resultant load lies in the center of gravity of the intensities of the load, also in the middle of the uniformly distributed load. Its magnitude will be their sum, the area of the diagram:

$$P = q \cdot L \text{ (N)}$$

For a load that is distributed like a triangle along a cantilevered beam we find: The location of the resultant force is 1/3L from the fixed end (center of gravity in the triangle), and its magnitude is equal to the area of the triangle.

$$P = 1/2q \cdot L \text{ (N)}$$

*The dead load of the beam as weight for each portion. The load is symbolized by a series of load arrows of the same magnitude.*
*Such a load is called a linearly distributed load.*

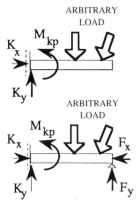

*Top: Statically determinate cantilevered beam with three unknown load reactions corresponding to the three conditions of equilibrium.*
*Bottom: Statically indeterminate and supported beam with five unknowns (statically indeterminate to the second degree).*

## 2.9 STATICALLY DETERMINATE AND INDETERMINATE STRUCTURES

We used the three general equilibrium equations to find all of the forces acting on the cantilevering beam. For this beam, under arbitrary loads, we generally have three unknown reactions to find:

• horizontal load reactions from the wall
• vertical load reactions from the wall
• the moment in the beam

We have three general terms for equilibrium at our disposal, and just as many equations as unknown magnitudes. We call a

structure where these conditions are satisfied a statically determinate structure. If the beam, in addition to being cantilevered, is supported at it's other end, we will also have a reaction force there. Thus in such cases we have four or more unknown magnitudes that we must find, and consequently we require help from several more equations than the three equilibrium equations. These systems are called statically indeterminate. To find all of the reactions, the system's deformation must be considered.

## 2.10 DISTRIBUTION OF FORCES AS A MEANS OF ARCHITECTURAL EXPRESSION

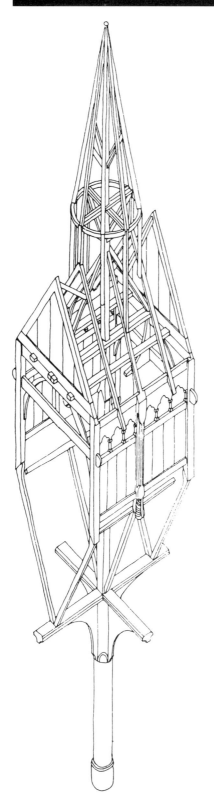

*Nes stave church. Ca. A.D. 1100. Isometric of the spire by Håkon Christie.*

Advances in technology have made it possible for us to enclose large spaces with long and deep simple beams, some of which result in a uniform and unarticulated architectural expression.

But long spans can be subdivided, columns can be split up, and a structural system can be used to create a varied and rich architectural expression.

Talented architects and builders through time have incorporated these principles in the design of wood structures.

The Nes stave church in Hallingdal, dating from the 1100s, is one of the few examples of a middle-masted church. After long deterioration, the church was demolished in 1864. Architect Håkon Christie from the Norwegian Central Office of Historical Monuments and Sites has produced a series of drawn reconstructions, so that we can better visualize how the church must have looked.

The floor plan is quite simple and consists of a rectangular nave with four corner posts and a mast at its middle. The middle mast extends up to the rafters and is connected to four beams stiffened by half arches. Diagonal struts from this level support the points of the gables, other struts, and the roof's spire. Scissor trusses support the roof, while the primary task of the middle mast is to bear the spire.

A thorough examination of the church is beyond the scope of this book, but we see how a 650-year-old structural system works and gives a building its character. It is the method of design and construction that creates architectural expression.

Alvar Aalto's (1898-1976) courthouse in Säynätsalo was inaugurated in 1952. The multiform complex, in red brick, is deployed around a central courtyard that is

*Alvar Aalto.*
*Town Hall*
*Säynätsalo, Finland.*

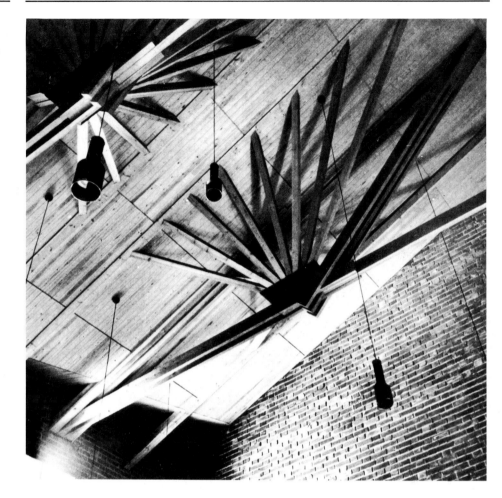

*Nes stave church.*
*12th century.*
*Model by architecture*
*students*
*Olav Dalheim,*
*Svein Hoelseth, and*
*Jan Petter Seim.*

elevated with respect to the surrounding terrain. The main hall of the courthouse is nearly cubic in form, as height is reflected in width. The roof, with a span of almost 10 meters (33 feet), bears two structural suspension elements in wood. From the suspension elements' shearing point a bundle of struts fan out and support the roof trusses from their undersides.

The cross section of the bottom chord of the roof trusses is reduced, because the bundles of struts actually shorten the length of the free span. The actual bundle of struts could have been supported by a column that transferred the loads downward, but Aalto chose to hang the construction of tension struts so that roof loads are transferred to the top of the bearing walls at the perimeter. Note that the joint for the 16 struts is designed as a steel trough.

The Commons (Allhuset) at the University in Stockholm, built in 1981, is a service building for students and guests. Here Ralph Erskine (born 1914) demonstrates his version of variations on a theme. A screen-like roof, with extended eaves, directs the disposition of the free plan and is borne by laminated diagonal-wood masts. But unlike Aalto's project, the loads are directed down to the ground through sculptural concrete foundations. In the corner foundation, which supports three masts, the axial loads intersect each other at one point, nullifying all bending moments. The masts that function as pendular columns are pointed and flashed with galvanized pin joints at their tops and bottoms. Because the diagonal masts support the roof beams from their undersides, the danger of deflection is not present, something that normally exists with roof overhangs.

It is the method of construction, the dominant roof borne by the diagonal masts, that gives character to the complex.

In the project for an indoor swimming pool at Peblingesø in Copenhagen (1979), architect Jørn Utzon (born 1918) shows how he mastered a theme and gave it his own special interpretation. Different from Erskine's more wild, growing world of ideas, we have a complex that is characterized by structural order. A large raftered ceiling is carried by two parallel rows of bundles comprised of diagonal struts. The bundles rest on cruciform concrete foundations running parallel to the long sides of the swimming pool. Each wood bundle supports and subdivides four rafters that can be very slim in relation to their length. Further creation of bidirectional struts and purlins form immovable triangles between rafters so that the structure is well stiffened. Concrete foundations with wide bases stand firm. The columns, with their branching crowns, bear the roof, and the reflection in the water mirrors the main idea of the complex.

*Ralph Erskine. The Commons at the University of Stockholm, Sweden. 1981.*

*Jørn Utzon. Project for a swimming hall at Peblingesjø, Copenhagen, Denmark. 1979.*

# Chapter 3    TRUSSES: A SYSTEM OF MEMBERS

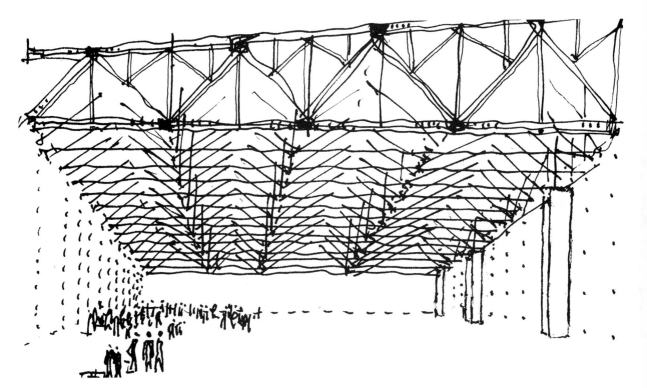

*Hangar for Oslo Airport, Fornebu, built by the Germans in 1941.*
*The roof structure is built with flat trusses of massive quadratic wood timber with a span of 30 meters (120 feet). It was systematically detailed with plates connecting simple and double members. Over the doors, the wooden trusses are carried by a steel truss that rests on concrete columns.*

**3.1 EXAMPLES FROM HISTORY**

**3.2 ROOF TRUSSES FROM EAST AND WEST**

**3.3 FORCE, STRESS, AND ELASTICITY**

**3.4 A SYSTEM OF MEMBERS**

**3.5 THE POMPIDOU CENTER**

**3.6 PIANO AND ROGERS**

**3.7 FORCE FOLLOWS FORM**

**3.8 A TURNING POINT IN BUILDING**

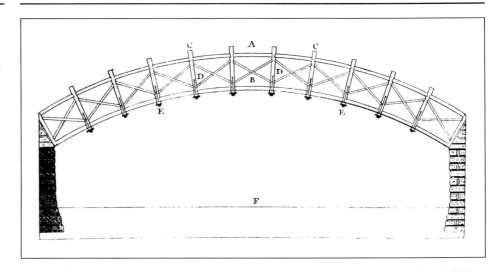

# 3.1 EXAMPLES FROM HISTORY

Trusses were developed to span greater distances than the lengths of massive wood beams. At first, master builders explored methods for combining several members in order to maximize the structural possibilities of the material and to span greater distances.

The system of members is primarily a construction for wood or steel. Linear elements of limited lengths and strengths are combined to create effective systems with enormous bearing capacity and at the same time a high grade of openness. The trusses can be straight or curved beams, slabs, arches, frames, or columns.

We are going to take a quick look at two historic structures, both of which are arched-truss constructions. The first is in wood, the other in iron. Principally, the arched-truss can be formed by implementing shorter members on its underside than the corresponding members along the top. In reality this construction would define a section of a many-sided polygon. As an alternative we could, especially in steel and iron, bend the top and bottom members.

Andrea Palladio (1508-1580) had studied forerunners for truss structures from antiquity and published in 1570 a project for a curved bridge with wooden members and simple iron connector plates for bolting the members together. The detailing of the joints shows which members are assumed to be in tension and which are to take up compression loads. By letting the radially placed middle members bear the tension loads and the diagonal members the compression loads, the simplest joint detail was achieved.

Almost three hundred years later, Henri Labrouste (1801-1868) introduced iron structures as the dominant bearing system in a monumental building. After designing the Biblioteque St. Géneviève (1843-1850), he reached full maturity as an architect with the Biblioteque National in Paris (1858-1868).

The reading room in the Biblioteque National is covered by nine domes that rest on sixteen iron arches. The arches are comprised of curved iron profiles connected by straight and diagonal members. The whole construction rests on slender iron columns.

The iron structure's riveted connections are beautifully expressed by the rivets and are as such incorporated in the trusses' ornamental design. Sunlight, highlighted on the glass mosaic-tiled domes, reflects farther down through the open-webbed, arched truss structure.

*Biblioteque National
in Paris. 1858-1868.
The natural light is
reflected by glass
mosaics and is spread
through the open truss
construction.*

*Biblioteque National.
Reading room.
Architect: Henri
Labrouste.*

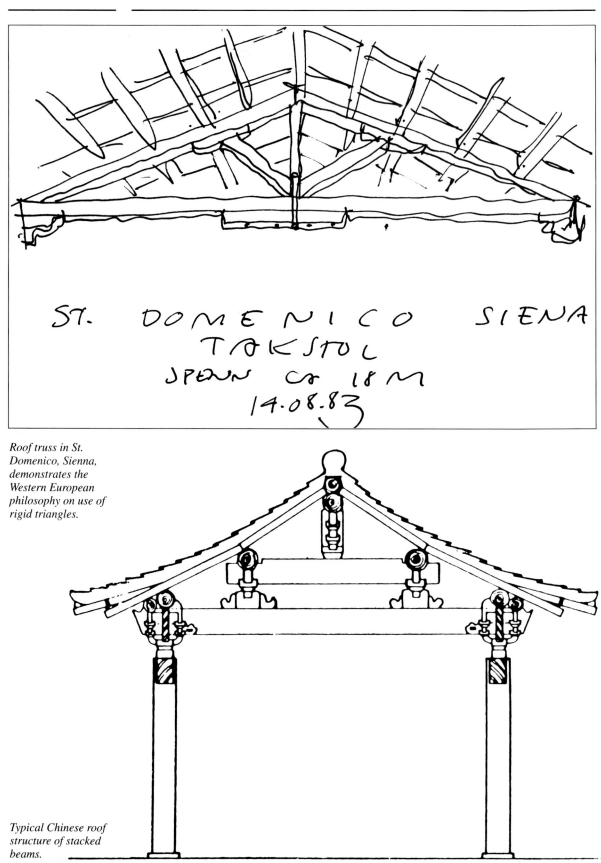

ST. DOMENICO SIENA
TAKSTOL
SPENN CA 18M
14.08.83

*Roof truss in St. Domenico, Sienna, demonstrates the Western European philosophy on use of rigid triangles.*

*Typical Chinese roof structure of stacked beams.*

# 3.2 ROOF TRUSSES FROM EAST AND WEST

Wooden roof trusses, such as those that span the twelfth-century nave of St. Domenico in Siena, exemplify a structural form that is widely used in Europe. Roof trusses are incorporated in the simplest barns and the largest basilicas. Leon Krier used them extensively in his projects of the 1970s.

The roof trusses function as a system of connected inflexible triangles. The weight of the roof is transferred through the trusses as pure compression and tension forces. The length of the span can be up to 18-20 meters (60-65 feet) depending on the length of available timber. At St. Domenico the horizontal bottom member needed to be spliced at its middle with a double plate connector, so the one-piece, sloping upper member would then determine the width of the nave. If the addition of a second side aisle was desirable, preferably it would have a trussed shed roof that would stand independent of the main roof.

Roof forms in Asia were developed in accordance with other principles. In China, the static potential of wood structures were either unknown or not employed. Instead, a roof consisted of a stack of propped-up beams. The length of the span was determined by the bearing capacity and length of the bottom beam. If the space's width needed to be increased, an extra row of columns was erected.

The roof was accorded significant meaning in Chinese architecture. The numerous and sloping roof forms are often associated with Chinese pagodas and temple complexes. Variation and nuances in bracketing and beam design create the basis for the sloping roof forms.

When we compare the typical Eastern and Western roof forms, we are struck by the lack of similarity. The construction principles incorporate quite different methods and bear witness to different philosophies. In the East Asian building tradition, the beams are stacked one on the another without concern for efficiency or quantities of materials, but instead for order and the beauty of the order. The beams become gradually shorter and shorter as the structure increases in height. The long span is bridged with a series of shorter spans.

In Europe, we have created stiff triangles that are again combined to comprise one triangle. The triangles make for a lightweight and effective structure that may be a bit boring in its precision. The singular members accept their portion of the load, none of them receiving significantly more or less than the other. In short, they distribute the work evenly among themselves.

The European tradition has been documented since the late Roman Empire, but it is possible that its building methods begin in Greek antiquity. In either case, we can say that the Western roof truss represents a structural ideal, an even distribution of loads.

The Eastern roof tradition seems to express a structural hierarchy. The bottom beam must bear all of the other beams, while the next one is responsible for one less layer.

*March de la Madeleine. 1832. Engineer: Gabriel Vengny. We recognize the typical roof truss motifs, but here it is built in iron.*

## 3.3 FORCE, STRESS, AND ELASTICITY

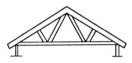

*Roof truss for a small house.*

In a bearing system that is built only of linear structural members, the members can be arranged in such a way that each member will receive either pure compression or pure tension forces. This will insure an efficient and economical bearing system that is likewise light and airy in appearance. A standard wooden roof truss that is used in house building is such a system, as are the light, open-roof structures we associate with steel industrial buildings.

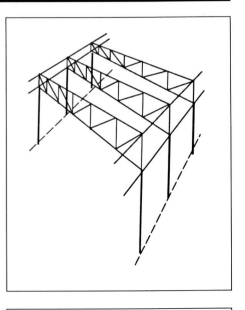

*Principle for trusses in industrial buildings.*

Each linear element in such a bearing system is called a member. Members are acted on by tension or compression forces at each opposite end and along their axes.

The most important requirements with axial loading in a bearing element and in other structural elements, such as beams, columns, arches, etc., are that they have adequate strength and stiffness. In practice this means that the component under stress doesn't collapse or deform beyond allowable limits.

The component's ultimate strength can be defined as a property of the material and be expressed by the component's ability to withstand maximum stress without failing.

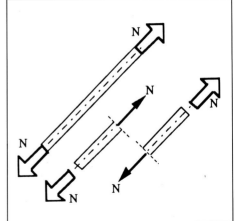

*Outer loading and inner axial force in a linear member.*

Stress is measured as the force's magnitude or intensity per square unit.

$\sigma = N/A$ where

$\sigma$ = the stress in the cross-sectional area A, acted on by the force N ($N/mm^2$) (psi)

A = the area of the cross section acted on by $N/mm^2$ (psi)

N = the acting force (N) (lb.).

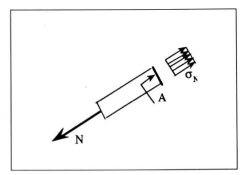

*Stress is force per square unit.*
*The stress is constant over the cross section in the linear member.*

What is the tensile stress in a cross section of $A = 100mm^2$ under an axial tensile load of $N = 5kN$?

$$\sigma N = N/A = 5000N/100mm^2 = 50N/mm^2$$

The tensile stress is constant over the

*The wooden floor can give in under high stresses. Both the load and the area of the load is decisive.*

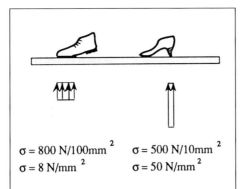

$$\sigma = 800 \text{ N}/100\text{mm}^2$$
$$\sigma = 8 \text{ N/mm}^2$$

$$\sigma = 500 \text{ N}/10\text{mm}^2$$
$$\sigma = 50 \text{ N/mm}^2$$

whole cross section.

In the following example we can see how critical stress, not necessarily force, is in a building material: A parquet floor is susceptible to scratching and gouging. A person weighing 176 lb. (80 kg) walks on the floor with flat shoes. Another person with a weight of just 110 lb. (50 kg) walks with high-heeled shoes and gouges the floor. It is the small loading surface that results in large stress, and therefore it is critical.

The greatest stress a material can withstand is called the material's ultimate strength. Ultimate strength varies for most building materials under such loads as tension, compression, bending, and shear. Concrete, for example, has an ultimate compressive strength approximately ten times greater that its ultimate tensile strength. For practical purposes, the ultimate compressive strength is considered the material's ultimate strength. A similar condition exists for masonry, while steel exhibits the same ultimate strength in both compression and tension.

A material's elastic properties are important to consider when discussing load bearing capabilities. It is critical that the deformation of a bearing element under normal bearing conditions can be nullified after the bearing load is removed. Without this quality, which is called the material's elasticity, repeated loading would cause an ever-increasing deformation. The bearing element would, therefore, eventually collapse because of the build-up of deformation damage.

Whether or not the deformed body returns to its original form after the load is removed is determined by the capacity of the inner forces between the molecules comprising the material. As long as the molecular strength is not exceeded under loading, we can say that the material is within its elastic range. When the limit of elasticity is reached, some of the material's molecular connections will be broken. Some elements will then break in two; the binding of molecules is destroyed and cannot be repaired. This type of material is said to be a brittle material. Some examples are nonreinforced concrete and masonry.

In ductile materials, an overstepping of the limits of elasticity leads to movement of molecules to new positions and molecular connections remain in those positions. The material may still be permanently deformed, but it will remain whole, with nominal reduction of bearing capacity. An example of ductile materials is steel.

The overstepping of a material's limit of elasticity places it in a so-called plastic state. Molecular displacement also causes an increase in deformation without requiring an equal increase of the stresses.

The application of an axial tension load in an elastic material will cause deformation in the form of elongation. The relative elongation, elongation per unit of length, is called the strain:

$$\Delta L / L = \varepsilon \text{ where}$$
$$L = \text{the original length}$$
$$\Delta L = \text{the change in length}$$
$$\varepsilon = \text{strain as a result of the applied load}$$

The elongation will at the same time lead to

*The linear member acted on by tension force experiences elongation. Simultaneously the cross-sectional area is slightly reduced.*

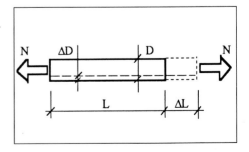

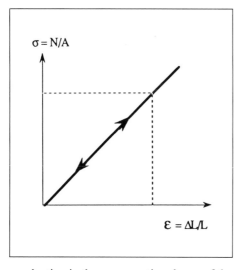

$$\sigma = N/A$$

$$\varepsilon = \Delta L/L$$

a reduction in the cross-sectional area of the material under tension:

$\Delta D/D = -n\varepsilon$ where
    $D =$ the original diameter,
    $\Delta D =$ the change in diameter, positive or negative
    $\varepsilon =$ the axial strain
    $n =$ the material constant, a numerical value for cross-sectional contractions or expansion

In practice, $\varepsilon$ will be so small that the reduction of the cross section is unimportant. Therefore it is assumed that the cross-sectional area will be the same, even after deformation along the longitudinal axis.

If we consider the relative elongation or the strain of the rod by the tension force N, we see that the magnitude of the strain is dependent on tension force N, the rod's cross section A, and the property of the material. If we can observe a direct correlation between $\varepsilon$ and N, it is said that the material in the rod is elastic. If the strain is proportional to the axial force in the rod, the material is said to be linearly elastic. We can then assume that the rod is minimally deformed. Additionally, we can further see that a larger cross-sectional area results in a smaller relative elongation and vice versa. The strain is therefore the inverse of the area of the cross section, A. We therefore have:

$$\Delta L/L = \varepsilon = 1/E \cdot N/A,$$

where E = the material constant: modulus of elasticity (N/mm$^2$) (psi) or Young's constant.

We can introduce the notion of stress in the previous formula and write:

$\varepsilon = \Delta L/L$ and $\varepsilon = \sigma \cdot 1/E$ (A positive $\varepsilon$ is related to elongation)

This equation is very important for a full understanding of the deformation of structural elements where loads are acting along one axis. We call the equation Hooke's law, named after Robert Hooke (1635-1703), the English mathematician and astronomer who formulated the stress/strain relationship in 1678.

We can graphically depict the relationship between stress and strain. A linear, elastic material will be represented as a straight line. The incline of the line is precisely the material's modulus of elasticity E:

$$E = \sigma/\varepsilon$$

A graphic depiction of the relationship between stress and strain of a material is called a working diagram. Hooke's law is valid for linear elastic materials and for the linear portion of the working diagram for other materials.

|  | E[N/mm$^2$] | n |
|---|---|---|
| STEEL | 210,000 | 0.3 |
| ALUMINUM | 70,000 | 0.25 |
| CONCRETE | 25,000 | 0.15 |
| WOOD | 10,000 |  |
| MATERIAL CONSTANTS (AVERAGE VALUES) | | |

*Typical working diagram for a few materials.*

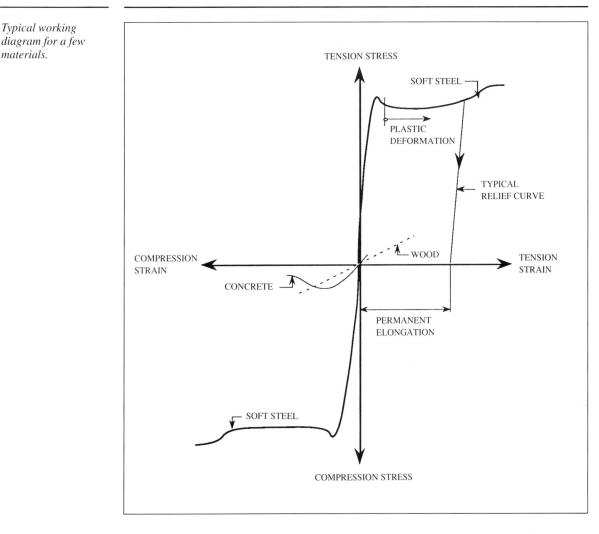

TENSION STRESS

SOFT STEEL

PLASTIC DEFORMATION

TYPICAL RELIEF CURVE

COMPRESSION STRAIN

WOOD

TENSION STRAIN

CONCRETE

PERMANENT ELONGATION

SOFT STEEL

COMPRESSION STRESS

## 3.4 A SYSTEM OF MEMBERS

The simplest roof truss we can imagine is a system of members that makes up a closed triangle. If a load is applied at the top of the triangle (ridge), the forces in the roof truss will either push, as in the angled top members, or pull, as in the horizontal bottom member.

For this to be correct, the following conditions are necessary:

• the load must be applied at the members' points of connection or joints

*Principle for simple roof truss with a ridge load.*

• the weight of the members themselves must be ignored (in practice this will be nearly achieved as long as the applied loads are decisively larger than the bearing system's own weight)

• the joints must be pin joints, that is to say the members must be able to rotate in relation to each other.

These three stipulations hinder the members of the roof truss from being acted on by moments (see also chapters 2 and 4). Because the forces are transferred through the system as axial forces, the members can be thinner and lighter than conventional bearing systems that must withstand bending moments. We call a structure of this type a planar truss.

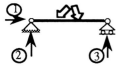

*Statically determinate beam: Three unknown load reactions.*

The truss is a system of axial members that are connected by pin joints and combined so that as a whole, they constitute a rigid structure. We will have a rigid truss if the members are combined to make triangles. Closed triangles result in rigid, form-holding elements, which are the basic components in a truss.

We shall concentrate on statically determinate trusses, that is, structures that can be analyzed with the help of the three laws of equilibrium (see chap. 2). A bearing system is externally statically determinate if there are as many unknown forces in the system as there are equilibrium equations. A sim-

ple beam supported at both ends by pin-joint connections is therefore statically determinate if the one support can transfer both horizontal and vertical loads while the other accepts horizontal movements but not vertical movement. The latter means that this support can only transfer vertical forces.

For the trusses we shall study, we must therefore require that they are externally statically determinate. Likewise, the new unknown axial forces in the members must be determined only by the use of the laws of equilibrium.

Let's take a look at a few examples. The three systems in the diagram are all externally statically determinate. In the first case, the system has four members that represent four unknown axial forces. These come in addition to the three unknown reactions, resulting in seven unknown forces. For each of the four joints, which are pin joints, we can formulate two laws of equilibrium, that is, equilibrium of forces in the horizontal and the vertical directions. With eight equations of equilibrium and seven unknown forces, the system is said to have one degree of freedom. We call such a system a mechanism, and this one could fall sideways under a minimal horizontal load.

If we call the total number of members in

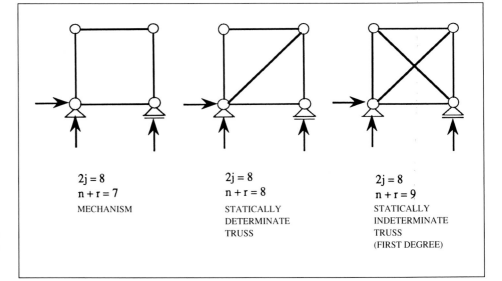

*Three structures formed by linear members: mechanism, statically determinate, and statically indeterminate truss.*

$2j = 8$
$n + r = 7$
MECHANISM

$2j = 8$
$n + r = 8$
STATICALLY DETERMINATE TRUSS

$2j = 8$
$n + r = 9$
STATICALLY INDETERMINATE TRUSS (FIRST DEGREE)

the system n and the total number of joints j, we have for this mechanism:

n = 4 and j = 4
total number of equations = 2j = 8
total number of unknowns = n + 3 = 7

In the next example, there is an extra member inserted, the diagonal member. We have the following:

n = 5 and j = 4
total number of equations = 2j = 8
total number of unknowns = n + 3 = 8
thus the system is statically determinate.

Finally, the system is braced with two crossing diagonal members. The final member gives an added unknown:

n = 6 and j = 4
total number of equations = 2j = 8
total number of unknowns = n + 3 = 9

We now have one unknown more than the total number of equations. The system is statically indeterminate to the first degree. Generally we call the total number of external reactions r. Thus, we can formulate the conditions for any truss to be statically determinate:

2j = n + r

If the total number of members, n, is less than 2j - r, we have a mechanism. If the total number of members is greater than 2j - r, the system is statically indeterminate.

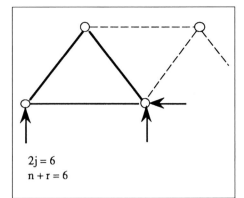

2j = 6
n + r = 6

The simplest statically determinate truss is also a triangle. From triangles, we can build statically determinate trusses. For each new joint we have two new equilibrium equations, and one new joint also requires two new members, that is, two unknown forces.

Let's now look at the joints, where the members meet. For a truss to act only in pure compression or tension, we have seen that the joints must be designed not to transfer bending moments. We call such joints hinged joints or pin joints. The background for this name can be traced back to the cast iron structures of the 1800s. With cast iron, it was simple to mold the members with holes in them at both ends, so that the problem of connection was solved by threading a bolt (a pin) through the holes at the overlapping of each member. In this way, a truly movable connection, a pin joint, was achieved.

Modern wooden and steel trusses use bolt connections with several bolts or welded

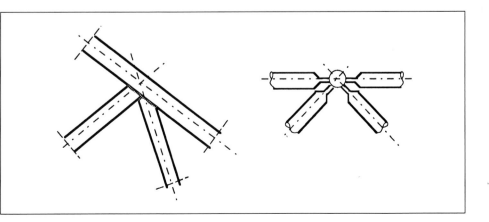

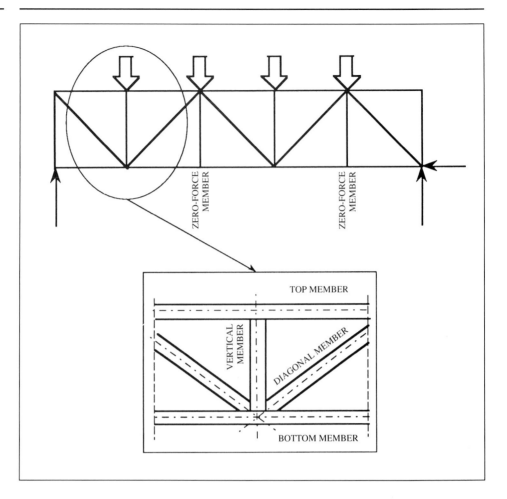

connections. The material of the member, however, is usually adequately flexible to achieve the required rotation. It must also be noted that the member's axes meeting in a joint also pass through the same point. In this way, bending moments due to distorted or eccentric forces will be avoided. Our line drawings of trusses represent the axis lines of the members in a system.

Trusses are described in fixed terms. The members that define the structural perimeter of trusses are called top and bottom members. In between are diagonal and vertical members.

In the diagrams above, there are two vertical members that meet the bottom member at a right angle. If these members carry compression forces from external loads, these forces will require the bottom member to act in bending. There is no possibili-

ty to transfer the load over to the bottom member as an axial load. However, the members of the trusswork by definition are thin because we suppose they are acted on only by axial forces. A lateral loading of the bottom member, from above, causes it to deflect and bend. Therefore, the external load is instead directed through the diagonal members, which will be stiff and not easily give way. This is because the magnitude of the axial deformation in diagonal members is generally less than bending deformation in the bottom member.

The vertical members described here are called zero-force members because they normally do not carry any loads. They still can be meaningful as visual elements or assist in holding a thin bottom member from deflecting due to its own weight. In addition, a zero member that under normal loading of a truss will not carry a force can

*The Eiffel Tower.*
*Robert Delaunay.*
*1926.*

become loaded if the deformation of the truss is excessive. Excessive downward bending may lead to a change in the angle between the zero-force member and the top and bottom members, resulting in the possible transfer of axial forces through zero members. Such a member can therefore be of structural significance in a sort of "secondary loading situation" or after the displacement of the second order, as it is called.

A truss that spans between two columns and is loaded with a vertical load acting downward will have a compression force in the top member and a tension force in the bottom. It can, in this case, be advantageous to use a spatial truss with a double top member. The compression force will then be divided between two members, and this means better resistance against lateral buckling.

If the bottom member experiences only tension forces under all loading conditions, it can take the form of a steel cable or wire, a structural element that cannot withstand compression forces. This, in combination

*Simply supported*
*truss with*
*compression along the*
*top member and*
*tension along the*
*bottom member.*

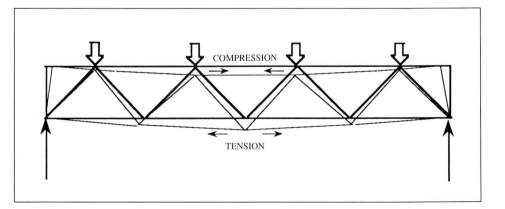

COMPRESSION

TENSION

with top members and vertical members in wood, is a commonly used marriage of materials in trusses.

Trusses can be planar or they can be spatial. Both types have a one-way span and enclose space, as trusswork does, by an additive repetition of equal structures.

The spatial truss has a horizontal cross section that stretches out in plan, contrary to the planar truss whose cross section is linear. The vertical cross section of a spatial truss has preferably a triangular form or a form that is comprised of rigid triangles.

A system of members with a two-way span will be a fully three-dimensional truss. It is called a space frame and is a structure that has the ability to withstand a load acting from any direction, dispersing it through the system of members.

Joints in space frames can have three possible translational directions: We can thus formulate three requirements for equilibrium that demand rigidity in the x, y, and z directions.

*Planar and spatial trusses.*
*Left: slab structure of planar trusses, planar beam, arch, and frame.*
*Right: space frame, spatial beam, arch, and frame.*

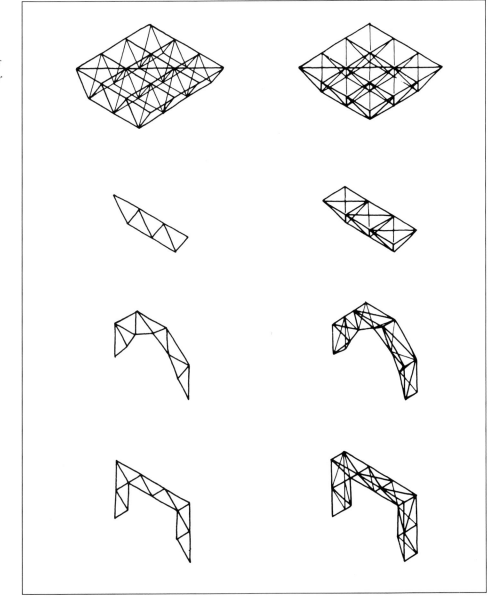

*Pompidou Center.*
*Model by architecture*
*students:*
*Guy Fehn and*
*Vegar Voraa.*

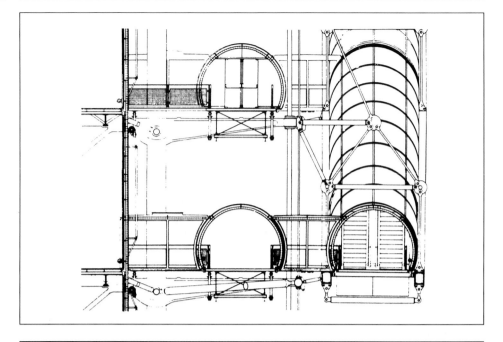

## 3.5 THE POMPIDOU CENTER

The Pompidou Center, with its library and collection of modern art, is one of a handful of monuments that we associate with Paris. In the same way as Notre Dame and the Eiffel Tower, the Pompidou Center protrudes up over the strictly zoned boulevards and cornice lines of building masses. It provides a vision and view over the city landscape. Each of the three buildings mentioned represents a high point and is possibly the culmination of its epoch in the art of building.

While the Eiffel Tower sums up the previous century's "iron age," the Pompidou Center, with an outstanding employment and demonstration of modern steel technology, is our modern hallmark. Common for the three monuments is the exposure of the structural assemblage. We remember them for their method of construction.

The Pompidou Center competition, with 681 contestants, was won by the architects Renzo Piano and Richard Rogers with the engineering firm Ove Arup & Partners. The grand opening of the center took place in 1976.

By concentrating the building mass on the rue de Renard, and by having the building reach higher than those of the other contestants, a public plaza could be built toward the west. The plaza at the Pompidou Center, which soon became the stage for genteel public life, slopes downward and is oriented toward the Pompidou Center. The concept is based on six column-free floors with a 48 x 166 meter (157 x 545 foot) footprint. In addition, a 6-meter-wide (20 foot) zone on each of the long sides functions as "structural thickness." The zone facing the public plaza contains vertical circulation—escalators and elevators—while the other side, toward rue de Renard, handles technical services.

The floors are carried by 3-meter-high (10 foot) trusses with an impressive span of 48 meters (157 feet). They are coupled to cantilevered arms, so-called gerberettes, named after the eighteenth-century German bridge builder Gerber. The gerberettes are threaded onto and fastened around steel columns that are held in balance with the help of tension rods connected to underground anchors.

Besides being a visual clarifier for the transmission of the horizontal and vertical elements, the gerberettes insure, in their outstretched balance, that the considerable load of the trusses is transferred down the center axis of the columns. Without this arrangement, the columns would be vulnerable to skewed loads and large bending moments.

The main structure is comprised of a limited number of elements: columns and stays, gerberettes, and lattice girders. An extensive use of cast steel, which in contrast to cast iron can withstand great tension loads, has made it possible to give structural details the correct form and precision.

The assembling of the elements was planned as a giant building set "produced off-site" and coupled together on-site. The 48-meter-long (157 foot) trusses were produced at Krupps Steelworks in Germany, sent on trains to Porte de la Chapelle at the outskirts of Paris, and towed by semitrucks with police escort to the building site at night.

The size and weight of the trusses are near their limits for this type of construction. With a span of over 50 meters (164 feet), the weight of steel required is so great that it would be natural to consider alternative structural forms.

*Pompidou Center. System sketch of trusses, load bearing column with the so-called gerberette, together with the prestressed stay.*

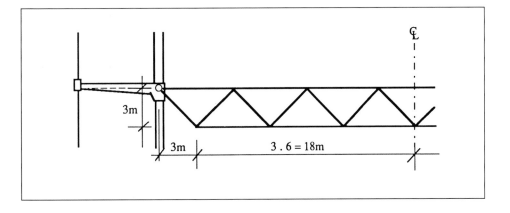

## 3.6 PIANO AND ROGERS

Let's take a closer look at the main bearing structure of this modern museum. Trusses make it possible to have a column-free span of over 40 meters (130 feet). In an architectural context, this is a relatively large structure. The most obvious advantage of the webbed system is that materials are placed exactly where there is the greatest need. The webbed system is open between the members: thus the structure is light and airy. The alternative of using a massive beam would result in a totally different architectural expression with a different distribution of forces. The benefit of openness and lightness, however, leads to the need for deeper structural dimensions.

There are several methods for determining which forces, either compression or tension, are present in each singular member in a truss and also the magnitude of the forces. One method is the so-called joint method, which requires equilibrium at each joint: The sum of all intersecting vectors of the axial forces at each connection must be equal to zero (see chap. 2).

In the 1800s the most commonly used method for lattice girder design was the graphic method (Cremona plan). Today, with calculators, personal computers, and large computers, numerical methods have completely taken over. The graphic method is as follows: Based on the member's direction, known forces can be drawn to a scale representing the magnitude of the force.

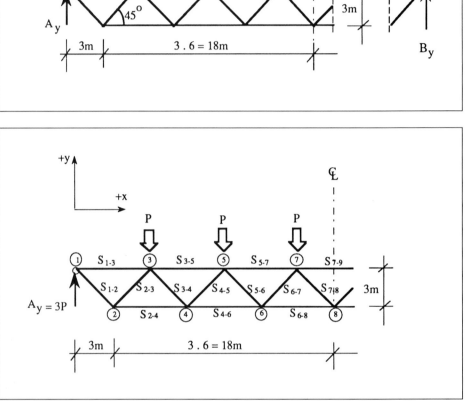

*Loading situation with concentrated loads on the joints.*

*Identification of the members and joints with letters and numbers.*

Unknown forces are found with their correct magnitudes in force polygons that must be closed in order to achieve equilibrium in the joint. The forces' directions for axial forces are concurrent with the direction of the members.

An effective alternative is the so-called section method. Here, we analyze directly the forces in desired members with the help of an imaginary section through the truss. The one or more forces acting in the section must maintain rotation and translation equilibrium with the external forces that act on the truss. The truss as a whole is then considered to be rigid and undeformable.

The truss of the Pompidou Center is statically determinate.

We count the total number of members and find the sum to be $n = 27$. The total number of unknowns is the sum of the member forces and the external reactions, $n + r = 27 + 3 = 30$. For the system to be statically determinate, the sum of the joint must be 15.

$$2j = 2 \cdot 15 = 30, \quad n + r = 30.$$

Since the truss is symmetrical, we can focus in and study only half of it. We assume that all loads are acting at the joints and that there are only vertical forces; therefore, we can conclude:

$$A_x = 0$$

For the sake of order, we assign names to the joints and vector forces: Joints 1 to 8

*Joint 1.*
*Forces on the joint.*

*Joint 2.*
*Forces on the joint.*

*Joint 3.*
*Forces on the joint.*

and vector forces $S_{1-2}$, $S_{1-3}$, etc.

Vertical equilibrium gives:

$\Sigma K_y = 0$, so that $A_y - 3P = 0$, $A_y = 3P$

We'll use the joint method first and begin by formulating equilibrium equations for the joints with the most known forces:

*Equilibrium in joint 1:*

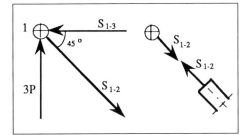

$\Sigma K_y = 0$, so that $3P - S_{1-2} \sin45° = 0$

$S_{1-2} \sin45° = 3P$

$S_{1-2} = 3P/0.71 = 4.24\ P$

We have a positive sign in our calculation. The direction of the force is therefore as indicated in the figure, so that the force in the member $S_{1-2}$ is a tension force. If you are not sure of this, you can solve the joint from the vector diagram as the figure shows:

The force pulling on the joint has a counter-force acting on the member. This tension force pulls on the member.

$\Sigma K_x = 0$, $S_{1-2} \cos45° - S_{1-3} = 0$

$4.24P \cdot 0.71 - S_{1-3} = 0$

$S_{1-3} = 3.00\ P$, compression, as expected.

*Equilibrium in joint 2:*

$\Sigma K_y = 0$, so that

$S_{1-2} \cos45° - S_{2-3} \sin45° = 0$

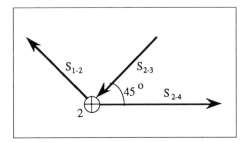

$S_{2-3} \sin45° = S_{1-2} \cos45° = 4.24P \cdot 0.71$

$S_{2-3} = 4.24\ P$, compression, as expected.

$\Sigma K_x = 0$, so that

$S_{2-4} - S_{1-2} \cos45° - S_{2-3} \cos45° = 0$

$S_{2-4} = 4.24\ P \cdot 0.71 + 4.24\ P \cdot 0.71 = 6.0\ P$, tension, as expected.

*Equilibrium in joint 3:*

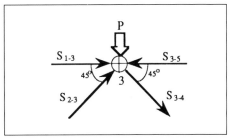

$\Sigma K_y = 0$, so that

$S_{2-3} \sin45° - S_{3-4} \sin45° - P = 0$

$S_{3-4} \sin45° = 4.24\ P \cdot 0.71 - P$

$S_{3-4} = 2.82\ P$, tension, as expected.

$\Sigma K_x = 0$, so that

$S_{1-3} + S_{2-3} \cos45° + S_{3-4} \cos45° - S_{3-5} = 0$

$S_{3-5} = 3.0\ P + 4.24\ P \cdot 0.71 + 2.82\ P \cdot 0.71 = 8.0\ P$, compression, as expected.

*Equilibrium in joint 4:*

$\Sigma K_y = 0$, so that

*Joint 4.*
*Forces on the joint.*

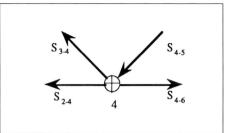

$$S_{3-4} \cos45° - S_{4-5} \cos45° = 0$$

$S_{4-5} = S_{3-4} = 2.82\ P$, compression, as expected.

$\Sigma K_x = 0$, so that

$$S_{4-6} - S_{2-4} - S_{3-4} \sin45° - S_{4-5} \sin45° = 0$$

$$S_{4-6} = S_{2-4} + S_{3-4} \cdot 0.71 + S_{4-5} \cdot 0.71$$

$$S_{4-6} = 6.0\ P + 2.82\ P \cdot 0.71 + 2.82\ P \cdot 0.71$$

$= 10.0\ P$, tension, as expected.

Now we can see a pattern in the path of the forces. The diagonal members alternate between compression and tension and the magnitude of the forces gets smaller as we move toward the middle of the truss. The magnitude of the force changes for every joint acted on by external loading. Further calculations, as those above, show that the diagonal members in the middle will not be under stress. The upper members will all experience compression forces and these forces will increase toward the middle of the truss. The lower members take up the tension forces that also increase toward the middle. At the middle of the span, the upper and lower members have equally large but oppositely directed forces.

The center line of the truss is a line of symmetry. The force diagram for the other half will be exactly the same as in the first half.

Now we can check the vector forces at the

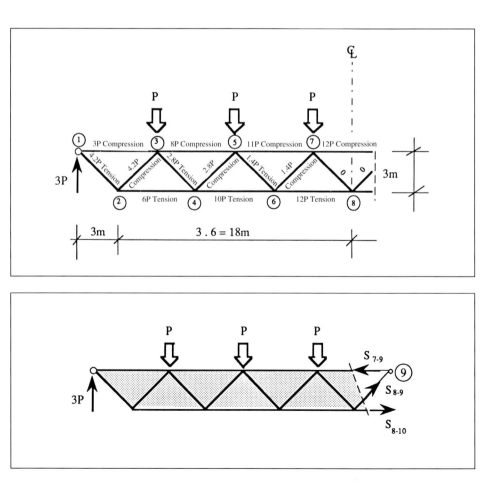

*Result of the force analysis. The line of symmetry for the truss is also the line of symmetry for the forces.*

*The section method considers the structure to the side of the section as a stiff plate and requires force and moment equilibrium for the entire plate.*

center. When we wish to find the forces in specific members of a truss, the section method is most practical. A section cut is made just to the right of the center line, and we cut through three members altogether. The rest of the construction is treated as an undeformable and rigid plate.

We must require that the construction as a whole does not rotate or move in its own plane. Rotation does not occur as long as the sum of the moments is equal to zero. To find $S_{8\text{-}10}$, it is advantageous to find the sum of the moments acting on joint 9.

$\Sigma M_9 = 0$, so that

$3\,P \cdot 24 - P \cdot 2 - P \cdot 6 - S_{8\text{-}10} \cdot 3 = 0$

$S_{8\text{-}10} = 3\,P \cdot 8 - P \cdot 4 - P \cdot 2 = 12\,P$, tension.

Vertical equilibrium results in:

$\Sigma K_y = 0$, so that

$3\,P - P - P - P + S_{8\text{-}9} \cos 45° = 0$.

$S_{8\text{-}9} = 0$

Horizontal equilibrium results in:

$\Sigma K_x = 0$, such that $S_{8\text{-}10} - S_{7\text{-}9} = 0$,

$S_{7\text{-}9} = S_{8\text{-}10} = 12\,P$, compression.

This confirms the use of the joint method. The section method is quick in examining, for example, top and bottom members, which often have maximum force along their center lines. $S_{7\text{-}9}$ and $S_{8\text{-}10}$ create a force pair with a moment arm equal to the depth of the truss (3 meters [10 feet]). They are the only forces acting in the midsection because the diagonal members are not under stress. The pair of forces gives the truss as a whole a bending moment, but each structural member is only affected by axial forces.

Let's look at the consequences that the present forces have on the design of the trusses. All of the members are circular in cross section, naturally fire protected, and jacketed in

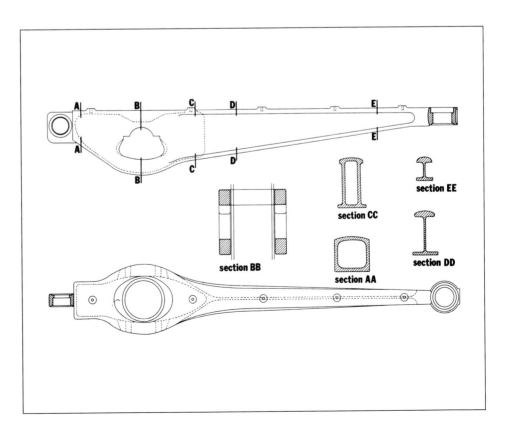

*Pompidou Center.*
*Paris.*
*Renzo Piano and*
*Richard Rogers.*

stainless steel. The top members have the greatest dimension, even though the compression forces are not greater than the tension forces in the bottom member. The same goes for the diagonal members under compression. This is done to prevent buckling problems that can develop in the compression members under large compression forces.

We can also observe that all of the members in compression have hollow circular cross sections, while all of the members in tension are solid. In a member under tension forces, we are able to utilize the strength of the material to it's full potential. Every square millimeter of material is used to withstand the tension force, and how the material is distributed around the axis of the member, is not crucial for bearing capacity.

Therefore we can concentrate all of the material in the center, in order to make the outer dimension as small as possible.

For compression members, it is different. The tendency for the material to buckle is reduced by pulling the material as far as possible from the center axis of the member in order to obtain the best results. Thus, the form with a hollow cross section is the most efficient.

The members are welded at the connection joints with the help of a transition element. This is done with cast steel, a steel with a high carbon content that makes it possible to melt the steel into a liquid state. In this state, the steel can be molded, and difficult geometries are easily formed.

*Hollow compression members and massive tension members. The compression members have the largest cross-sectional area.*

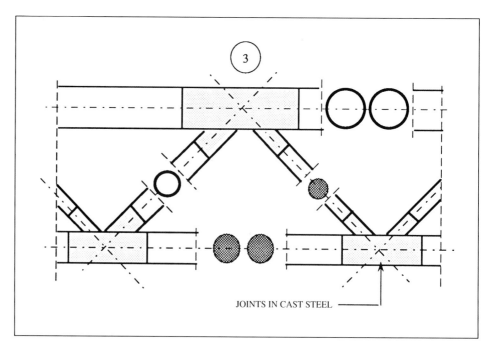

JOINTS IN CAST STEEL

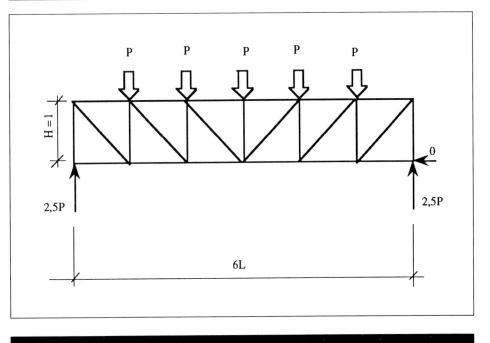

# 3.7 FORCE FOLLOWS FORM

The zigzag diagonals of the Pompidou Center, with their alternating tension and compression forces, can help us understand two other quite ordinary forms of trusses.

Look at a truss with interchanging diagonal and vertical members where the two outer diagonal members are not directly connected to the support. The diagonal members slant in the same direction until the center line of the truss, where they "turn."

This truss can be loaded either from the top or the bottom depending on the position of the roof. The truss contains 28 unknowns and has 14 connection joints, and therefore

it can be resolved with the help of the laws of equilibrium. Use of the section method can tell us the types of forces in the individual diagonal members.

$\Sigma K_y = 0$, so that

$2.5\,P - P - S_D \cos 45° = 0$

$S_D = 1.5\,P/\cos 45° = 2.12\,P$, tension.

It is important to recognize that the diagonal members are subjected to tension force. If we examine the truss to the right of its center line, we find the force in the diagonal member slanting in the opposite direction:

$\Sigma K_y = 0$, so that

$2.5\,P - P - P - S_D \cos 45° = 0$

$S_D = 0.71\,P$, tension.

The effect of letting the angle of the diagonal members slant in opposite directions on each side of the center line is that the members then have the same type of force, which in this case is tension. We will also see this in a direct consideration of symmetry.

*Detail of the truss. Seeking the equilibrium of forces produces the member forces.*

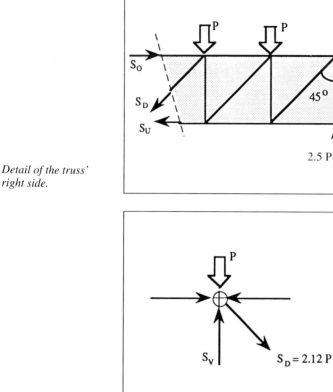

*Detail of the truss' right side.*

*Joint on the truss' left side.*

A study of the equilibrium of the joints with external loading will provide the answer to the force in the vertical members:

$\Sigma K_y = 0$, so that

$S_V - P - S_D \cos 45° = 0$

$S_V = P + 2.12P \cos 45° = 2.50\ P$, compression.

The vertical members are, in other words, always in compression.

We have, in the next truss, rotated the direction of the diagonal members. We can examine section A:

$\Sigma K_y = 0$, so that

$2.5P - P - S_D \cos 45° = 0$

$S_D = 1.5P/\cos 45° = 2.12P$, compression.

For joint B:

$\Sigma K_y = 0$, so that

$2.12\ P \cos 45° - P - S_V = 0$

$S_V = 1.5\ P - P = 0.5\ P$, tension.

The effect of turning the diagonal members' direction is that they will be under compression force while the vertical members are under tension force.

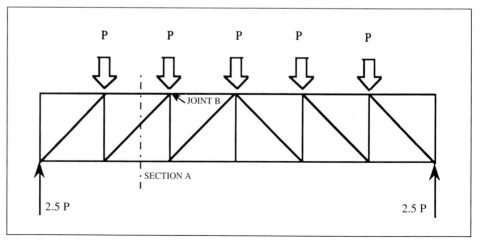

*Truss with alternating vertical and diagonal members.*
*The diagonal members meet the supports.*

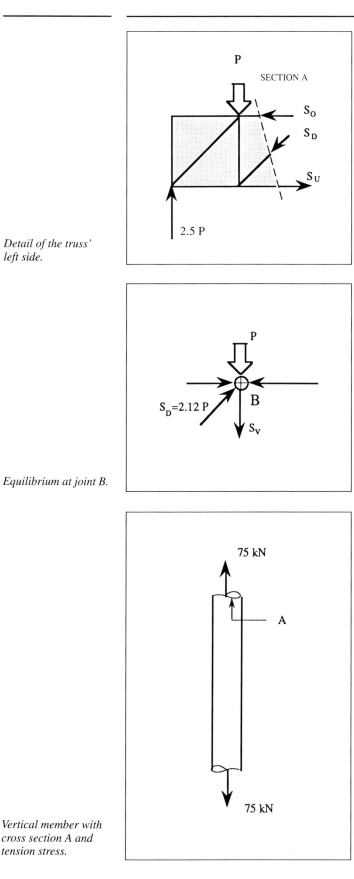

*Detail of the truss' left side.*

*Equilibrium at joint B.*

*Vertical member with cross section A and tension stress.*

Theoretically, we can surmise, for the last truss, that the diagonal members will be thicker than in the first design, even though the load and the width of the span are equally large. The reason is that the compression force can cause buckling. Since the diagonal members are longer than the vertical members, the diagonal members under compression will require a larger cross section than the vertical under compression force. This will require a greater amount of material in the construction of the last truss.

The principle for determining the dimensions of a member in a truss can be found by limiting ourselves to the simplest members, namely, tension members. Let's look at the last vertical member we sketched before. We found:

$S_V = 0.5$ P, under tension force.

If P is the weight of the roof structure and snow loads acting on the joints, we can say:

P = 150 kN (667 kips), so that $S_V$ = 75kN (333.5 kips)

The stress in the member will be:

$\sigma_s = S_V/A = 75$kN/A, tension stress,

where A = the members cross-sectional area.

The truss is built in steel. The greatest tension stress this steel quality withstands, its ultimate strength, can be said to be:

$f_{sd} = 200$N/mm$^2$ (29,000 psi)

We require that the acting tension stress, $\sigma_s$, shall be less than the ultimate strength, $f_{sd}$:

$\sigma_s = 75000$N/A $< f_{sd} = 200$N/mm$^2$

A > 75000N/200N/mm$^2$ = 375 mm$^2$

The member's cross section must, in other words, have a minimum cross-sectional

*Hollow circular cross section in steel. Two profiles that have different diameters and wall thickness but the same cross-sectional area.*

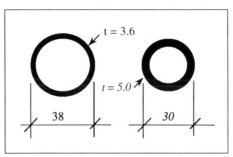

area of 375 mm$^2$ (0.6 in$^2$).

For a circular solid member we have:

$$A = \pi r^2 = 375 \text{ mm}^2$$

$$r = \sqrt{375/3.14} = 11 \text{ mm}$$

It is more common to use hollow cross sections. Steel tables can give information on circular hollow sections. We are searching for a cross section that has the desired area and we can use the following examples:

$30 \cdot 5$ mm with an area = 393 mm$^2$

$38 \cdot 3.6$ mm with an area = 389 mm$^2$

*Exhibition Pavillion for IBM. 1982. Architect: Renzo Piano. Arched trusses without linear members. The trusses are established using pyramids of polyethylene. The edges of the pyramids have the required stiffness and function as members.*

The dimensioning of the compression members is accomplished in a similar way. The difference is that the steel's ultimate strength cannot be fully utilized owing to the danger of buckling. Therefore, a reduced ultimate strength and the buckling stress must be calculated on the basis of the compression member's length and the shape of the cross section.

# 3.8 A Turning Point in Building

Konrad Wachsmann (1901-1981) contributed considerably to the development of industrial building processes, both as an educator and as a catalyst of research projects.

His career parallels that of other great architectural personalities, such as Walter Gropius and Ludwig Mies van der Rohe. Wachsmann was born in Germany and emigrated to United States in the late 1930s.

A research project for the U.S. Air Force led to his most meaningful work, the development of a structural system for large hangars. In contrast to Pier Luigi Nervi's famous hangar with a concrete skeleton, Wachsmann's choice of material was steel. The goal for the development work, which was done at the Chicago Institute of Design in the latter part of the 1950s, was a building system for long spans and cantilevers based on the use of standard elements of minimal variation.

He chose a space-frame system based on addition of tetrahedrons, pyramids with a rectangular base. Because the triangles are rigid, there is no need for rigid joints.

The space frame was already known through Alexander Graham Bell's experiments, but it was Wachsmann who first used the system in an architectural setting.

The practical problem with the use of the space-frame system lies in finding an effective joint. The solution, in this case, was a spherical joint in chromium steel that could take up to 20 steel pipe members. Connection was achieved by using a simple wedge principle where the wedges were pounded in place with a hammer.

The space frame rested on a number of stable polygons with the same construction as the roof. The projects carried the message of a new architecture with a free dynamic space of, at that time, unknown dimensions and lightness.

This kind of structure is best suited for use in a great hall. The nature of the space frame is based on an uncompromised geometric principle for order, with clear game rules for the addition of secondary building parts as roof, facades, and installations. Only the most capable of architects can understand and master this game.

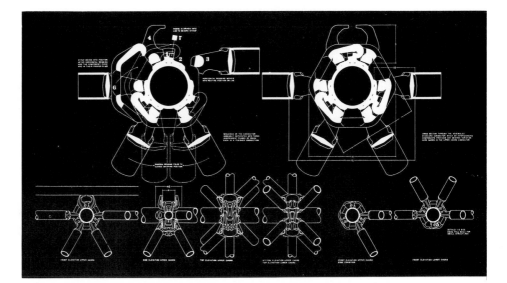

*Konrad Wachsmann.*
*Project for a hangar.*
*1959.*
*Typical joints.*

*Konrad Wachsmann.*
*Project for a hangar.*
*Model photographs.*

# Chapter 4 THE BEAM

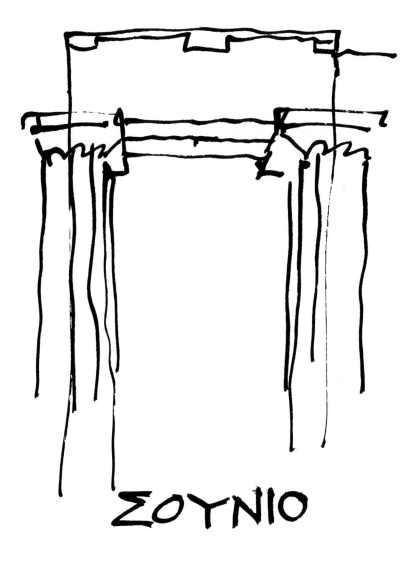

*The Temple of
Poseidon.
Sunion, Greece.
5th century B.C.*

ΣΟΥΝΙΟ

*Stonehenge, England.
1000-1400 B.C.*

## 4.1 THE PREHISTORIC BEAM

It is reasonable to assume that the beam was the first bearing element. In a prehistoric rain forest, a fallen tree may have coincidentally made it possible to cross a river. A beam resting on two columns is the simplest port or space marker; it represents the beginnings of architecture. A lintel with two supports can serve universal existential needs.

The beam/columns concept characterizes two buildings of monumental character, Stonehenge in England and the so-called valley temple, the middle-most of the pyramids at Giza in Egypt. The building material is stone, other materials crumble away over the centuries, or at best, are discovered as fragments in excavations.

The structures display an almost absurd massiveness. The stone beam's dimensions are overwhelming, taking into account the span. This expresses the beams' underlying problem, which will be discussed later.

Stonehenge is a cult building site at Salisbury in England. The complex, which is comprised of concentric circles of rock formations, was built in phases around 1000 to 1400 B.C. Construction and orientation make it reasonable to assume that the site was used for worshipping the sun and for astronomical calculations in connection with the changing of the seasons and farming. The innermost ring is marked by sandstone "dolmens" of enormous dimensions. The supports, which extend 6.5 meters (21 feet) into the air, are partially buried and weigh over 40 metric tons (39.3 tons). The stones are roughly carved and portray much of their natural stone character. The dolmen stands by virtue of its immovable weight.

*Pharaoh Chefren's
valley temple.
Giza, Egypt.
Ca. 2400 B.C.
Processional
entrance.*

*Bård Breivik. Pylon.*
*1986.*

In Pharaoh Chefren's valley temple in Giza, from ca. 2400 B.C., we find a processional passage of sandstone monoliths. In keeping with the Egyptians' preference for clear basic forms, this is a column/beam/slab structure with precisely cut elements. In defiance of the dimensions and mysteries of the pharaoh's tomb complex, this passage has the air of a set of reliably simple building blocks.

The Norwegian sculptor Bård Breivik's (born 1941) work from 1986 captures the column/beam theme in an interesting way. The material is black granite with an exciting contrast between the roughly carved profile and the polished sides. The sculpture, which evokes many associations, shows that the theme is universal without being connected to epoch or place.

"Great-stone atmospheres" was historian H. P. Lorange's characterization of the atmosphere around such rock structures.

# 4.2 THE TROUBLE WITH BEAMS

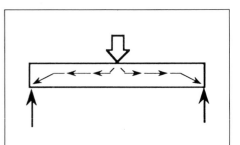

*The flow of forces in the beam are perpendicular to the direction of the load.*

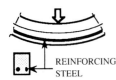

*Principle for reinforcing a concrete beam.*
*Reinforcing steel, which easily withstands tension forces, is placed on the tension side of the beam, but the concrete itself withstands the compression forces.*

*Graphic illustration of the variation in force from the top side to the bottom side of a beam consisting of a linear, elastic material.*

*An effective cross section in a beam is achieved by "moving" the material from the middle section to the top and bottom sides.*

*Examples of I-shapes in steel, concrete, and wood.*

The task of the beam is to bear the load perpendicular to the load's direction, and it is actually quite a difficult task since it deals with bending. Bending creates, from the start, the main problem with beams, the inefficient utilization of the material.

Let's imagine a beam with a compact, rectangular cross section of a malleable material. A point load at its center introduces downward bending in the beam. The beam has a deformation that is greatest under the load. The fibers of the material experience tension owing to elongation along the underside. In the upper surface of the beam, the contractions increase as the fibers of the material experience compression. The material fibers of the middle region experience little stress, and the stress is equal to zero at the center line of the beam. The axis that is unaffected by tension or compression stress is called the neutral axis. The neutral axis lies in the beam's center of gravity, which generally coincides with the centroid of the beam's cross section if the cross section is uniform in geometry and if the beam's material is uniform in quality throughout the cross section. Steel is such a material.

Around the neutral axis, the material is barely active, and therefore we can remove as much material as possible from that region and move it to the over and underside where it can be put to better use. In this way, the beam has enormous bearing capacity but the same amount of material. The design of such a beam (for example, the I-beam) is well known and can be made in different materials, such as steel, concrete, and wood. There are limits to the amount of material that we can remove from the midregion. The top and bottom flanges of the beam must be connected in order for it to work. Even though the midsection of the beam, the web, takes up little of the bending forces, it is decisive in the beam's ability to withstand lateral forces or shear forces.

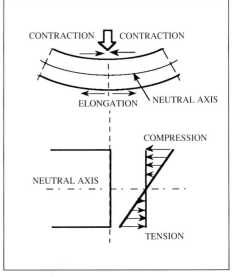

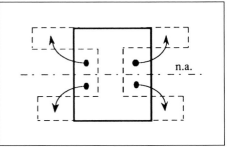

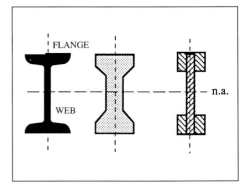

*The comparison between expanding spans and decreasing bearing capacity in beams, by Leonardo da Vinci.*

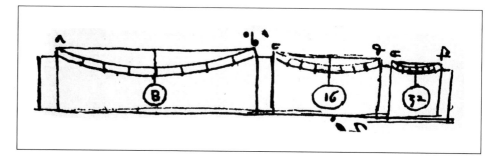

*Perpendicular cross sections of the beam will also be perpendicular after the beam is bent.*

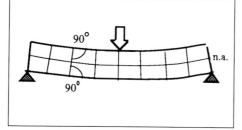

Let's take a closer look at the reactions of beams under bending. To understand this process better, we can draw evenly spaced vertical lines along the length of the beam. The contraction of the beam's top side and elongation of the bottom side reveals that the distance between the vertical lines will be respectively smaller and larger with the bending of the beam. Along the neutral axis the distance between the lines will remain equal. Contraction and elongation are directly associated with compression and tension stresses. Where the fibers are inactive, along the neutral axis, no force is present.

Furthermore, we can note that the vertical lines along the beam that represent the theoretical sections through the beam, are straight and perpendicular to the top and

bottom of the beam even though the beam is bent. This realization is very important in understanding why beams bend.

Leonardo da Vinci (1452-1519) was aware of this but Galileo worked on the problem and presented the first but incorrect conclusion in 1638 (*Due Nouve Scienze*).

It was the Frenchman Louis Marie Navier (1785-1836) who corrected Galileo's error and published the first correct solution for bending in beams in 1826. He based his theories on the assumption, "planar sections will remain planar" under bending. This assumption is called Navier's hypothesis. Later it was proven that this hypothesis was true for all structural materials. All specifications in physics and mathematics concerning what actually transpires under the bending of a beam are based on Navier's hypothesis.

Study what happens to the beam after deformation. At any section, we find that the upper half of the beam is exposed to compression and condensed, while the lower half is under tension and will be elongated. The compression and tension forces

*Strain ($\varepsilon$) and stress ($\sigma$) in the cross section of a beam vulnerable to bending moments. Linear elastic material.*

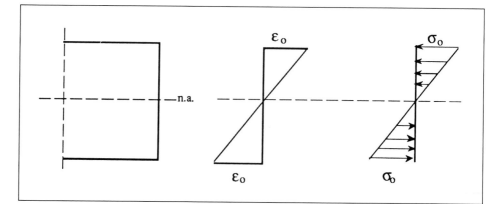

in a cross section act in square units as compression and tension stresses.

We know that Hooke's law shows the correlation between stress and the resulting deformation for linear, elastic materials. There is also a straight line correlation between force per square unit in a cross section and a beam's relative change in length. Since Navier's calculations concluded that deformation was linear through the section ("planar sections will remain planar"), the stresses for such materials also are divided by straight lines.

Stresses are at their highest level at the top and bottom sides of a beam, which, respective to compression and tension, have equal values in a symmetrical cross section.

Let's study the effects of the stresses in a cross section of, for example, a rectangular laminated wood beam with depth h and width b. The volume of the stresses on the compression and tension sides represents the respective forces that are equally large but oppositely directed: a force pair. The force pair creates an internal moment with a magnitude as follows:

$$M_i = C \cdot a = T \cdot a$$

where a is the distance between the forces:

$$a = h - 2 \cdot 1/3 \cdot h/2 = h - h/3 = 2h/3$$

The forces will be equal to the volume of the stress triangles:

$$T = C = 1/2 \cdot \sigma_0 \cdot h/2 \cdot b = \sigma_0 b \cdot h/4$$

So that:

$$M_i = \sigma_0 \cdot b \cdot h/4 \cdot a = \sigma_0 \cdot b \cdot h/4 \cdot 2/3h = \sigma_0 \cdot b \cdot h^2/6$$

We see that the internal moment is proportional to the stresses in the outermost fibers. The constant of the proportioning is only dependent on the dimensions of the cross section. The constant is called the cross section's resisting moment W ($mm^3$) ($in^3$), and for a rectangular cross section, the constant is equal to $bh^2/6$ as follows:

$$M_i = \sigma_0 \cdot W$$

For H- and I-formed steel profiles, we can quickly find the approximate expression for W. We estimate that the thickness of the flange is minimal in relation to the depth of the cross section and that all of the compression and tension forces are contained in the flanges. The width of the flanges is equal to b. We seek to resolve the internal moment:

$$M_i = T \cdot a = C \cdot a$$

$$M_i = \sigma_0 \cdot b \cdot t(h - 2t/2)$$

$$M_i = \sigma_0 \cdot b \cdot t(h - t)$$

The approximate resisting moment, W, for such cross sections will be:

$$W = b \cdot h \cdot t - b \cdot t^2$$

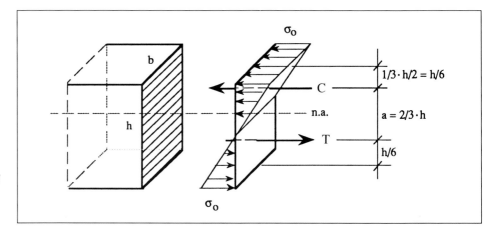

*Disposition of bending stresses through a rectangular cross section.*

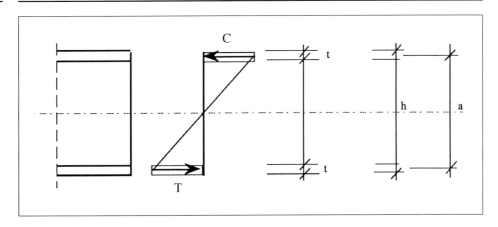

*To find H and I beams resisting moments (force pair), the compression and tension forces are assumed to be compiled in the top and bottom flanges. The force arm is the distance between the forces.*

The resisting moments for all normal cross sections of structural materials are found listed in their respective tables. Here we have found the resisting moments for symmetrical cross sections. If the cross section is not symmetrical, the neutral axis will not go through the centroid of the cross section, as the center of gravity has moved. With that, the compression and tension stresses will be of different magnitudes. This means that again we must assign a resisting moment to the upper element and one to the lower element.

If we have an asymmetrical cross section or frequently wish to find the relationship between moment and stress at a given point in the cross section of a beam (until now we have examined the commonly strained outer fibers), we see that resisting moment (W) is proportionally opposite to the distance (y) from the neutral axis, so that W = I/y.

This new constant I $(mm^4)$ $(in^4)$ is called the cross section's moment of inertia. This is an absolute value for the cross section and is normally calculated from the center of the gravitational axis. We find that:

$$M_i = \sigma_y \cdot I/y$$

which represents the relationship between moment and stress at any distance from the neutral axis. I and W are designated in the same way in the profile tables.

In a symmetrical cross section with a depth h and set y = h/2 in the expression, we again have the relationship between M and s, where the stress is acting on the upper and lower edge of the beam.

$$M_i = \sigma_y \cdot I/(h/2) = \sigma_o \cdot W$$

What is the reason for wanting to look at the inner moments in a cross section of a

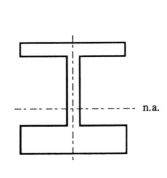

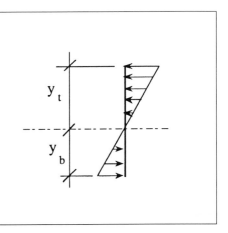

*In an asymmetrical cross section the neutral axis is moved from the center axis. The stresses will be different in magnitude on the compression and tension sides.*

*Fixed beam with a simple load.*

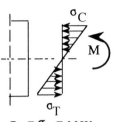

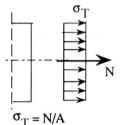

$$\sigma_T = \sigma_C = M/W$$

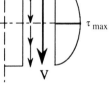

$$\sigma_T = N/A$$

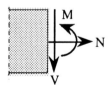

$$\tau_{max} = 3V/2A$$

*Stresses in a section of a rectangular beam. A is the cross-sectional area. W is the moment of resistance.*

*Three general force reactions in a cross section of a beam.*

*Distribution and magnitude of shear stresses in an H section.*

beam or of other structural elements that are susceptible to bending? In chapter 2 we saw that the cantilevering beam was acted on by a moment that in stress was equal to the magnitude of a point load multiplied by the distance of that load from the wall. This is the outer moment, which must be counteracted by the inner moment so that equilibrium can be maintained.

In chapter 2 we also studied the internal moment in a cross section in general terms. The information above shows us that the requirement for equilibrium between external and internal moments allows us to find which stresses the load places on the material. This is essential in choosing dimensions and ensuring that the bearing capabilities of material and size are not exceeded. Thus:

$$M_{ext} = M_{int} = \sigma \cdot W$$

In the next section, we shall make it clear that bending moments from an external force can be found along the entire length of a beam. We need these in order to find the magnitude of the stresses in the entire bearing element. When we understand the properties of structural materials (how great a force a material can withstand), we can finally determine the beam's form both in length and cross section.

We shall now focus on how the shear force produces stress in a cross section. We call to mind again the cantilevered beam from chapter 2. To satisfy the requirements for the sum of the forces acting in a vertical axis to be equal to zero, there must be a force from the wall acting on the beam that is equal in magnitude to the external load but in the opposite direction. This transverse force is called shear force. Generally, in a section of a beam or other structural elements vulnerable to bending, three magnitudes of force are present:

• bending moment M (symbolized by a curving arrow indicating the direction of the pair of forces)

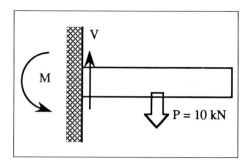

• normal force N (which results in either compression or tension)

• shear force V (which has a transverse action in a cross section)

The bending moment has the same, normal compression and tension stresses (bending stresses) in cross section. Axial forces also have the same, normal stresses in cross section, but shear forces in the area of the section result in forces parallel to the face of the section. Shear is indicated by the Greek letter $\tau$.

Shear spreads itself over the section's face in a parabolic shape. It has its greatest magnitude at the neutral axis and is always equal to zero at the top and bottom edges. In a rectangular cross section with the depth h and width w we have:

$$\tau_{max} = 3V/2bh \ (N/mm^2) \ (psi)$$

where V is the magnitude of the shear force.

For I and H profiles, the transition between web and flanges will result in a large jump in the shear force's magnitude, because stress is inversely proportional to the width of the cross section. Because the width of

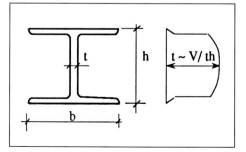

*The shear force as it acts on an infinitely small element in the beam subjected to bending. The vertical shear force must be in translational equilibrium with the load. The horizontal shear force will prevent the element from twisting. Together, the shear forces impose on the small element compression and tension forces along the diagonal.*

*Top: The tendency for fracturing of the beam from vertical shear stress.*
*Bottom: The tendency for fracturing in the beam from horizontal shear stress.*

the flange is much larger than the thickness of the web, the shear stresses in the web will be much greater than in the flanges. That is, shear stress will be resisted by or taken up in the web. The bending moment, in contrast, will be taken up by the pair forces in the flanges.

A small element is cut out of a cantilevering beam (see diagram). First we note that a shear force is required to achieve vertical equilibrium of the element that has an external, vertical load. But together these forces create a force pair that tries to rotate the element. To counterbalance the rotation, two forces that are rotating in opposite directions must be found. They are shear reactions that are acting along the length of the beam. In a beam with bending moments, shear force and shear stresses act both vertically and horizontally.

At the corner of the extracted section, the shear forces will combine two by two and cause tension or compression loading on the element along its diagonals. In other words, this means that shear forces structurally are the same, with their tension and compression normally acting on each other at a 45° angle to the direction of the shear force.

The following example shows clearly that the shear force has a horizontal component in cross section that is vulnerable to bending.

Lay two planks on top of each other and let them span freely between two supports. With a drill, bore holes through both of the planks, not too far from the supports. Stick a pencil halfway into the hole and have a colleague sit on the planks. The pencil will break or try to break as the two planks slide away from one another, showing the effect of the horizontal shear forces created by the bending of the planks.

Up to now, we have noted that bending stresses result when the beam is loaded and bending downward. As Hooke's law shows, the bending stresses and material's elongation with downward bending are related and are dependent on each other

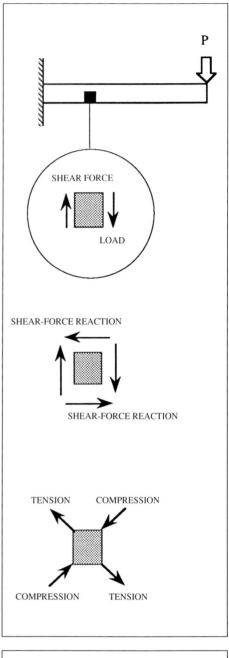

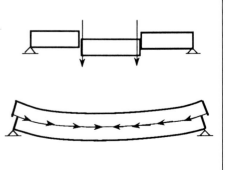

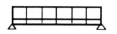
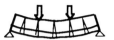
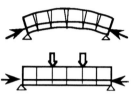

*Top: Reinforced beam, unloaded and with an external load.*
*Bottom: Prestressed beam, unloaded and with an external load. The prestressing can eliminate tension stresses and reduce deflection.*

and on the beam's stiffness (S). The principle of stiffness is mechanically defined in the fraction:

$S = E \cdot I/L$ where
    E is the material's modulus of elasticity $(N/mm^2)$ (psi)
    I is the cross section's moment of inertia $(mm^4)$ $(in^4)$
    L is the beam's length (mm) (in)

Intuitively, we can say that a beam with little downward bending, resulting from a known load, is stiffer than a beam with great downward bending from the same load. We assume that they have the same length. The beams have either different cross sections (I different), different elasticities (E different) or both. In case E and I are equal for the two beams but the length of the beams varies, we will find that the shortest beam will be stiffer under loading. The stiffness is inversely proportional to the length. The shortest beam has the least downward bending.

Therefore, the amount of downward bend-

ing is inversely proportional to the stiffness. The greater the stiffness, the smaller the downward bending. We call the amount of downward bending d (mm) (in). Thus:

$\delta_{max} = k \cdot M_{max} \cdot L/S$
$= k \cdot M_{max} \cdot L^2/EI$ where
    M is the beam's largest moment
    L is the beam's length
    S is the stiffness
    k is the constant dependent on the load's form and the beam's makeup.

As an example, the bending at the end of a cantilevering beam with a concentrated load will be:

$\delta_{max} = 1/3 \cdot M_{max} \cdot L^2/EI$, and since

$M_{max} = P \cdot L$, we have

$\delta_{max} = 1/3 \cdot P \cdot L^3/EI$.

Now we shall go on with the principals for finding bending moments in a beam exposed to different loads.

*The development of the cast-iron beam and its form up until ca. 1800.*
*Much of the material is located in the lower region where it normally is under tension.*
*The reason for this is cast iron's low tensile strength in relation to compression strength.*

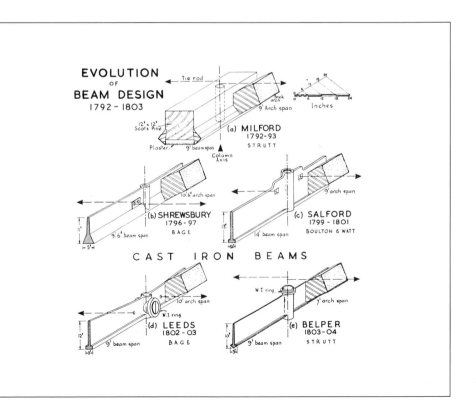

## 4.3 MOMENT AND SHEAR DIAGRAMS

*Galileo found that the
moment of resistance
for a rectangular
beam was $W = bh^2/2$
and not $bh^2/6$ as we
have found. The
problem with Galileo's
formula was that he
believed the bending
in the beam acted
about the bottom side
and not about the
neutral axis.*

Even though Galileo's conclusion for general bending in a beam was not correct, he still had some answers correct. In his studies of the cantilevered beam, he came forward with the correct expression for the magnitude of the bending moment. Later studies were interpreted in conjunction with Galileo's cantilever. At the end of the 1600s, the Frenchman Edné Mariotte determined the relationship between the bearing capacity in a cantilevering beam and in a simple beam based on experimentation. Only after Navier could such beams and other statically determinate beams be treated theoretically.

A simple beam is one supported at both ends and free to rotate under loading. This

general support condition is called a joint or bearing joint. Under this condition force pairs are not possible at the transition point between the beam and supports. A simple beam, with bearing joints at both ends, could not have bending moments at its end points. No matter what type of load, the moment, at the ends, will be equal to zero.

We can study a simple beam with bearing joints and a span equal to L. The beam has a distributed load q (kN/m) (kips/ft). In addition, both ends of the beam can rotate and one end slides freely in the same direction as the length of the beam. The other end is fastened against vertical and horizontal translation of forces and therefore can develop reactions in both directions against eventual loads. The floating bearing joint can withstand just forces in the vertical direction. Therefore, there can be just three unknown reactions acting on the beam when it is loaded. The beam, as specified, is statically determinate, since we have just as many equilibrium equations as unknown reactions.

*A simply supported
beam with a uniformly
distributed load.
Three unknown force
reactions make the
beam statically
determinate.*

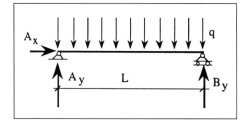

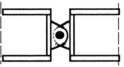

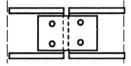

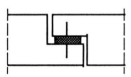

*Pin joints in beams. Top: Hinged joint. Middle: Plate joint without the flanges being joined, that is, the connection is unable to transfer moments. Bottom: Console for a concrete beam.*

Equilibrium equations give:

$\Sigma M_A = 0$, which says that

$q \cdot L \cdot L/2 - B_y \cdot L = 0$

$B_y = q \cdot L/2$

$\Sigma K_y = 0$, which says that

$A_y + B_y - q \cdot L = 0$

$A_y = q \cdot L - q \cdot L/2 = q \cdot L/2$

The vertical reactions will be equal because of symmetry. Together they act against the external load.

$\Sigma K_x = 0$, so that $A_x = 0$

The distribution of forces has now been found. Generally, in a section of the beam, one can find bending moments, shear force, and axial force. We examine a section with distance x:

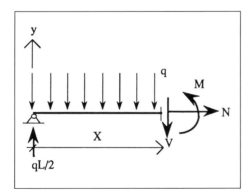

*In a section, with the distance x from the support, we can have both moment, shear, and normal forces.*

$\Sigma M_{section} = 0$, which says that

$q \cdot L/2 \cdot x - q \cdot x \cdot x/2 - M = 0$

$M = q \cdot L/2 \cdot x - q \cdot x^2/2 = (L - x) \cdot q \cdot x/2$

Here we find an expression for the moment and its variation in the long axis. It is a general equation for a parabola, since X appears in both first and second powers.

*Moment diagram for the simply supported beam with a uniformly distributed linear load.*

By placing x at determined points in the beam, we can find the value of the bending moments along the length of the beam:

| X | M | |
|---|---|---|
| 0 | 0 | |
| L/4 | $q \cdot L/8 \cdot (L - L/4)$ | $= 3q \cdot L^2/32$ |
| L/2 | $q \cdot L/4 \cdot (L - L/2)$ | $= q \cdot L^2/8$ |
| 3L/4 | $3q \cdot L/8 \cdot (L - 3L/4)$ | $= 3q \cdot L^2/32$ |
| L | 0 | |

The diagram is drawn in relation to the length of the beam:

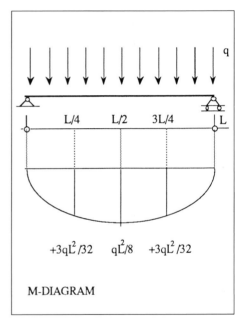

$+3qL^2/32 \quad qL^2/8 \quad +3qL^2/32$

M-DIAGRAM

We have now found the simple beam's moment diagram for uniformly distributed loads. With help of this diagram, the bending moments can be read for any beam point along the length of the beam, and with that, the bending stresses for the material are also given. Furthermore:

$\Sigma K_x = 0$, so that $N = 0$ and

$\Sigma K_y = 0$, so that $q \cdot L/2 - q \cdot x - V = 0$

$V = q \cdot L/2 - q \cdot x = q \cdot (L/2 - x)$

This is the variation of the shear forces along the beam. Since x exists just in the first power, the equation describes a

*Shear diagram for the simply supported beam with a uniformly distributed linear load.*

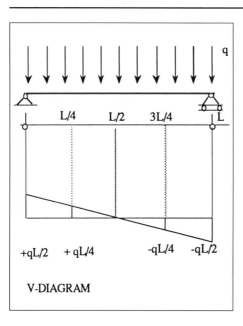

**V-DIAGRAM**

straight line. The variation will be:

| X | V | |
|-----|---------------------|---------|
| 0 | $q \cdot L/2$ | |
| L/4 | $q \cdot (L/2 - L/4)$ | $= qL/4$ |
| L/2 | 0 | |
| 3L/4 | $q \cdot (L/2 - 3L/4)$ | $= -qL/4$ |
| L | $q \cdot (L/2 - L)$ | $= -qL/2$ |

When drawn in the form of a diagram for the length of the beam, we have the beam's shear force diagram.

We note that the shear force has its highest value at the end points, where the moments are equal to zero. The shear force itself is equal to zero at the center of the beam where the moment has its highest value. The interdependence between M and V is generally valid for simple beams, regardless of the magnitude or the direction of the load. Moreover, the expression for the variation in shear forces with x is always one power lower than the expression of moment. This means that if the moment diagram has a parabola form, the shear diagram is a straight line. With a straight line moment diagram, the shear diagram is constant.

*Identification of positive section forces:*
*Positive moments result in tension along the lower half of the beam.*
*Positive shear forces attempt to turn the beam clockwise.*
*Positive normal forces result in tension stress in the cross section.*

*Positive shear forces are drawn over the line that represents the beam, while negative shear forces are drawn under. The moment is drawn on the tension side of the beam. Tension in the lower half is positive, while negative tension is in the upper half of the beam.*

In this situation, the sign for shear changes at the middle. It is normal to assign positive values to shear forces above the horizontal line and negative values to shear forces below the horizontal line. For the moment, the diagram is drawn underneath the beam as tension forces, as, for example, underneath a simple beam's own weight. The bending tension along the bottom half of the beam is considered positive. If the tension occurs along the top half of the beam (for example, a cantilevered beam), the moment diagram is drawn over the beam and has a negative sign.

How will we know that the beam has tension forces on the top or bottom half? It is not always immediately easy to see. Therefore, we choose the positive direction for the forces and moments we investigate in the area of a cross section. If the analysis results in a negative sign, we know that the moment or the force is acting in the opposite direction. (These signs must not be combined with positive or negative directions in the summation of external moments and forces in the requirements for equilibrium. It is customary to consider the forces in the direction of the x and y axes as positive, and also clockwise rotating moments.)

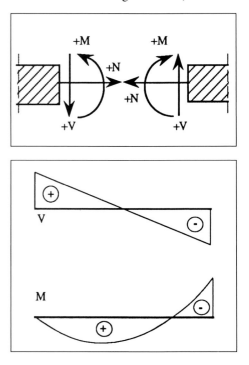

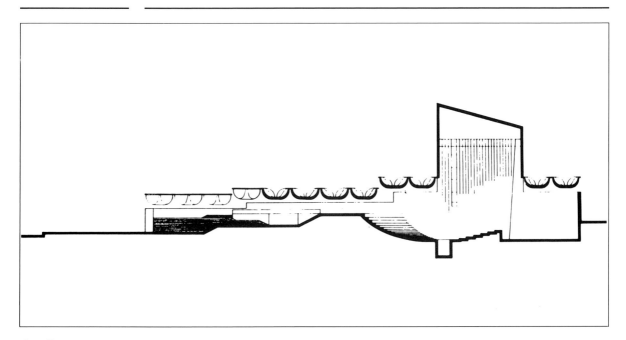

## 4.4 UTZON'S MOMENT BEAMS

Jørn Utzon was fascinated by the plateau as an architectural idea. On study tours to Central America and the Far East, he noted how plateaus in many variations and sizes created the spine of many powerful architectural compositions. From this central idea, Utzon created a series of projects in the 1950s and 1960s, few of which were ever built but that live on through marvelous architectural drawings.

The horizontal plane solved a series of problems. Traffic and other service-oriented functions could be placed below the plateau so that a pure building structure could rise above it. But a flat roof did not support the idea of a plateau. Varied roof forms allowed room for different heights and experience with substance, and it created contrast in relation to the flat plateau. (Mies van der Rohe also raised his buildings on plateaus, but his world of ideas was quite different.)

Utzon's roof forms were an investigation of concrete's structural possibilities. A series of competition projects show variations on the theme, that is, the Confederation of Trade Unions (LO) school at Helsinki in 1958, a project for the World Expo in Copenhagen in 1959, a theater in Zurich in 1962, and a theater in Augsburg in 1964. (A comprehensive presentation of these projects is found in the Italian publication *Zodiak*.)

The roof construction should have been built as folded beams with varying cross sections but with a constant height. At the supports, the profile of the beams was nearly a T-shape, while the middle of the span formed a U. In this way the beam's mass was moved to the region of the cross section where there was most use for it. At the span's middle, where the moment was greatest, the mass was concentrated at the bottom to take up the tension in the beam's underside. When the moment diminished as it neared the supports, the bottom width of the beam's profile was reduced, and the mass was elevated as the profile neared the T-form.

There is a conformity between the beam's form and structure. The richness in the project is achieved through structural expression. It is striking to see Utzon's ability to interpret proficient bearing ideas from historic building works of different cultures.

*Jørn Utzon.*
*LO-school.*
*Elsinore. 1958.*
*Competition project.*
*Section.*

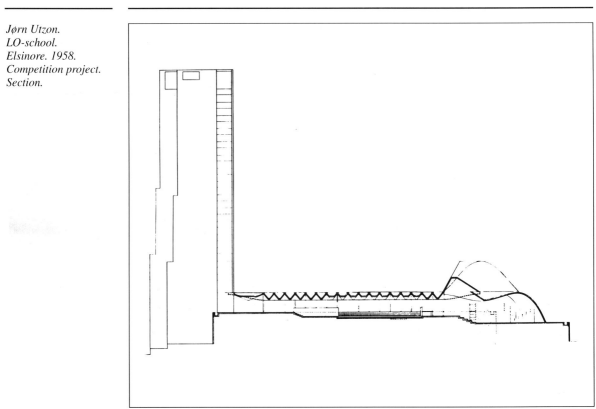

*Jørn Utzon.*
*LO-school.*
*Elsinore. 1958.*
*Competition project.*
*The roof plan shows*
*the moment beams*
*that span the*
*classrooms.*
*The tower housing*
*the student dormitory*
*is to the left.*
*To the right is the*
*auditorium.*

*Jørn Utzon.*
*The World Exposition.*
*Copenhagen. 1959.*
*Competition project.*

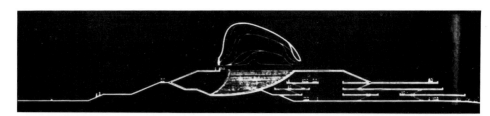

*Jørn Utzon.*
*The World Exposition.*
*Copenhagen. 1959.*
*Competition project.*

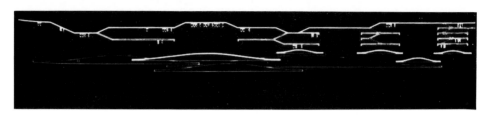

*Jørn Utzon.*
*The World Exposition.*
*Copenhagen. 1959.*
*Competition project.*
*Roof plan.*

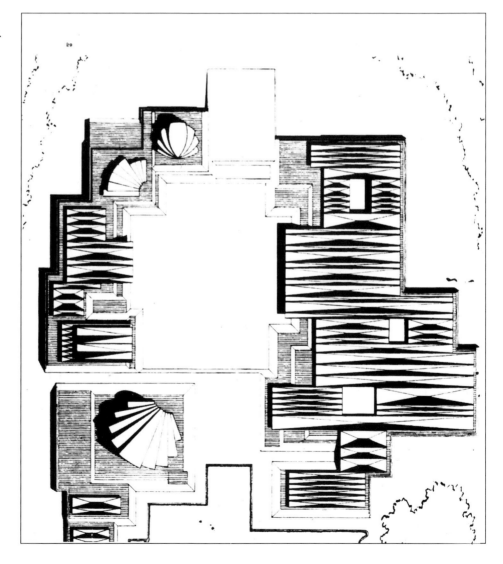

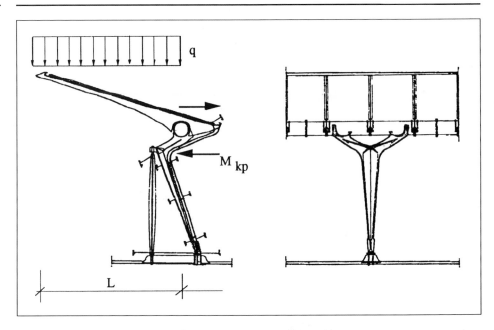

## 4.5 FORCES AND FORM

We have seen that the moment in a beam varies with the square of the span, while the shear force varies with the span. This means that with the increase of the span, there is a dramatically greater increase of moment than shear force. Therefore, the moment's magnitude most often determines the beam's form and dimension, while the shear force normally requires a control calculation of the chosen cross section.

A cantilevered beam is hindered from rotating at its fixed end. It is often firmly defined by the variation in the bending moment. An example is the powerful and bristling canopy that the Spanish architect and engineer Santiago Calatrava (born 1951) designed for Stadelhofen Train Station in Zurich. The organic skeletal construction is repeated along the curving platform and forms the support for a light roof.

The fixed ends of cantilevered beams wrap around and are welded to a steel pipe that spans horizontally between the pairs of columns. A force pair, $M_{kp}$, works here, hindering the beams from twisting. The vertical load on the beam results in bending

moments along the whole length of the beam (wind and snow loads will be taken into account later). Even though the thickness of the beam changes, we are simplifying, so that the load from the beam and roof is calculated to constant q (kN/m) (kips/ft).

We require that the moment is to be in equilibrium around the fixed ends along the pipe:

$\Sigma M_{cant} = 0$, gives us:

$+M_{kp} - qL \cdot L/2 = 0$

$M_{kp} = qL^2/2$

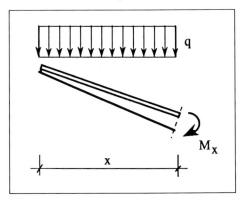

*Stadelhofen Train
Station. Zurich. 1989.
Architect: Santiago
Calatrava.*

Now we know the moment in the fixed end of the cantilevered beam. To find the variation along the beam, we look at a detailed section:

$\sum M_{section} = 0$ gives:

$+M_x - qx \cdot x/2 = 0$

$M_x = qx^2/2$

appear in every section of the beam. This is the structural interaction that gives it its vigorous and resilient expression.

If we look at the direction of the beam in relation to the vertical load, we understand that the load must have a component that acts laterally on the beam and one that acts along the length of the beam. The first gives the shear forces, the second gives normal forces in the beam. We shall find these for

*Moment diagram with tension in the upper half of the cantilevered beam. The variation is parabolic with the largest moment at the fixed end.*

*Shear diagram with a linear variation. The largest shear stress will be at the fixed end.*

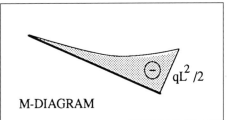

**M-DIAGRAM** $qL^2/2$

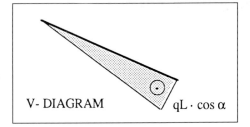

**V- DIAGRAM** $qL \cdot \cos\alpha$

When x = 0 we are at the outer end of the beam and in accordance with the previous expression the moment will be equal to zero. ($M_x = 0$ when x = 0). When x = L, we have the fixed end with the moment $qL^2/2$.

If we compare the moment diagram's form with the actual form of the beam, we see that they agree. The beam has a parabola shape, just as the moment diagram. The moment diagram is drawn above the beam, so that it forms a mirrored projection of the beam's form.

As we can see, the beam has the same sloping form as the moment diagram, starting from nearly zero depth at the free end and sloping to its maximum depth over the support. This form is also very effective in withstanding the bending stresses that

the sloping beam with the angle $\alpha$.

The sum of the lateral forces in the beam must be equal to zero:

$V - qx \cdot \cos\alpha = 0$

$V = qx \cdot \cos\alpha$

The shear force V has the direction shown in the figure above. It is negative because it attempts to twist the section of the beam counterclockwise. The shear force will be equal to zero at the outermost end and has a maximum value at the fixed end, where x = L. Since x exists in the first power, the variation will be linear.

Along the beam we must require equilibrium.

$-N + qx \cdot \sin\alpha = 0$

$N = qx \cdot \sin\alpha$

*Detail of the beam showing shear and normal forces in the section area.*

*Normal force diagram. Linear variation of the compression forces with a maximum force at the fixed end.*

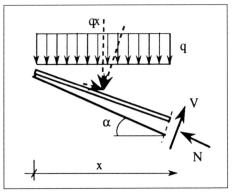

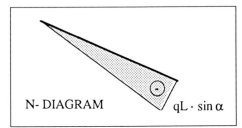

**N- DIAGRAM** $qL \cdot \sin\alpha$

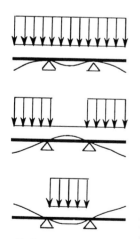

*Luksund Bridge. Hordaland, Norway. 1986.*
*Contractor: Selmer-Furuholmen.*
*Planners: Department of Bridges.*
*The bridge is a so-called straightforward concrete bridge.*

*Simply supported beam with two cantilevered spans.*

*Deformations figures for varying loads for the beam with two cantilevering spans.*

*Detail of the beam used to examine section forces.*

The normal force also has the direction shown in the figure below and results in compression in the cross section. Compression is defined as negative normal force. The variation is, as for the shear force, linear from zero to $qL \cdot \sin\alpha$.

Now we shall look at a beam over two columns with two overhanging ends. The beam is loaded with a uniformly distributed load. We count on the beam deforming as shown in the figure. The overhanging ends will press down and create tension along the top side. The middle section bends downward, though not as much as in a simple beam, and experiences tension along the bottom side.

We estimate that the deformation figure is dependent on the load's location and size, together with the relationship between the spans. If the load is especially large on the overhanging ends and the overhanging ends are large in relation to the middle span, the beam can be lifted up in the middle and have tension along its top side. Let's look at a beam with uniformly distributed loads, q:

$$\Sigma K_y = 0$$

$$A_y + B_y - q \cdot (2L_1 + L_2) = 0$$

$$A_y + B_y = q \cdot (2L_1 + L_2)$$

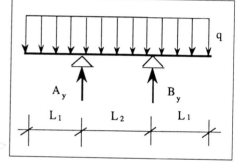

For reasons of symmetry, $A_y$ and $B_y$ must be equally large, therefore:

$$A_y + B_y = q/2 \cdot (2L_1 + L_2)$$

When the reaction forces are found, we can seek the bending moments. By taking a cross section in the middle, we get:

$$\Sigma M_{section} = 0$$

$$q/2 \cdot (2L_1 + L_2)x - M - q(L_1 + x)^2 \cdot 1/2 = 0$$

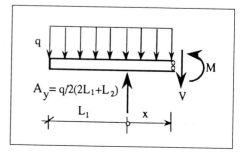

*Moment diagram for a uniformly distributed load along the entire beam.*

$M = q/2 \cdot (2L_1 + L_2)x - q/2 \cdot (L_1 + x)^2$

When the general arrangement of the forces is found, we can seek the parabola, since the span's variable exists in the second power. For a closer study of the variation in the moment along the beam, we set the value for x. The moment at the supports is set for x = 0:

$M = -q \cdot L_1^2/2$ so that tension is found to be on the top side.

For the middle section, we find:

$x = L_2/2$, so that

$M = q/2 \cdot (L_2^2/4 - L_1^2)$

At the right support $x = L_2$, and we get:

$M = -qL_1^2/2$, with tension acting on the top side.

We shall examine how the relationship between the spans must be for the moment at the middle section to be negative, resulting in tension on the top side:

$L_2^2/4 - L_1^2 < 0$ so that $L_1 > L_2/2$

The calculation shows that the moment at the midsection of the major span experiences tension at the top side, that is, is neg-

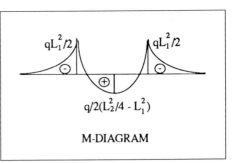

$qL_1^2/2$ $qL_1^2/2$

$q/2(L_2^2/4 - L_1^2)$

**M-DIAGRAM**

ative, if the overhanging span is larger than half the midsection. Thus the beam is lifted up at the middle.

What about the depth of the beam at the overhang and the middle span? Structurally, it should be constant if the bending moments are equal over the columns and the mid span.

With the chosen load, it is again the relationship between the spans that is determinant. These bending moments are equal if:

$q/2 \cdot (L_2^2/4 - L_1^2) = q/2 \cdot L_1^2$

$L_2 = \sqrt{8L_1} = 2.8\,L_1$

This means that the bending moments over the column system and the middle section of the major span will be approximately equal if the spans are about 1:3:1. The prerequisite is that there must be uniformly distributed loading.

*Left: Principle for moment diagram for the beam if the center span is lifted.*

*Right: Moment diagram with a span ratio of 1:3:1 and with a uniformly distributed load along the whole beam. The moments over the supports will be equal to the moment in the middle of the span.*

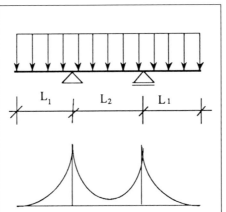

$L_1$ $L_2$ $L_1$

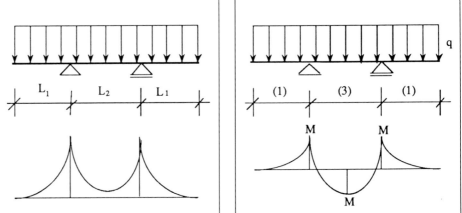

(1) (3) (1)

M M

M

q

*Medical Center. Philadelphia. 1956. Architect: Louis I. Kahn.*

*Medical Center. Philadelphia. 1956. Kahn uses a so-called Vierendeel beam where the top and bottom portions of the beam have a rigid connection to the vertical "members." These are connected at the top and bottom flanges and are rigid, securing transmission of horizontal shear forces. The vertical elements of the beam can thus function almost as diagonal members in a truss.*

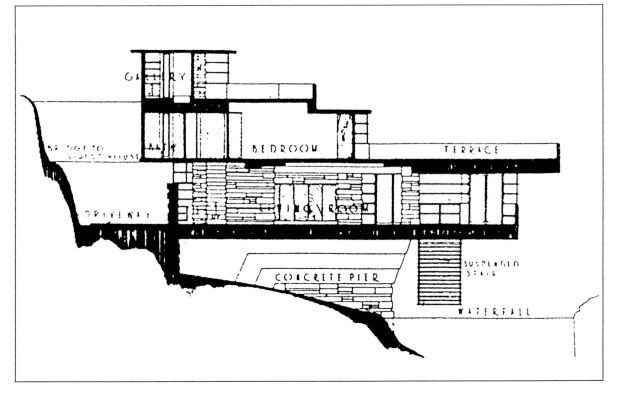

GALLERY

HATCHED GUEST HOUSE

BEDROOM

TERRACE

DRIVEWAY

LIVING ROOM

CONCRETE PIER

SUSPENDED STAIR

WATERFALL

*Frank Lloyd Wright.*
*Falling Water. 1936.*
*Section.*

## 4.6 FRANK LLOYD WRIGHT'S FALLING WATER

Falling Water, one of Frank Lloyd Wright's most famous and admired works, was completed in 1936 as a weekend house for Edgar J. Kaufmann, somes miles outside of Pittsburgh, Pennsylvania. The site is a natural area with deciduous forest, wild rhododendron, and rapids. Built on a sandstone embankment, the house was erected as a series of overhanging terraces over falls.

The architect describes the house as: "an extension of the cliff beside a mountain stream making living space over and above the stream upon several terraces upon which a man who loved the place sincerely, one who loved and liked to listen to the waterfall, might well live."

For Wright, the principle of cantilevering was a very personal solution, as natural as a branch that grows from the trunk of the tree or an outstretched arm. Used with insight and ingenuity, the structure had many possibilities. It could set free spaces and create new plans parallel to the ground.

The main terrace of reinforced concrete with slate flooring was at that time a highly advanced structure with a cantilever of over 5 meters (16 feet). The concept was based on the interaction between the beams in the deck and the concrete folded edges. Donald Hoffman's book, *Frank Lloyd Wright's Falling Water and Its History* furnishes a good insight into the difficult and at times dramatic planning stages and building process. Several times, the daring and visionary Kaufmann expressed serious doubt on the bearing ability of cantilevers and had his engineer check Wright's dimensions. Furthermore, he had him measure the bending deflection of the terraces at regular intervals as long as he lived. But the house, as we know, still stands and is considered a major work in architectural history.

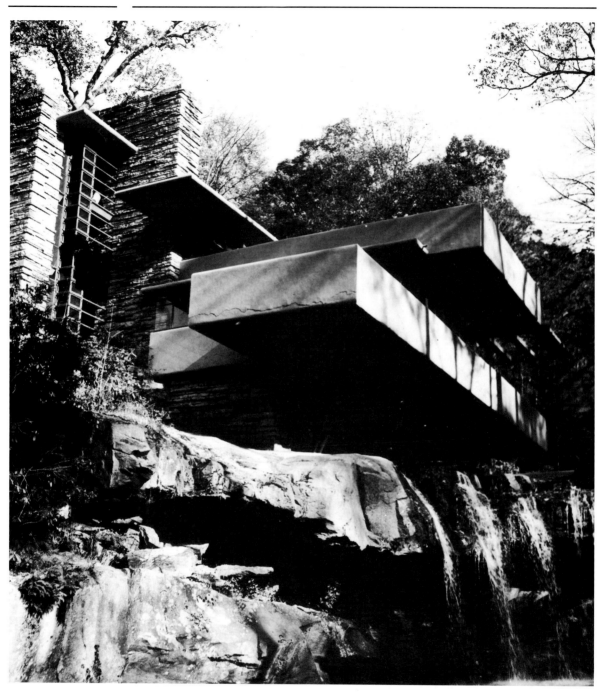

*Frank Lloyd Wright.*
*Falling Water. 1936.*
*Photograph taken*
*October 1987.*

104

*Continuous beam over several equal spans. With uniformly distributed load over the whole beam, an inner span will be prevented from rotating at the ends. These will therefore be subjected to bending moments equal to the beam with two fixed ends.*

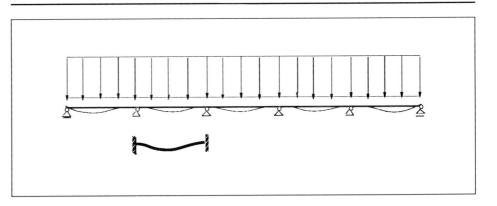

## 4.7 CONTINUOUS BEAMS AND GERBER BEAMS

A beam that uninterruptedly spans over three or more supports is called a continuous beam. In several cases, it is natural to let a beam be carried by several columns without splicing it. This has production-related (and economic) advantages because the continuous beam generally has lower bending moments. With that, we can save on the depths of the beams.

A continuous beam, over many equal spans and with a uniformly distributed load, will be deformed as shown in the figure above. In the middle region, as in the other regions, we have natural bending occurring between the supports. Directly over the supports the beam will have a tendency to rotate owing to the fact that the load at one side of the support will be working against the other side's tendency to rotate. The reason for this is the symmetry in both load and span. As a result, the beam will be prevented from rotating. We have previously called this cantilevering. This type of middle region of a continuous beam can also be considered as beams over a span with two fixed ends, as long as the load is uniformly distributed over all similar spans. A comparison between a beam with both ends fixed and a simple beam shows that the greatest bending moment will be 1.5 times larger in the simple beam. In addition the deformation will be 5 times larger.

Let's look again at the simple beam. The support at one end is a column that, for example, is set on a foundation plate in

*Moment diagrams for a simply supported beam and a fixed beam with the same span and load. The first has a moment 1.5 times larger.*

*Deflection figures for the simply supported beam and the fixed beam. The first has a deflection 5 times larger.*

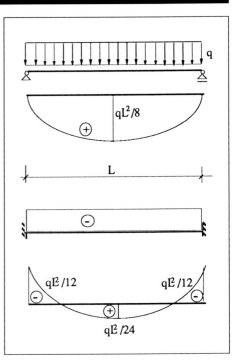

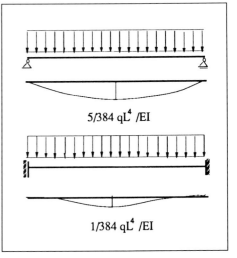

$5/384 \, qL^4/EI$

$1/384 \, qL^4/EI$

*Displacement of the support doesn't lead to bending in the statically determinate beam. In the statically indeterminate beam, a shifting of the support will produce bending moments.*

*Top: Statically indeterminate, continuous beam. Bottom: Statically determinate Gerber beam.*

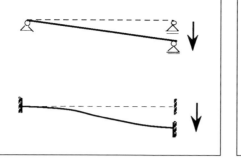

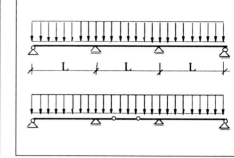

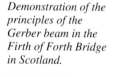

*Demonstration of the principles of the Gerber beam in the Firth of Forth Bridge in Scotland.*

clay. If the one column sinks because of settling of the clay, the beam will shift at the top of the column and position itself in a state of equilibrium. The beam is still straight and undeformed. If the same would happen to the fixed end of a statically indeterminate beam, it will have to twist in order to assume its new position. Fixed ends are, by definition, unyielding against torsion. With that, bending moments are introduced in the beam. These moments come in addition to the moments of the external loads. A simple beam or any other statically determinate bearing element can be vulnerable to shifting (shear) without resulting in additional forces in the element.

The wish to reduce the effects from the settling of the supports of continuous bridge beams and the knowledge of the differences between the statically determinate and the statically indeterminate beam systems was the basis for the development of the continuous type of beam. The statically determinate beams of the German engineer Heinrich Gerber (1832-1912), called Gerber beams, were created by using rotation free joints in each alternating span of the continuous beam. Gerber beams are understood and treated as a series of simple beams with cantilevering side spans. The coupling element is a simple beam that hangs between the cantilevering spans and places a load on each of their ends.

*Firth of Forth Bridge.*
*Scotland. 1890.*
*Span 1708 feet (521 m).*

## 4.8 A GRID OF BEAMS AND SLABS

The normal beam is seen as an isolated one-way or one-axis bearing element, that is, it bears a load along a line from A to B. We can make the most of this simple fact if we cover a rectangular space with a beam construction. Since the bearing capacity is inversely proportional to the square of the span, we normally arrange the beams so that they have the shortest span.

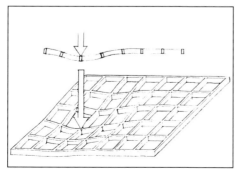

*The deformation of
the beams in the two-
way grid with rigid
moment joints.*

To span a space that is nearly square, we can consider adding a beam in each direction. This will result in a greater bearing capacity, and hence require shallower beams. If the beams in the two axial directions are joined to each other, the system will have bearing capabilities simultaneously in both directions. This type of beam structure is called a framework of beams (two-way beam structure).

A point load at the intersection of two beams will result in a bending of the two beams in addition to all adjacent beams. Thus, such a structure yields great load resistance. If the beams have rigid moment connections, the loaded beams will be in pure bending, while the adjacent beams will, in addition to bending, experience torsion. This is due to the rigid moment con-

*Slab/beam structures of concrete.*

*From the top:*

*Flat slab for spans from 5 to 8 meters (2 to 3 1/8 feet).*

*Slab strengthened at the columns. The maximum span is about 14 meters (45 feet).*

*Slab with underlying beams for a one-way span direction, up to about 15 meters (49 feet).*

*Beam/slab structure for a two-way span direction of 10 to 20 meters (32 to 65 feet).*

*Underlying beams in one direction for a slab carrying large loads.*

*Normal two-way slab structure, waffle slab for span from about 8 to 20 meters (26 to 65 feet).*

*Dom-i-no. 1914. Architect: Le Corbusier. Sketch project for a house with slab/ column bearing system.*

nections at the points of intersection and the tendency of the adjacent beams to follow the deformation.

Many cross sections of beams, for example, closed cross sections such as in a steel pipe, have a considerable resistance to torsion. It will take a large load to deform a two-way beam structure because of bending and torsion. Torsion is a moment that also can appear, in addition to bending moments, as shear force and normal force. For beams with torsion stiffening, the torsion moment will result in cross-sectional resistance with stresses in the cross section's plane, as well as shear stress.

We can imagine the spacing between beams in a framework of beams becomes increasingly less until the beams melt all together, and we end up with a slab structure or a deck. For slabs in residential building, reinforced concrete is the most important material. The slab works structurally like a framework of beams. It will be vulnerable to bending, shear, and torsion if it spans in two directions.

Slabs can be constructed with moderate spans. At a certain length, an increase in the slab thickness to enhance the bearing capacity results in a large increase in actual weight that "eats up" the increase in strength. For long spans, reinforced slab structures are made by combining the beam and the slab in several different ways and using prestressed concrete for very long spans.

The flat slab has obvious advantages in relation to slabs with beams underneath. In multiple-unit housing, the flat slab results in a finished ceiling, whereas in an office building it makes it very easy to mount piping and wiring. In Le Corbusier's idea-project "Dom-i-no" (1914), the flat slab could rest directly on the columns and form the structural concept for rational building of housing. This thought later influenced the development of concrete as bearing material in housing and office building.

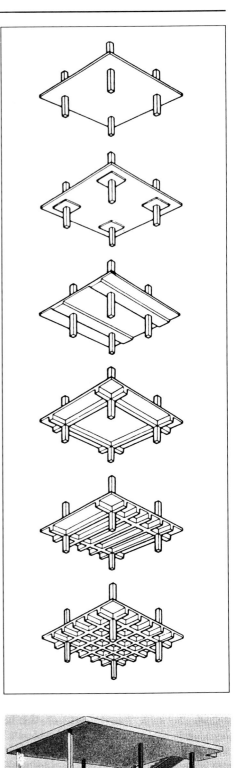

# Chapter 5

# THE COLUMN

*The Doric Temple
of Aphaia.
Aegina, Greece.
5th century B.C.*

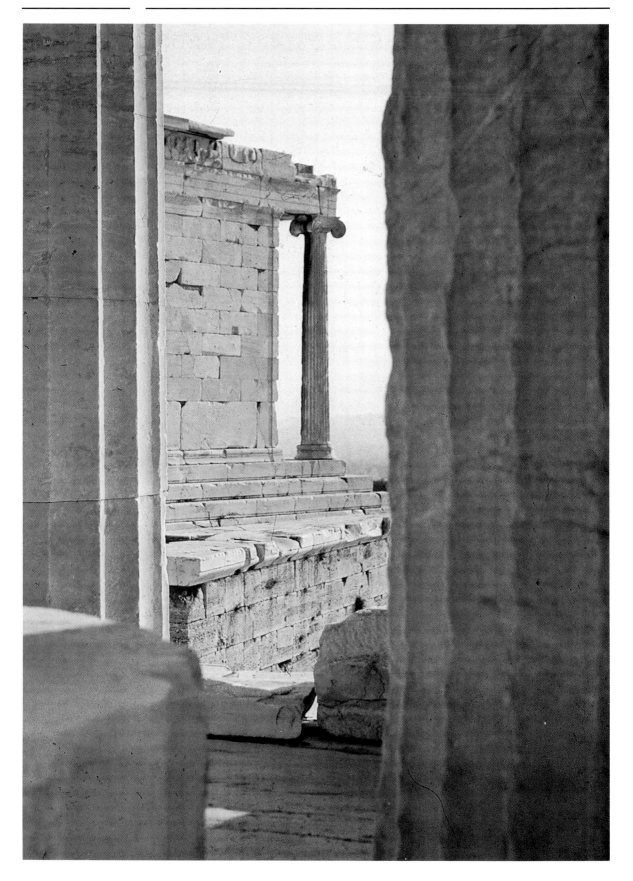

## 5.1 ON THE THRESHOLD OF THE ACROPOLIS

Standing with your back to Areopagos you can look up at the west front of the Acropolis. "There is just one entrance to the Acropolis, no others can be found because the embankment is so steep and all around their is a tremendous wall," wrote the Roman traveler and author Pausanias in the second century A.D.

Then, as now, a ramp leads up to the Propylaeum that forms the entrance into the Acropolis. From the threshold to the Acropolis one can turn to the right and, between the Propylæum's Doric columns, get a glimpse of the little Ionic Temple of Nike standing obliquely on top of a protruding bastion. The temple, which is dedicated to Athena and identified with the goddess of victory, Nike, was built in 435 B.C. The walls of the temple's cell are retracted to free the corner columns. These Ionic marble columns, which stand proudly over the infernal noise of Athens, a city of millions, have all of a column's essential and highly developed elements. The columns stand as an eternal paradigm, both positive and negative, for all of the "column builders" since.

The column has an articulated base that mediates the transition between the foundation of the temple, the stylobate, and the shaft of the column. The column's shaft, which consists of several stacked sections, has fluted, vertical profiles where light and shadows describe the circular cross section and enhance the impression of height and tension.

The profile of the column is not quite perpendicular but forms a convex curve from the base to the capital. The difference between the straight line and the curved is called *entasis*, which can be measured down to just a few millimeters. Entasis gives the added and accurate visual contribution needed to suggest power and bearing capacity.

The capital is formed to accept and concentrate the load from the beam over and down the shaft of the column.

In *Centrum and Periphery*, H. P. Lorange writes of the Ionic capital: "As an expressive measure of compression, the volute piece of the Ionic capital between the beam and the shaft of the column and the volute's elastically taut stream of lines reflect the play of forces in the blocks inward—this seemingly springy resistance in the stone's innards, here lies open to our eyes."

## 5.2 THE CAPITAL

The design of the transition joint between column and beam, the capital, has always attracted attention. The different properties of materials and the level of technical know-how sets limits to and creates new possibilities in capital design, but the problem is always the same: The forces that are to be transferred from the beam and down through the shaft of the column are always there.

The Doric Aphian temple at Aegina, dating from the beginning of the fifth century B.C., is a complex of gray limestone. The

*The Metro Line 2
(subway) in Paris.
Cast iron capital.
1910.*

building's components have a rough fabric-like appearance quite different from the finely sanded marble of the Acropolis. The broadly formed capital grows out, in a way, from the shaft of the column, while the horizontal contour captures and concludes the fluting. The abacus lies between the echinus and the architrave. Here all of the elements are correctly formulated. The stones are precisely fitted to each other. As compression distributors for the forces from above, this capital is perhaps the most beautiful and most expressive we know.

At the turn of the century, Paris got its Metro (subway) system. Line 2, which runs over the boulevards, was designed as a

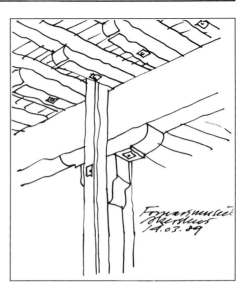

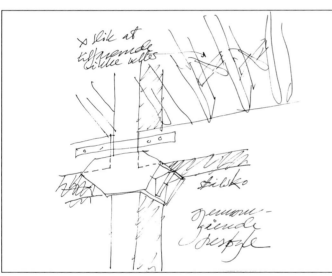

*Logo of the Society for the Preservation of Norwegian Ancient Monuments.*

bridge system of steel trusses with riveted joints. The compression joints' reversed Ionic capital with a globe and two cylinders rests on top of Doric columns. Here one can freely dip into history's well to find an elegant treatment of the many problems with the transferring of forces in cast iron.

Traditional timber structures offer many interesting variations on a theme. The Military Museum at Akershus Fortress in Oslo, Norway, designed by the architects Schirmer and von Hanno, was completed in 1860 with brick facades and timber joists. The main beams are carried by columns with side brackets. The main beams are continuous, but the columns are joined at every floor. The connection between the columns and the joists is secured by a pair of vertical braces that are held together by forged-through connecting bolts. Even though the brown patina of the timber is not always impressive, the construction contributes to a number of high-grade spaces rich in character. Massive timber, with its rectangular cross section, has a reasonably good fire resistance when the outer surface is charred in the course of a fire, and the charcoal outer layer protects wood's inner bearing core and lengthens the life of the column.

Parallel to the famous skyscraper experiments in steel at the First Chicago School in the 1880s, Chicago's buildings were built of brick with wooden columns and joists. The columns, in the Chicago version, are continuous through all of the floors. A cast-iron capital (or maybe a two-sided bracket is a more accurate description), threaded down the column, forms the support for the simple beams. Special time-consuming preparation of the wood was not required, and the cast iron brackets were mass produced. The demand for quick, effective fittings resulted in simple and robust solutions.

In the 1965 design of an exhibition hall for machines in Monza, Italy, the architect Angelo Mangiarotti (born 1921) attempted to display the design potential of prefabricated concrete elements. In this type of project, which often consists of just one space, the conditions are ideal for a simple and well-refined structural system. The number of elements present here are three: column, beam, and deck. The capital of the column is a hammerhead form where angled tongue-and-groove interlocking joints insure a solid connection for the system of beams.

The *pilz* (mushroom) column is concrete architecture's contribution to the forming of the capital where the column turns into a cone. An example of this is seen in James Stirling's (1926-1992) 1971 project for Olivetti at Milton Keynes in England. A perspective drawing by Leon Krier in his apprentice period with Stirling shows how the pilz column meets the flat concrete deck and is also consistent with the undulating facade. The principle is employed with many variations, but often the capital disappears behind a casually hung ceiling system.

In church building of the Middle Ages, the messages and accounts from the Christian Bible were transmitted through pictures. We must remember that most of the congregation could not read. Accounts from daily life and plant and animal motifs were also part of this picture world. In Urnes stave church, from the 1130s, the free-standing masts are topped with the so-called die or cushion capitals with carvings of fabled beasts.

It is not difficult to find parallels in European stone and wood architecture of the Middle Ages. In the crypt of the Canterbury Cathedral, we find the same type of four-sided capitals with fabled beasts carved in sandstone.

It seems as though medieval building ornament occurred mostly at entrances, window openings, and structural joints to accentuate and articulate these building elements. Later, ornament found its way to walls, ceilings, and roofs.

## 5.3 THE WAY THE COLUMN WORKS

*Oh, what a wonderful day when the wall parted and the column was born.*

*—LOUIS KAHN.*

The column is an important shaper of space. Its task is to define and stabilize the horizontal plane that is elevated over the plane of the ground and to establish an architectural space. With that, the column takes on the structural responsibility for holding up the elevated plane. The column must bear the load.

The structural task of the column is simpler than the beams, because the direction of the column generally is the same as the direction of load, that is, vertical. A column is more or less a level bearing element that is vulnerable to loads with direction most often equal to that of the column itself.

For the most part, axial loading seldom occurs in columns. The column most often has a point of loading not on the center axis. This is called an eccentric load. The eccentric load, which has a distance from the point of loading to the center axis, will give the column a bending moment.

In addition to the column's primary structural task, which is to bear the vertical load, the column often experiences horizontal loads in the form of lateral forces at the head of the column. An example of this is a column in a facade, which in addition to bearing the floors also experiences wind loads. These columns will be vulnerable to combincation loads with bending moments from wind loads and eventual moments from eccentric vertical loads plus the vertical load itself.

The column can, in addition, be connected with the beam so that, together, they form a bearing system capable of taking horizontal forces. This system is called a frame and is covered in the next chapter.

## 5.4 THE SHORT COLUMN

Let's look at the short column of a linear elastic material with centric loading. A so-called short column is a column with a large cross section in relation to its height. The area of the column's cross section is equal to A, and the centric load, the axial load, is called N. This gives the cross section of the column compression stress $\sigma_c$ (c for compression) that is uniformly distributed over the cross section. The load on such a column can be increased within the compression stress limits of the material. This limit is called the material's compression strength, $f_c$ (N/mm$^2$) (psi). When this is exceeded, the column will collapse due to compression fractures.

*A. Column with concentric vertical load.*
*B. Column with eccentric vertical load, results in the moment $M = P \cdot e$ along the whole column.*
*C. Column with combined loads; acts partly as a column and partly as a beam.*

When the load N exists off the center axis of the column, the column has a moment in addition to the vertical load. The compression stress will be the sum of the stresses from the two loads. In order to avoid compression fracturing, the stress must be less than the compression strength.

With the introduction of eccentricity and, therefore, a bending moment in the column, we see that the compression stress is no longer uniformly distributed over the area of the cross section. The bending moment

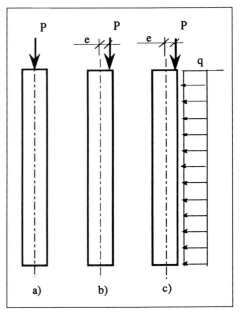

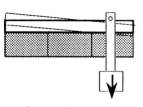

*Foam rubber with load outside the middle third of the cross section. "Cracking" on the opposite side.*

gives compression and tension stresses that must be added to the compression stress from the vertical load. If the eccentricity is minimal, the tension stress will be so small that the result will be compression stresses over the whole cross section, but with a reduced area on the side of the column that is opposite the load. This is true as long as the vertical load is acting within the inner third of the cross section. The tension stresses will be less than the compression stresses so that the resultant will always be compression. This is of minor significance with today's materials that are poor in tension, such as nonreinforced concrete and masonry, but was of great significance in the past with materials that were poor in tension, such as masonry.

If the material cannot withstand tension stresses or has a low tensile strength $f_t$ (t for tension) (N/mm$^2$) (psi), the column crumbles when the vertical load is eccentrically placed, that is, outside the inner third of the cross section. The inner third of the cross section is called the core of the cross section. A simple model from physics can verify this. The load on a wooden plate with a foam rubber sublayer will induce "cracking" at the opposite end of the loading point when acting outside the core of the cross section.

In a Gothic cathedral, for example, the resultant of the compression forces from a flying buttress and the weight of the buttress' pier will normally lie within the core of the cross section at the foundation of the pier. Thus, bending and tension stresses are in check and the whole flying buttress can bear the compression forces alone.

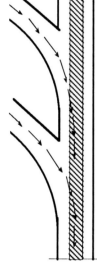

*The resultant of compression forces in a flying buttress falls within the middle third of the cross section.*

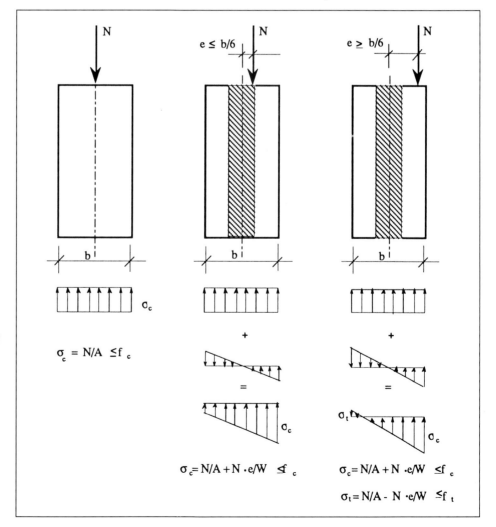

*Short column under three different loading conditions*

*Charlie Chaplin.*

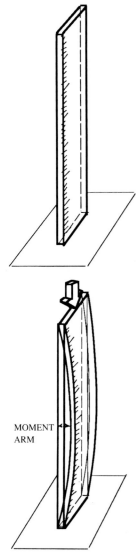

MOMENT
ARM

*Sudden bending of a loaded plastic ruler.*

## 5.5 THE SLENDER COLUMN AND BUCKLING

In modern column structures of reinforced concrete, wood, or reinforced masonry, tension stresses in the material are not a significant problem. The tendency has been to build sleeker, more economical modern structures that still can withstand moments with tension stresses, but that can experience another type of deformation due to compression loads—buckling.

We saw that the short column could collapse because of failure of the actual material. The deformation is solely dependent on the cross-sectional area of the column and the strength of the material. Slender columns can deform with uncontrollable bending or buckling. This deformation type in its purest form is dependent on the elasticity of the mat̶ ̶ ̶, the height and cross-sectional form̶ ̶ ̶ ̶olumn, as well as on the require̶ ̶ ̶ ̶e column's joints, that is, the ̶ ̶ ̶h it is connected at its top and ̶ ̶re buckling is also independen ̶ ̶gth of the material.

Let's study th̶ ̶ ̶g characteristics of a straight plastic ̶ ̶.̶ ̶ ̶r. If we stand it on end like a column and place a load on it with our finger, the ruler more or less gives up and suddenly bends outward. If we continue applying more load, the ruler will bend further until it breaks in two. We can determine that the same will happen to an absolutely straight column. With an excessive load along the central axis, it will suddenly bend outward and eventually collapse.

If the bending of the plastic ruler doesn't happen suddenly, but gradually, this means that the ruler is not absolutely straight and/or that the point of loading is not exactly centric. The ideal condition just described is difficult to attain and in real structural situations it seldom appears. Therefore the column often "starts" with an unintended moment caused by eccentric placement of the load and/or previous crimping of the column. This initial moment results in bending of the column. If we then increase the vertical load, the bending will be a force arm for the load, and we have a new moment. This moment results in a new bending that creates a new moment, reoccuring until the deformation of the column is so great that it buckles. Therefore, if the column's load is kept under a certain magnitude, determined by the stiffness of the column, this chain reaction will not occur. This loading limit is called the column's critical load or allowable unit stress ($P_{kr}$).

The buckling reaction starts with the allowable unit stress ($P_{kr}$). This load is independent of the column's stiffness. Still, buckling most often leads to rupture of the material, because extreme bending results in the buckling of the column. We shall now look a little closer at the condition that determines the allowable unit stress.

## 5.6 LEONARD EULER'S DISCOVERY

The strength of the material of a column does not determine the bearing characteristics of a slender column that buckles and collapses under a certain vertical load. It does, however, determine the column's stiffness. We have defined stiffness in the previous chapter as:

S = EI/L, where
  E = the material's modulus of elasticity

($N/mm^2$) (psi)
I = the cross section's moment of inertia ($mm^4$) ($in^4$)
L = the length of the bearing element (mm) (in)

We will first look at a column that has translation fixed ends at both top and bottom. The column can also freely rotate at its ends. If the column has a previous bending

($y_0$), the load (P) will give the column a moment

$$M = P \cdot y_0.$$

What occurs further depends on the magnitude of the load P and the column's stiffness, which is $EI/L_k$. How the simple magnitudes relate to each other was investigated by the German mathematician Leonard Euler (1707-1783) in 1757. He presented the following relationship between the load that caused buckling of the column and the stiffness properties of the column:

$$P_{kr} = \pi^2 \cdot EI/(L_k)^2 \text{ where}$$

$P_{kr}$ = the allowable unit stress (also called the Euler load)

$\pi$ = the circle constant 3.14

$L_k$ = the effective column length in relation to bending or the column's bending length that is not necessarily equal to the actual length of the column.

The equation is the oldest in statics that is still in use. The expression is correct for very slender and placid columns or compression rods but must be modified for normal columns in architecture.

In the example, we looked at a column with rotating joints at both ends, a so-called pendulum column. It will bend outward from the end points as shown in the drawing below. If we have a column with a fixed end at its foot but with the same length and elasticity, we will have another bending form. For the same load, the bending will be less. The column is held back by the fixed end at its foot. The column's bending will be equally great for a pendulum column with a length of just 0.7L of the fixed end column. With these end conditions, we say that the effective column length is equal to 0.7 times the column's actual length. The effective column length is also generally equal to the length of the pendulum column with bending equal to the bending of the

*Three stages in the loading of a slender column with an initial deflection:*
*If P is less than the critical load, the stiffness of the column prevents further bending.*
*When P is equal to the critical load, many equilibrium situations can be created where the moment from the vertical load is held in equilibrium by the stiffness of the column.*
*If P is greater than the critical load, the moment will produce deflection until the column collapses.*

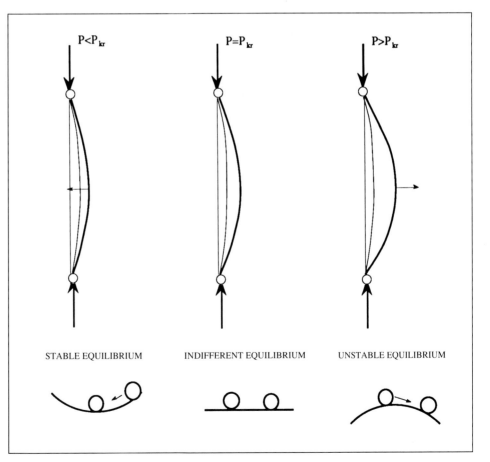

illustrated columns. Therefore, the effective column length will be the distance between the points of the column where the bending figure turns, that is, the bending moment changes its sign from acting in compression from the one side to be in tension on the same side. At the point of change, the bending moment must be equal to zero (as with the column's end points). These turning points are called inflection points.

The amount of bending is also important in determining the slender column's bearing capacity or the allowable unit stress ($P_{kr}$). Therefore, it is not just the column's actual length that plays a role but also the end conditions. The bearing capacity of the column with the fixed end point at its foot and with a length L will therefore be larger than the pendulum column's bearing capacity with the same length. For the column with a fixed end, we write:

$$P_{kr} = \pi^2 \cdot EI/L_k^2 = \pi^2 \cdot EI/(0.7L)^2$$

$$= \pi^2 \cdot EI/0.49L^2 \sim 2\pi^2 \cdot EI/L^2$$

With a fixed end at the foot of the column, the bearing capacity in regard to buckling is doubled.

In Leonard Euler's equation, the material's modulus of elasticity E ($N/mm^2$) (psi) is included. The smaller the E-modulus is, the softer the material is, and with that, bending is increased. Increased bending means lower allowable unit stress. $P_{kr}$ is therefore proportional to the material's E-modulus. With testing, for example, we will find that a steel column of high-quality steel (high strength) bears more than a steel column with lower material quality, as long as it is shorter. With similarly slender columns of

*Column with two hinged joints, pendulum column. The column has an initial deflection $y_o$.*

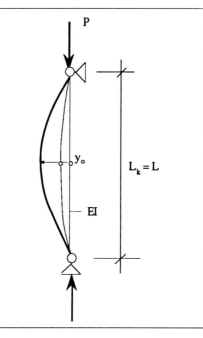

*Deflection diagram for the column with a fixed foot joint.*

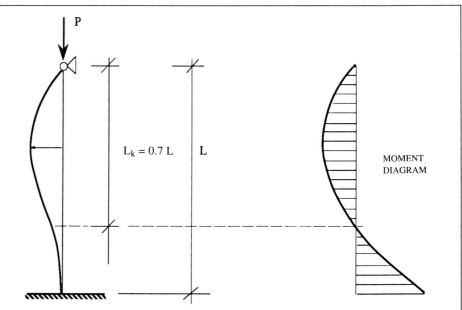

*Four columns of equal
length but with
different joint
conditions. Varying
critical lengths and
critical loads.*

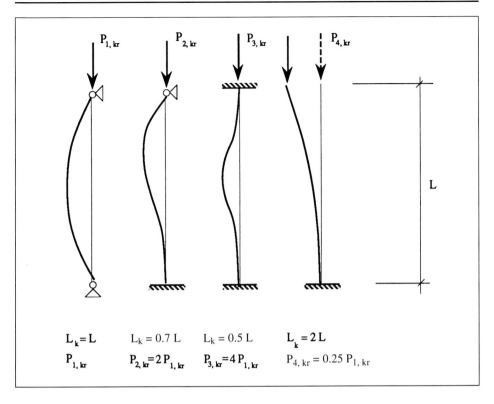

the same length where buckling determines the bearing capacity, the two columns will bear approximately equal amounts because the E-modulus for steel changes very little with different steel qualities.

The last magnitude that is incorporated in the Euler formula is the cross section's moment of inertia I $(mm^4)$ $(in^4)$. The size says something about the form of the cross section.

Let's consider putting two columns under a compression load with the same column length and end conditions. Both of the columns have the same cross-sectional area, but one is flat while the other is round. The circular cross section has the largest moment of inertia around the bending axis, and the column has the least bending and, with that, the greatest bearing capacity $P_{kr}$. The allowable unit stress is also proportional to the cross section's moment of inertia. In order to counteract buckling, the cross section needs to have a large moment of inertia. This is determined by the cross-sectional area, but, more important, by the distribution of material. As with beams, it helps to have more material along the cross

section's outer edges.

We have now labeled columns as "short" and "slender" without specifying in detail what these terms mean. It has become apparent that the expressions refer to the way that they collapse. We can say that the short column is a column where bearing capacity is determined only by the strength of the material, while the slender column is one that experiences collapse through buckling.

The breaking load causing buckling relates to a breaking stress that is called the Euler stress $(\sigma_k)$.

For the column with cross section A we have:

$$\sigma_{kr} = P_{kr}/A = \pi^2 \cdot EI/AL_k^2 =$$

$$\pi^2 \cdot E/(AL_k^2/I) = \pi^2 \cdot E/\lambda_{kr}^2$$

We have introduced a new term that sets a numerical value for the column's degree of slenderness—slenderness ratio. Slenderness ratio $\lambda_{kr}$ will then be:

*Deflection diagram
and critical load for
two columns with
different cross-
sectional forms.*

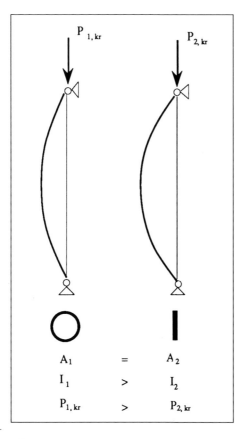

$$\lambda_{kr} = L_k/\sqrt{(I/A)}$$

Again, it is practical to combine the terms in new sizes. We introduce now:

$i = \sqrt{(I/A)}$ = the column's inertia radius, or radius of gyration (often given in handbooks as "r"), (mm) (in), and thus we can write:

$$\lambda_k = L_k/i.$$

The slenderness ratio is the relation between the column's effective length and the radius of gyration of its cross section.

These dimensions are compiled in profile tables for diverse column/beam cross sections in different materials. For rectangular column cross sections, we find that the radius of gyration is:

$$i = \sqrt{(I/A} = \sqrt{(1/12 \cdot bh^3)/bh} = \sqrt{1/12h^2} = 0.29h$$

*Gustave Doré.
Death of Samson.
Samson takes revenge
over the Philistines
and topples the
temple's columns
(Judges 13-16).*

For example, a rectangular pendulum column in wood with h = 200 mm (8 in) and length Lk = 4000 mm (about 13 ft) has the slenderness ratio:

$$\lambda_k = L_k/i = 4000/(0.29 \cdot 200) = 69$$

The bearing capacity diminishes drastically with the increase in slenderness ratio. For wood columns, an allowable slenderness is 170, while for steel columns 200 is acceptable.

In practice, most of the columns in architecture have a bearing capacity that is determined by both strength and stiffness, that is, they are intermediate columns between the short and the slender column. The breaking stresses for both the short and the slender column will be:

$$\sigma_{Br} = P_{Br}/A \text{ and } \sigma_{kr} = \pi^2 \cdot E/\lambda_{kr}^2$$

We can draw the results in the same diagram with the stress and slenderness ratio as variables. Thus, we say that with extreme slenderness ratio, material failure will determine the bearing capacity in short columns, while the Euler stress will set the upper limits in slender columns. In practice, there is a gliding transition between these breaking formulas, so that with the increase in slenderness ratio the buckling mechanism will increasingly influence the bearing capacity.

Finally, it must be noted that the phenomena of breaking has validity for all structural elements vulnerable to axial compression loads, for example, compression rods in trusses or the top flange of a beam with bending moments. In the latter case, the compression load can cause a lateral bending in the compression flange so that the entire profile of the beam twists. This form for breaking in beams is called lateral buckling and involves a combination of bending and torsion. The flange will be held in place as long as the beam is bearing a rigid, top-mounted slab or roof. In addition, lateral buckling can be prevented by welding stiffening plates to the steel beam.

# 5.7 THE FORM OF THE COLUMN

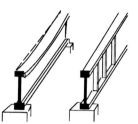

*Buckling of the compression flange of a loaded beam. In steel beams, this is prevented by welding in stiffening plates.*

It will be interesting to see what the formal consequences are in relation to the structural properties of the column. It is important to note that the column can buckle in both axes if it is not supported in any direction by walls, bracing, slabs, etc. Therefore buckling is, from the beginning, a spatial problem, and in determining the form of the column, we must remember to take this problem into consideration. In regard to form, the bearing capacity is determined by the cross-sectional area of the column, distribution of the load in that area, and the amount of bending that varies with the length of the column. Therefore it is a relationship between the column's structural mode of operation and its form, both in cross section and in length.

*The relation between the critical stress and the slenderness. Theoretical course for the slender and the short column, with a hint of the practical course.*

We will first look at the influence of the form of the cross section. For a short column with loading along its central axis, the bearing characteristics are determined solely by the material's strength and cross-sectional area. Such a column can be massive. The form of the column's cross section plays no role in this case. If the load moves or translates so that it reacts eccentrically, this will produce a bending moment in the column. If the vertical load is large in relation to the moment, a massive column will still be the wisest choice. With an increase in the moment, however, it will be best to move the material of the column to its outer edges. The material around the center line will not be as active, and increase in moment will create a problem similar to bending in a beam. Still, for the short column, the distribution of material in the cross section will play the most important role.

*A short column with a load acting along the centroid and with an eccentric load.*

We can now consider a slender column where the problem of buckling is decisive in determining the column's bearing characteristics. The column is loaded centrically and is not supported in any direction. Collapse resulting from buckling will happen along the axis that is weakest, that is,

along the short side of a column with a rectangular cross section. Increasing the dimensions of this side will increase the column's bearing capacity. It seems therefore reasonable that such a column should have a symmetrical cross section in both axes, for example, a square or a circular-shaped cross section. Since buckling determines the bearing capacity, this means that the cross section of the column that can handle buckling is suited for bearing the load. The area of the cross section, therefore, will ideally be distributed along the

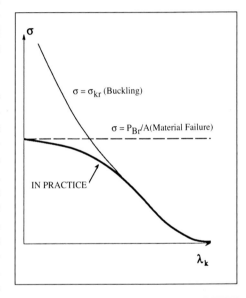

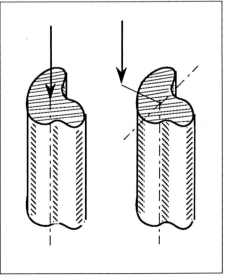

*The phenomenon of buckling as a spatial problem. Rectangular and quadratic columns.*

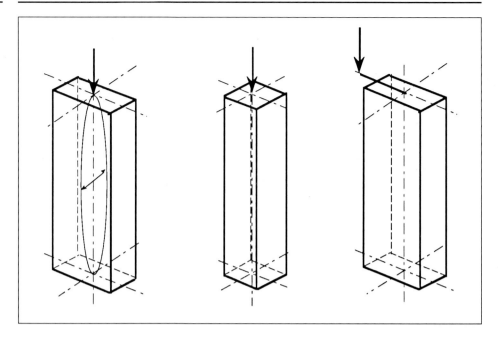

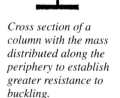

*Cross section of a column with the mass distributed along the periphery to establish greater resistance to buckling.*

*Mies van der Rohe. National Gallery in Berlin. 1969.*

*Typical facade column in steel. Strong axis perpendicular to the direction of the facade.*

edges in order to gain the greatest resistance to bending. In other words, a hollow column is most favorable. Hollow columns are most common in steel.

The cross section of a slender column with a moment in one direction will, as with a short column, be dependent on the magnitude of the moment in relation to the vertical load. If the moment is large, as, for example, in a facade column that bears beams from just one side and at the same time might experience wind loads, it would be appropriate to use a column with different characteristics in the two axial directions. The strongest axial direction is orientated perpendicular to the facade in order to take up the moments.

The form of the column is determined by a desired visual experience and by the column's bearing characteristics. Taking into account both of these conditions the column will, together with the other building components, be an active participant in creating architectural space. Let's look at Mies van der Rohe's National Gallery in Berlin (1969). Eight free-standing columns bear the large two-way steel beam system. The roof rests on rotation-free joints at the tops of the columns and thus transfers no bend-

ing moments to the columns. The columns are centrally loaded. In this situation, the columns could buckle outward in two axial directions and therefore have a doubly symmetric cruciform-shaped cross section. Perpendicularly placed steel plates terminate the main cross plates and distribute more of the material of the cross section to the outer edges. In addition, they will prevent the main cross plates from buckling.

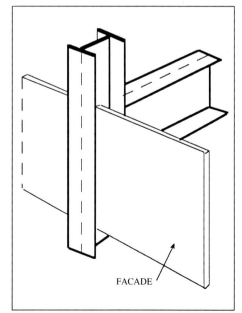

FACADE

*Mies van der Rohe.*
*National Gallery in*
*Berlin. 1969.*
*Spatial column.*

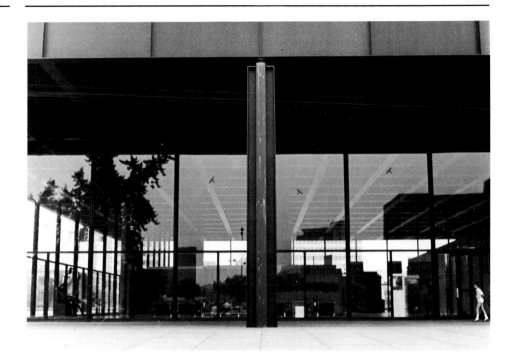

The column's cruciform shape is also consistent with the plan of the roof's two-way beam system. In this case, one axis is not more meaningful than the other.

In architectural theory, there is a quest for an idealized column that is visually the most slender and physically the strongest (see Thomas Thiis-Evensen's *Archetypes in Architecture*). With this in mind, we shall look at the round column and the square column. Both of the cross sections will be solid. First we will look at columns in which the length of the side of the square is equal to the diameter of the circular column. Before we look at slenderness, we shall determine the bearing capacity for the cross sections in the short columns. If they are made of the same material, the column with the largest cross section will bear the most:

$$A_1 = t^2$$

$$A_2 = \pi \cdot (t/2)^2 = 3.14 \cdot t^2/4 = 0.785t^2$$

$$A_1/A_2 = 1/0.785 = 1.27$$

The square column has a 27% larger cross sectional area and, for a short column, an equally greater bearing capacity.

We will now look at slenderness, which is an important value with regard to the bearing capacity of slender columns:

$$\lambda_{k,1} = L_k/\sqrt{(I_1/A_1)},$$

$$\lambda_{k,2} = L_k/\sqrt{(I_2/A_2)}$$

$$\lambda_{k,1}/\lambda_{k,2} = 0.87$$

The square column has a slenderness ratio that is just 87% that of the round column. Therefore, the round column with the same cross-sectional width is 15% more slender. Since the area is also less, the round column's bearing capacity will be considerably less than that of the square column. The latter column, with the same cross-sectional width, is "stronger."

We can also raise the question about the properties of the round and the square columns with equal cross-sectional areas, that is, equal use of material:

$$A_1 = t^2 \quad A_2 = \pi \cdot (d/2)^2$$

$$A_1 = A_2, \text{ so that } t^2 = \pi \cdot (d/2)^2$$

$$t = d/2 \cdot \sqrt{\pi} = 0.88d$$

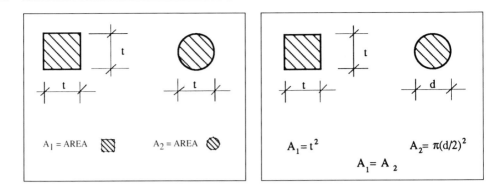

*Square and circular columns with equal cross-sectional dimensions.*

*Square and circular columns with equal cross-sectional area.*

As short columns, they clearly bear equally as much. Let's look at the slenderness:

$$\lambda_{k,1}/\lambda_{k,2} = \sqrt{[I_2/A_2]}/\sqrt{[I_1/A_1]} \sim 1$$

According to our definition, these columns have nearly the same slenderness ratio. With an equal cross-sectional area, they will, as slender columns, also have the same bearing capacity. The column type that visually appears the more slender is not necessarily the more slender structurally.

It must also be noted that while the circular column is symmetrical in all axes that pass through its center, the square column is not. Suppose, for example, that the axis passing through the diagonal is a bending axis, that would give the column exactly the same slenderness ratio as the above-mentioned column, since the area of the cross section remains the same.

The design of the column in vertical cross section is also important when determining its properties and bearing capacity. This is especially true for the slender column where the bending problem limits the bearing capacity. Since the type of deformation known as buckling entails uncontrollable bending, the profile of the column must be designed to prevent such collapsing.

Bending produces bending moments, and in response to these we saw that the cross-sectional dimensions could vary in such a way that the depth of a beam would be largest where the moment is greatest. It is the same for slender columns. If we choose

a column with uniform thickness, the cross-sectional dimensions must give adequate stiffness where bending is greatest. We therefore have a column that is over-dimensioned at all other points along the length of the column where bending is not the greatest. There are many examples in architecture where the cross sectional dimensions of a column vary in such a way that the column is thickest at its middle where bending is greatest and gradually tapers toward its ends. The column takes on a cigar shape, which represents a resourceful use of material and visually makes the column lighter. In addition, the protrusion expresses the bearing function of the column as it would seem to bulge under the vertical load it bears.

Buckling can be prevented with the help of protruding compression rods that are connected by a tension rod to the ends of the column. Bending in this region is effectively prevented. For a free-standing column, it will be necessary to establish this resistance spatially in order to prevent bending along both axial directions of the column.

We should touch on the column's relation to the wall: Structurally speaking, we choose to refer to the wall as an addition and combination of columns in reference to the introductory quotation of Louis Kahn.

It can be said that slender walls, as slender columns, can also experience buckling, though only in the plane of the wall. It is intrinsic to the nature of the wall to have an enormous buckling resistance in its long

*Kantonschule Wohlen. Argau, Switzerland. 1988. Architect: Santiago Calatrava Library. Column with a varying cross section.*

direction, the direction of its plane.

In walls, a combination of a pure wall and a free-standing column is called a pilaster. Pilasters work as localized wall stiffeners with a dramatic (local) increase in the thickness of the wall. Pilaster reinforcing increases the wall's ultimate strength. Such structures are used where the wall is to bear beams of great weight, and in such a way that the pilasters assist in bearing these beams, or where it is necessary to increase the wall's thickness locally to improve its rigidity against wind forces or earth loads.

The most distinctive structural difference between the wall and a corresponding row of columns lies not in the structure's bearing characteristics with respect to vertical loads but in their ability to resist horizontal loads, such as wind loads. Due to its planar rigidity, the wall has properties for transferring such forces directly to the foundations, but the row of columns eventually must work in cooperation with the beam above to form a rigid frame or incorporate the use of cross bracing to establish the same rigidity. The frame as a structural element is discussed in the next chapter.

*Column with lateral supports connected to tension rods between the midpoint and the column's top and bottom. The critical length of the column is cut in half and the critical load is four times as large. Renault Center in Swindon. Architect: Norman Foster.*

# 5.8 Entasis in a Broader Perspective

*A wall with pilaster strengthening and attached column results in significant increases in stiffness.*

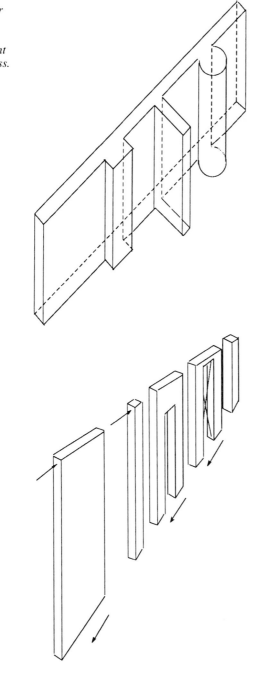

*The wall and the column as wind-bracing elements.*

Entasis, the thickening of the shaft of the column is usually considered, from an aesthetic point of view, an optical correction in response to the eye's requirements for beauty of proportions. The correction also has a practical and structural value: It increases the column's bearing capacity and its resistance to bending moments. In good architecture, structure and aesthetics meet in a natural way.

A few examples that are removed from classical Greek stone architecture can demonstrate the employment of entasis in the broadest applications.

Alvar Aalto's (1898-1976) private residence for the art collector Louis Carré was under construction from 1956 to 1959 a few miles south of Paris. At the entrance portico, we are met by a free-standing column that bears the cantilevered roof.

The material used in the column is unusual, a circular concrete cross section with four wooden fins. The fins are placed where the danger for bending is greatest, along the column's midsection. Aalto's main interest was statically correct structural forms, but the example shows how a great architect intuitively grasps the correct expressive solution.

The new triumphal arch at La Defense in

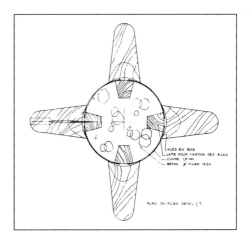

*Column cross section. Maison Carré. 1959. Architect: Alvar Aalto.*

*Tête Défence. Paris.*
*1989.*
*Basic element in the*
*external elevator*
*tower.*

*Top: The principle for*
*the column stabilized*
*with guys.*

*Middle: Bending in*
*the column without*
*stabilizers.*

*Bottom: Bending in*
*the column with*
*stabilizers.*

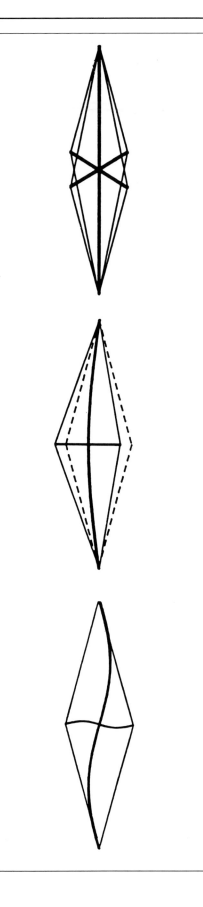

Paris forms the end point of the axis from Louvre through Place de la Concorde and Place de l'Etoile. The grand opening took place in 1989 during the bicentennial of the French Revolution.

Under the marble-sheeted monument, La Grande Arche, by architect Johan Otto von Spreckelsen (1929-1986) and engineer Erik Reitzel (born 1941), we find a free-standing elevator tower that carries its passengers up about 90 meters (300 feet) to the Jardin Suspendu.

The actual tower consists of a series of columns that form the shafts for the elevators. Each column consists of about 21-meter- high (70 foot) column elements that are stiffened with the help of tension rods.

The working method of the elevator tower can be compared to the mast of a sailboat where the extended crosstrees act as the entasis of the mast. As discussed earlier in this chapter, the resultant bearing capacity is multiplied by four.

The simple columns work together so that the tower forms a standing lattice structure. The tower is anchored laterally to the triumphal arch with horizontal elements. These elements are the wind bracing for the tower.

Based on the effective use of the properties of steel in a mast and guy wire system, a thread-like skeletal structure is formed in contrast to the triumphal arch's monolithic marble surfaces.

In the hazy sunlight of Paris, the tower's glittering polished stainless steel masts and guy wires can be seen from a great distance. This is the culmination of years of work with minimal structures by engineer Erik Reitzel.

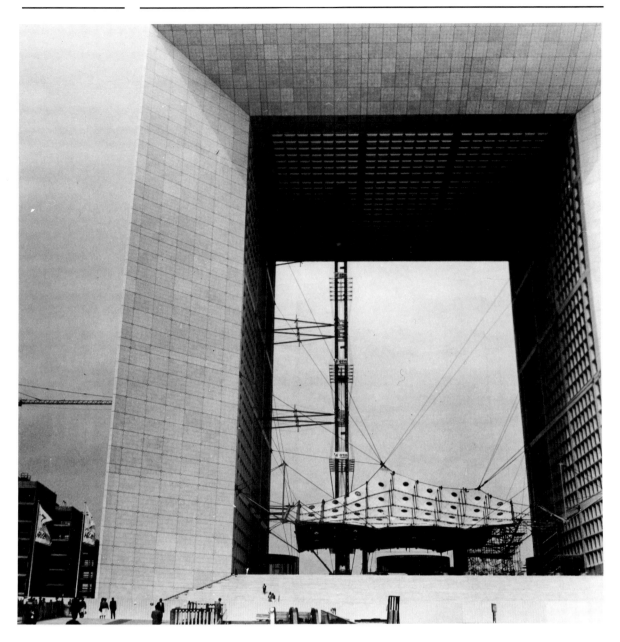

*Tête Défence. Paris.*
*1989.*

*Tête Défence. Paris.*
*1989.*
*The external elevator*
*tower.*
*CAD drawing by*
*architect Per Jacobi.*

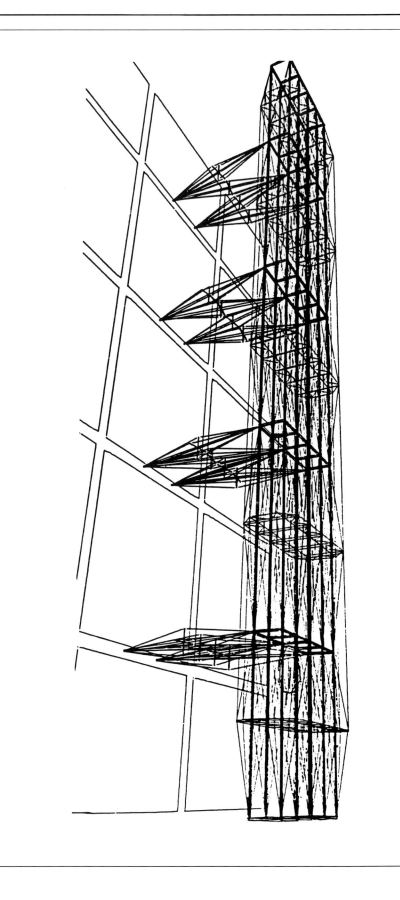

# Chapter 6    THE FRAME: COOPERATION BETWEEN THE COLUMN AND THE BEAM

*Storhamarlåven
Museum.
Hamar, Norway. 1970.
Architect: Sverre Fehn
(born 1924).
The new wooden
structures do not
interfere with the
masonry ruins from
the Middle Ages. A
simple frame carries
the weight of the
column and highlights
the auditorium doors.
The corners of the
frame are stiffened
with the help of inlaid
triangular steel plates
and bolts.*

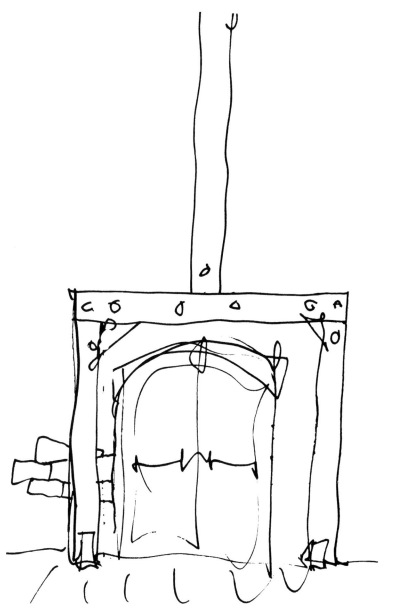

*The frame forms a complete figure. It's existence relies upon cooperation between the column and the beam. Therein lies its structural expression.*

—THOMAS THIIS-EVENSEN, *ARCHETYPES IN ARCHITECTURE.*

## 6.1 THE FUNCTION OF THE FRAME AS STRUCTURAL FORM

We have seen that the primary structural function of the beam and the column is to bear vertical loads, that is, dead loads and live loads. The beam resists such loads and transfers them horizontally to the supports. The direction of the load and its transport path are therefore perpendicular to each other. The beam is subjected to bending. The column resists vertical loads and transfers them directly to the ground. The column is thus subjected to forces acting primarily along the axis of the column: axial forces.

hindered from rotating on its edge, opposite to the force, owing to the twisting moment of the wall's own weight (G) around a point of rotation. Second, the wall must be built in such a way that it does not split up and slide laterally as a result of wind loads, that is, failure due to shear in the length of the wall must be hindered. Because of the possibilities for this form of failure, a wall used in wind bracing is called a shear wall.

The bending moment that arises in a wall as a result of the lateral load at the top of the

*The direction of the beam's span is usually perpendicular to the direction of the load.*

*The wall as a bearing structure for horizontal loads acting in the plane of the wall.*

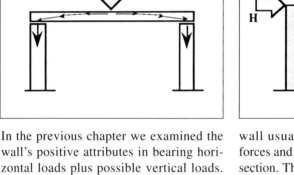

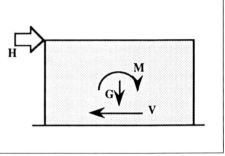

In the previous chapter we examined the wall's positive attributes in bearing horizontal loads plus possible vertical loads. The most important horizontal loads are windloads. It is critical for the stability of a building structure that some elements direct the windloads downward.

For the wall, there are two primary requirements that must be fulfilled so that stability can be maintained. First, the wall must be

wall usually causes small compression forces and tension forces in the wall's cross section. The reason for this is that the wall, by definition, has a large length in relation to its height.

For functional reasons, we might have to cut large openings in a wind bracing wall. We must think about stability and set the same structural requirements on the remaining structure as we had on the whole

*Wall bracing: Fracture possibilities in a wall with a horizontal load; overturning or shear failure.*

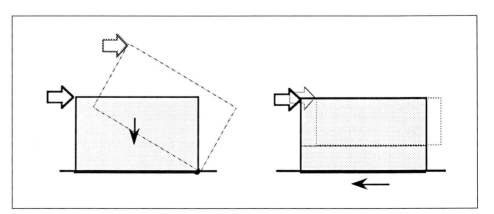

*A frame as though it were cut out of a wall.*

*If the frame is to act as wind bracing like the wall, the same conditions for stability are necessary.*

*Left: the wall. Middle: the frame. Right: static model diagram.*

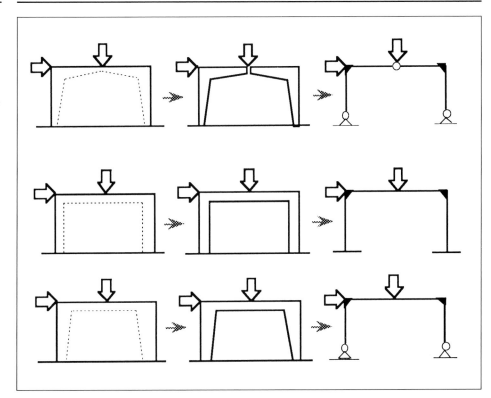

wall, that is, it must withstand the horizontal load. With the removal of large areas of the wall surface, we have formed horizontal and vertical bearing elements, that is, beams and columns. Together, they must form a structural unit that can stand rigid. This structural unit is called a frame. The frame, therefore, characterizes the cooperative efforts of the beam and the column in distributing horizontal and vertical loads.

We can say that the wall already contains the frame (that is, beams, columns, and arches). In contrast to the wall, bending moments will be of considerable importance to the frame.

Let's look at deformation in a double-jointed frame with rigid corners. If the column is loaded with a uniform lateral load, it will experience deformation due to bending.

*Stiff frame corners result in the deformation of the columns being transferred over to the beam and vice versa.*

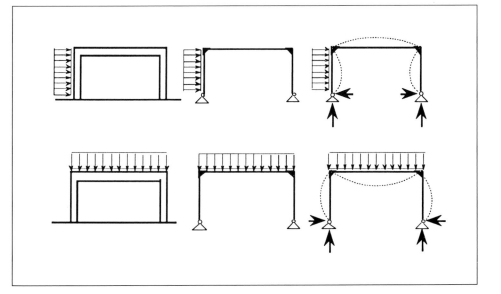

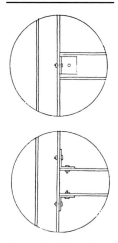

*Examples of bolted corner joints.*
*Top: Hinged joint.*
*Bottom: Fixed joint.*

*Examples of bolted corner joints.*
*Top: Hinged joint.*
*Bottom: Fixed joint.*

Since the corners of the frame are rigid, that is, unchangeable in form, the bending of the column will be transferred over to the beam so that the beam will also be deformed. Bending deformations produce bending moments, and this means that the transferred deformations are the same as the column's moments that are transferred over to the beam. In this case the beam will have moments present even though it is the column that is loaded. Moments in beams are then transferred over to the opposite column via the rigid frame corners.

If we load the same double-jointed frame with a uniformly distributed vertical load, we get a similar transfer of moments from the beam over to the columns via the rigid corners. Since the columns will be moment loaded, they also receive shear forces. These are horizontal and will be added to the horizontal reactions in the joints at the foot of the frame. The horizontal reactions remain, even though the outer loads are vertical. The force reactions are those that characterize the frame as static.

Stable frame structures are also characteristically comprised of no more than three free rotation joints. If there are several joints, the frame will be a kinetic chain that changes in form and thus collapses. A beam/column system with four free rotation joints must be made rigid with cross bracing or with a rigid diagonal. This system of braces is not actually a frame.

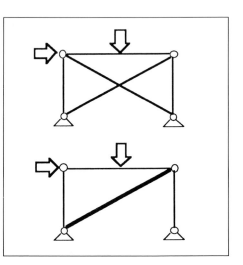

*Reinforced concrete frame construction. Theatre des Champs Elyses. Paris. 1914. Architect: August Perret (1874-1954).*

*The Great Coxwell
Barn.
England. 13th century.*

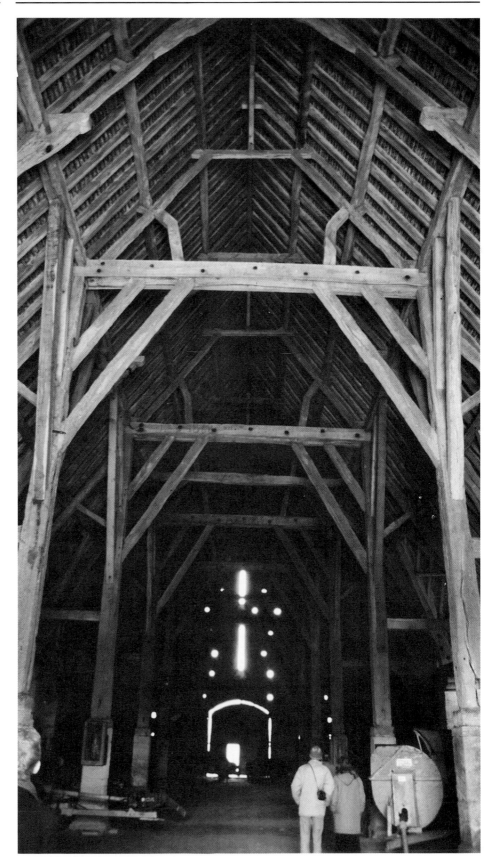

## 6.2 FINNISH FORM

The frame in its simplest form is, as we have seen, a beam connected to two columns, where the joint between the beam and the columns can form a rigid connection, a so-called frame corner. The comparison with a chair illustrates the principle of the connection between the seat and the leg of a stool, forming the corner of a frame. If the corners of the chair are not rigid enough, the legs of the chair will have a tendency to slide away from each other over a hardwood floor when someone sits on the chair. The chair will "do a split."

Wood is a universally used material. It is ideal for small structures, such as furniture, where the joints traditionally were completed with glued pin joints. With large frame structures in wood, the free rotation joints can be secured with several types of steel brackets.

Alvar Aalto experimented in the 1930s with wood's sculptural possibilities. These experiments led, after time, to practical solutions, such as pressed veneers and curving laminated wood structures. The experiments laid the groundwork for Aalto's classic series of curving wood furniture

The basis for most furniture is the stable frame forms. In the design of the actual frame corners lies Aalto's innovative genius, from simple bent-wood chair legs to the fan-shaped versions where the leg is composed of glued wedge-formed laminates. With one clean blow, the traditional solutions were replaced with a new unifying concept.

Aalto's work with furniture, over time, began to influence his later architectural works. Two projects can be cited in this connection, the auditorium of the Technical College in Otaniemi outside Helsinki from 1966 and Riolakirken in Italy from 1968. The arch-formed concrete frames incorporated in both of the projects constitute a synthesis of form and structure, as the earlier furniture experiments in bent-wood frames.

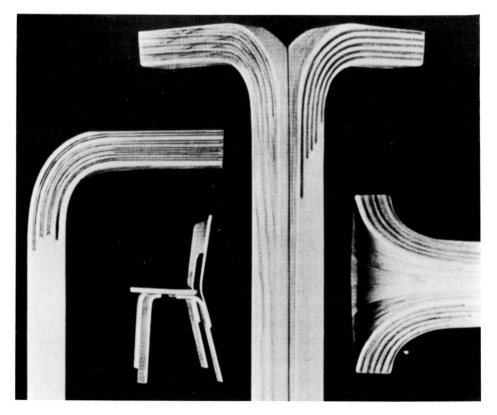

*Alvar Aalto.*
*Three variations of a*
*furniture leg.*

*Double concrete frame in the large auditorium of the Technical College, Otaniemi, Finland. 1966.*
*Architect: Alvar Aalto.*

*Riola Church. Bologna, Italy.*
*Architect: Alvar Aalto.*

*Comparison of statically determinate and statically indeterminate beams and frames, that is, with the same number of unknown forces.*

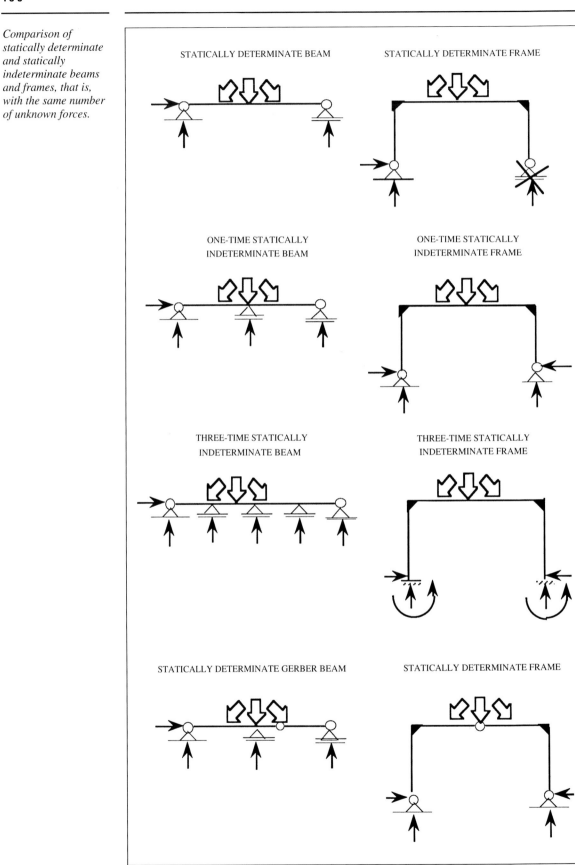

STATICALLY DETERMINATE BEAM

STATICALLY DETERMINATE FRAME

ONE-TIME STATICALLY INDETERMINATE BEAM

ONE-TIME STATICALLY INDETERMINATE FRAME

THREE-TIME STATICALLY INDETERMINATE BEAM

THREE-TIME STATICALLY INDETERMINATE FRAME

STATICALLY DETERMINATE GERBER BEAM

STATICALLY DETERMINATE FRAME

# 6.3 FORCES IN FRAMES

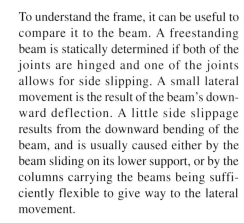

*Statically determinate beam.*

To understand the frame, it can be useful to compare it to the beam. A freestanding beam is statically determined if both of the joints are hinged and one of the joints allows for side slipping. A small lateral movement is the result of the beam's downward deflection. A little side slippage results from the downward bending of the beam, and is usually caused either by the beam sliding on its lower support, or by the columns carrying the beams being sufficiently flexible to give way to the lateral movement.

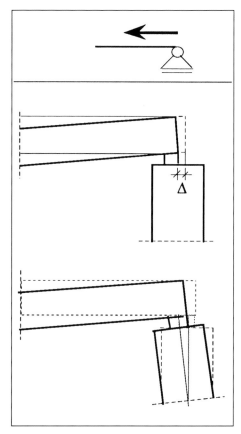

It is different for the frame. In practice, it is too difficult to build the foundations of the frame so that lateral movement is possible. This means that the frame has two fixed joints and is therefore statically indeterminate. Such a frame can be directly compared to a continuous beam with more than two spans. If the frame has two fixed columns, we have a structural system similar to a continuous beam over four spans.

*A small movement of the end of the beam can take place if the beam slides on top of the support or if the column is deflected.*

It is possible to build a statically determinate frame where the forces in the frame can be found through equilibrium formulas. We can achieve a statically determined frame if the frame contains three joints, a static system similar to the Gerber beam.

Now we shall find the forces in a statically determined port frame with three joints. The frame is loaded with a uniform vertical load, q. Vertical equilibrium and symmetry gives

$$A_y = B_y = qL/2$$

Horizontal equilibrium gives:

$$A_x = B_x$$

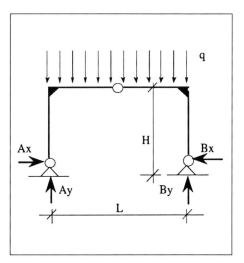

*Statically determinate three-hinged frame with a uniformly distributed vertical load.*

but the magnitude of the forces must be found by first considering the moments. We must "bisect" the frame into two parts through the joint in the beam and require rotation equilibrium for each half. In the hinged joint, we can have two forces, a ver-

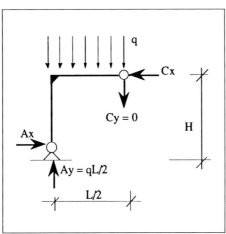

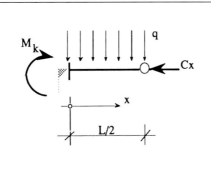

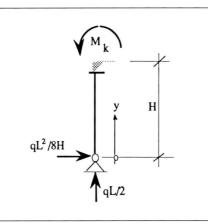

*Equilibrium of forces and moments in one half of a frame provides the forces acting in the support and in joint C.*

*Equilibrium requirements for a portion of the beam gives us the corner moment.*

*Equilibrium requirements for the column is used to find the moment variation along the column.*

tical and a horizontal reaction. In this case the vertical reaction, $C_y$, is obviously equal to zero, since $A_y$ is at equilibrium with the outer load.

$\Sigma M_{joint} = 0$   giving:

$qL/_2 \cdot L/_2 - A_x \cdot H - qL/_2 \cdot L/4 = 0$

$A_x = qL^2/8H$

$\Sigma K_x = 0$   gives: $C_x = A_x = qL^2/8H$

We can now find the bending moment, shear force, and the axial force diagrams for the whole frame. With the help of a section at the corner, we see that the moments in half of the beam will be:

$\Sigma M_{section} = 0$

$M_k + qL/2 \cdot L/4 = 0$

$M_k = -qL^2/8$

The moment will be negative, that is, opposite of that assumed, creating tension along the lower side of the beam. A control check on the column portion should give the same corner moment:

$-M_k - qL^2/8H \cdot H = 0$ gives $M_k = -qL^2/8$

The tension forces from the moment act opposite to that assumed, that is, on the outside, therefore negative sign. Variation along the column will be linear:

$M_{column} = (-qL^2/8H) \cdot y$, where $0 < y < H$

while the variation along the beam will be parabolic $(x^2)$

$M_{beam} = -q(L/2 - x) \cdot (L/2 - x)/2$

$= (-q/2) \cdot (L/2 - x)^2$

where x varies between 0 and L/2, so that for

$x = 0$   $M_{beam} = -qL^2/8$

*Vincent van Gogh.*
*Pont de l'Anglois,*
*Arles.*

*Frame structure as the means for "the well serviced shed." Sainsbury Center for the Visual Arts. 1979. Architect: Norman Foster Associates*

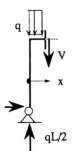

*Diagram used to find the shear forces.*

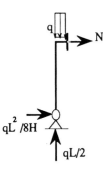

*Diagram used to find the normal forces.*

*Diagram for all of the forces acting in the frame; moments, shear, and normal forces.*

$x = L/2$   $M_{beam} = 0$.

That the moment at the middle of the beam will be equal to zero is a control of what we already knew, that the moment in every hinged joint is equal to zero.

Likewise for shear, we find:

$\sum K_x = 0$

In the column: $V = qL^2/8H$ (= constant).

In the beam: $\sum K_y = 0$, which gives:

$q \cdot L/2 - V - q \cdot x = 0$, and

$V = q \cdot L/2 - q \cdot x$.

For $x = 0$, $V = q \cdot L/2$

For $x = L/2$, $V = 0$.

And finally, for the axial forces:

In the columns: $N = -A_y = -B_y = -q \cdot L/2$ (constant compression).

In the beam $\sum K_x = 0$ giving:

$qL^2/8H + N = 0$   $N = -qL^2/8H$ (constant compression).

It is normally the magnitude and the form of the variations of moment that determine the frame's structural form and dimensions. Shear and axial variation are important for total control of the configuration of the forces. All of these forces vary with frame type and loads.

Finally, it should be mentioned that the frame types illustrated are straight and planar. In practice, other forms of frames and space frames are also valid solutions.

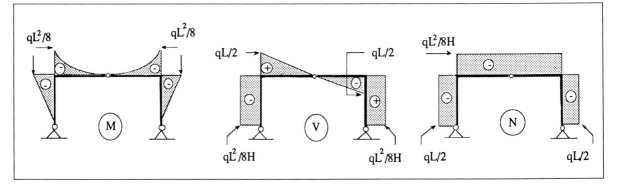

# 6.4 BEAM VS. COLUMN

The design and sizing of beams and columns have important consequences in how the forces will move through the frame. There will be mutual dependency between the column and beam in all statically indeterminate frames where their relative signs will determine each one's share in the absorption of forces.

We will look closer at the two statically indeterminate frames, two port frames with two hinged joints and rigid corners. The first has very rigid columns that support a shallow, "soft" beam. The other has thin columns connected to a rigid, deep beam.

The bending moments show their dependence on the design of the frame, in that they wander to the regions where the structure is stiffest and therefore incorporate the greatest resistance. The stiffer the columns are in relation to the beam, the greater the proportion of bending moments that will migrate to the columns, plus they can hinder twisting of the corner of the frame. For the beam this means that the closer this can come to a condition of fixed corners, the more the moments in the span of the beam are reduced.

The thinner the columns in relation to the

*Left: Frame with stiff columns and soft beam.*

*Right: A deep beam of significantly greater stiffness than the columns.*

*Bending moments are the greatest in the stiffest building elements.*

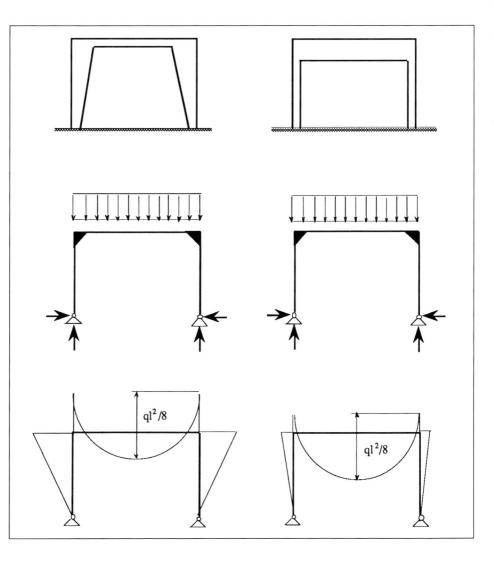

*Three-hinged steel frames. Galerie des Machines, World Exposition in Paris in 1889. Architect: Dutert. Engineer: Contamin.*

*Three-hinged steel frames. Galerie des Machines, World Exposition in Paris in 1889. Architect: Dutert. Engineer: Contamin.*

beam, the less resistance to corner rotation. With that, the frame effect for the load will gradually subside because the beam will approach a state with freely rotating ends, and a correspondingly large beam moment.

In both cases, the size of the beam's moment curve will be equal to $qL^2/8$ for this load, but the varying sizes of the corner moment will lift the curve up or down. In a design situation one can choose to increase the dimensions in column or beam in order to minimize the other building components.

Be sure to note the shape of the moment diagram for the columns. The moment increases from zero at the foot to a maximum value at the beam, that is, it follows a V-pattern. It is the same for the double-hinged frame even though the loading is horizontal. A natural starting point for

designing columns has been the shape of the moment diagram, so that the column also has the same V-form. The formal characteristics of the frame structure are in sharp contrast to the earlier points discussed regarding the transmission of forces down toward the earth. With frames, instead of expecting a thickening of the walls and columns as the load increases, we experience an actual constriction that results in the building meeting the ground "as light as a feather." The structural explanation lies in the importance of the bending moments and their variation. Before steel and reinforced concrete were developed, it was much more difficult to construct a frame with rigid corners. Masonry made it impossible to achieve a rigid moment in a natural way because of masonry's poor resistance to tensile stress. Pure tensile loads on masonry result in cracking and breaking between brick and mortar.

Let's look at Le Corbusier's "L'Unité d'Habitation" (1952). The apartment building is lifted up and rests on a series of concrete pillars that provide for a free ground plane. The pillars are connected to a set of double beams that together with the pillars creates a frame. The beams are hidden by concrete plates on the underside of the apartment building. The task of the frames is to stiffen the building laterally and help direct the wind loads to the ground.

The horizontal load produces bending moments in the V-shaped columns. If we study the moment diagram, we see that the moments are not equal to zero at the ground level, but they become minimal. In the lower portion of the column, the tension will be on the inside of the column for both of the loads. The reason that the moments are not absolutely zero is the width of the column itself, even at the foundations. This column width is necessary in a building of this size, but makes it difficult to have a completely free rotating foot as a joint. Therefore, the columns have, to a certain degree, fixed joints at the base.

*Cross section of l'Unité d'Habitation. Marseilles, France. 1952. Architect: Le Corbusier.*

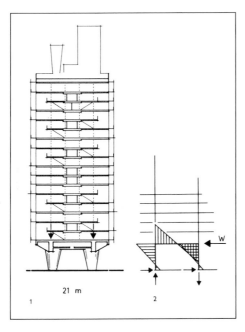

21 m

1

2

W

*Perspective of the frame structure that in reality is hidden from view.*

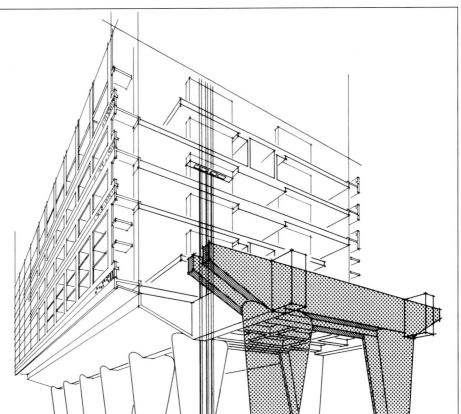

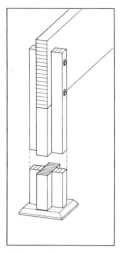

*Column/beam detail.*

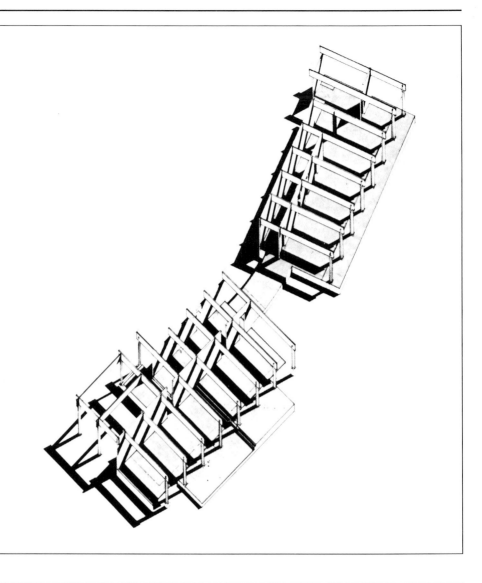

*The Perry House.*
*Surrey, England.*
*1967.*
*Architect: Ernö*
*Goldfinger.*

## 6.5 BRITISH WOOD

Laminated wood frames were the point of departure for a house in Surrey, England, designed in 1967 by architect Ernö Goldfinger (1902-1987).

Structurally, one of the most attractive features of the house are the cruciform columns consisting of three elements. Two of the "arms of the cross" stretch up and embrace the beam on top. They are fastened together by bolts. A ship (or open) joint is the term for such a solution.

We have a stiff frame corner that provides

an effective means for preventing the beam from tipping. The illustration at left shows that it is possible to rotate the direction of the beam 90 degrees. In this design, the technical solution found a sculptural expression.

A related solution to Goldfinger's house in Surrey can be found in Arne Jacobsen's St. Catharinas College in Oxford from the same period, but built of prefabricated concrete elements. In this case, the stability is achieved by fastening the column to the foundation.

*Crown Hall. Chicago.
1952.
Architect: Mies van
der Rohe.*

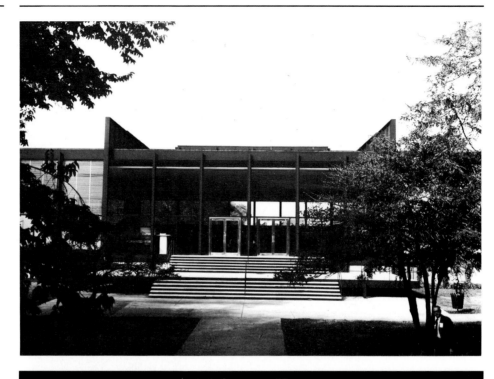

## 6.6 Crown Hall

Chicago gave Mies van der Rohe large building projects and the opportunity to realize his "European architectural ideas" in practice. In Crown Hall from 1952 at the Illinois Institute of Technology, the idea of a large universal space is clearly expressed.

The building's main plan, which contains the architecture and urban design department, has a column-free space that is 40 x 75 meters (132 x 246 feet).

Steel frames form the bearing structure. The roof consists of suspended bearing plates formed as tall I-beams. The web is stiffened with the help of welded plates that form the joints along the beam. The width of both of the flanges increases parallel the joints toward the middle of the span. The increase in width contributes to the strengthening of the flanges' ability to withstand the bending moment that, as we know, is the greatest at the middle of the span.

This solution also prevents the bearing plate and the compression flanges from lat-eral buckling. Since the bearing plates maintain a constant depth along the length of the roof beam, this solution increases the beam's bearing capacity. (In chapter 4, we described how Jørn Utzon's moment beams were designed with varying cross sections along the length of the span in order to increase their bearing capacity. In that case, the depth of the beams also remained constant.)

The bearing plates are supported by external columns and together form the primary frames. The outer walls are of glass, mounted in secondary steel profiles. On the interior, nonbearing walls are reduced to free-standing partitions covered with a rose-wood veneer.

It is characteristic of Mies' working method that once the structure is designed, all the other building parts will be secondary and subordinate to it. To strive for simplicity is demanding work. One of his clients, who understood this, said it in this manner: *"Macht es so einfach wie möglich, koste es was es wolle."*

*Crown Hall. Chicago.*
*1952.*
*Architect: Mies van*
*der Rohe.*
*Steel precision.*

*Crown Hall under*
*construction.*

# Chapter 7

# THE ARCH

*Cathedral. Chartres, France. Begun in 1194.*

*Tag Kisra.
Baghdad, Iraq.
300-600 B.C.
Vault structure in
sun-baked bricks;
span 25.5 meters
(84 feet).*

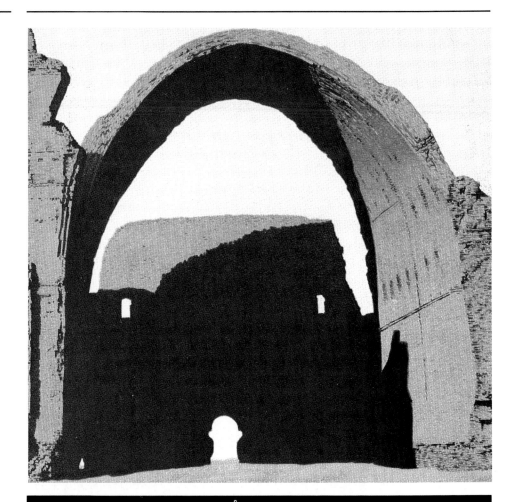

## 7.1 THE ARCH AS HISTORIC INDICATOR

The arch represents one of the most widely known forms of construction. The origin is lost in the ancient cultures along the Tigris and Euphrates rivers, centuries before recorded time. The development of a characteristic arch form is a common trait for later cultures.

The Romans, with their compulsion for simple geometric forms, developed the use of the semi-circular, or Roman, arch. The aqueduct, Pont du Gard (A.D. 100), which insured transportation to Vernausur (Nimes) in France, is one of the finest examples of how the Romans took advantage of the intrinsic potential in arched construction.

The pointed arch was introduced and seriously developed by the Gothic master builders in the Middle Ages. In a series of

French cathedrals that were actually pure structures, beginning with Chartres in 1194, Reims in 1211, Amiens in 1220, and Beauvais in 1247, the technique was further developed and taken to perfection.

The form of the arch in Islamic architecture is clear in our minds; it curves like an onion, not just outward but upward with its closure. We can find offspring of this arch form in Moorish palaces in Spain and Venice.

Other commonly known arch forms are compossed of portions of a circle, circle segments, and ellipses or combinations of several of these basic forms. In more recent times, the parabola-shaped arch has been industriously used. We will touch on the reason for this below.

*Triumphal arch,*
*Roman garrison city.*
*Volubilis, Morocco.*
*3rd century B.C.*

## 7.2 THE CHARACTER OF THE ARCH AND THE VAULT

The vault is an arched structure of three-dimensional character. The cross section of a vault is an arch.

In the northern European tradition, the vault is used for special building projects, spaces that service special functions. With the use of a vault, specific functions within a building complex can be highlighted. A vaulted structure also often requires an added contribution of expertise and resources.

The vault spans continuously from the first arch to the last one and forms a room. We do not experience a break, as with the ridge of a pitched roof. If we stand under a vault or face an arched window and look out, we see a little section taken from the outside world. The form of the arch gives us a complete picture of the world.

Architect Karl Friederich Schinkel (1781-1841) had, as a painter, often been preoccupied with the relationship between inside and outside. In his painting *Spreeufter bei Stralau* from 1817, we see how the vaulted bridge forms the foreground as well as the frame for the river landscape with the figures in the boat.

*Karl Friedrich*
*Schinkel.*
*Spreeufer bei Stralau.*
*1817.*

*Sketches by Leonardo da Vinci from his studies of horizontal reactions in arches.*

*Loading of a rope with a weight causing tension in the rope. The reaction forces attempt to pull the supports inward, and these must be resisted. In the same way, the opposite form subjected to a concentrated load is in compression. The reactions will press outward and must be counteracted with forces acting in the opposite direction.*

*The rope and the arch, with uniformly distributed loads along the arched form, result in a so-called catenary form. The rope carries with the help of tension, while the arch, of the same form, is subjected only to compression.*

Common for all types of arches is the curved haunch. The curve means that the load is borne in the form of compression forces rather than in the form of bending. As a construction, therefore, the arch can be historically described as the form that employs masonry materials—stone and bricks—in the best possible way. Masonry has poor bearing capabilities when it comes to bending tension and pure tension forces. For compression forces, however, the material is very favorable, and for spanning great distances, the arch was the most natural form, with its ability to bear compression loads.

In order to understand the arch, we will first analyze the rope, which can be considered a reversed compression arch, because the material can clearly bear only tension forces. (This is covered in closer detail in chapter 8.) With two hands, hold a rope with a weight hanging from the rope's midpoint. Tighten the rope to put it into tension. In addition to the mass of the weight, the hands will feel forces that attempt to pull them toward each other. In order to maintain the arch, we must pull with enough force to establish balance and equilibrium. If we now "freeze" the rope in order for it to be stiff or substitute it for another material, for example, wood, and invert the figure, the analysis will show that the form will bear under pure compression if the type of load is the same, that is, a simple load at the center point. This time, however, the form presses outward when it is loaded, and we must hold the structure to establish equilibrium. The arrow in the figure (bottom right) describes the direction of the load acting on the structure.

We can go one step further and look at a rope that bears a vertical load that is uniformly divided along the length of the rope, such as, the weight of the rope itself. The rope bears as before, only with the help of tension forces, and we see the same reactions at the supports.

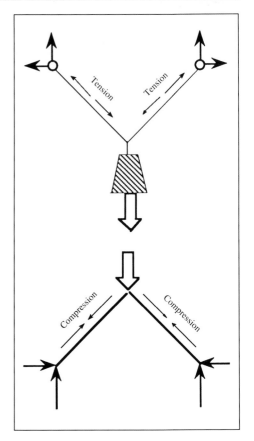

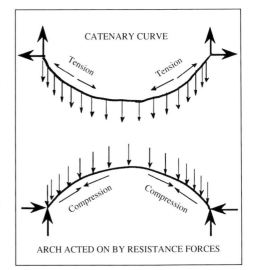

CATENARY CURVE

ARCH ACTED ON BY RESISTANCE FORCES

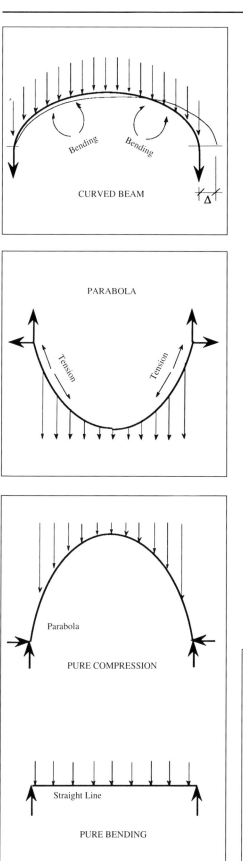

*Without counteracting forces, the arched form acts as a beam.*

CURVED BEAM

*With a load uniformly distributed along the length of the span, the rope will be parabolic in form.*

PARABOLA

Tension — Tension

*The parabolic form, as in the arch, will carry a uniformly distributed load by compression forces in the arch.*
*The same load acting on a straight line will result in pure bending in the structure.*

Parabola

PURE COMPRESSION

Straight Line

PURE BENDING

*The construction of a parabola.*
*The construction lines will be tangent to the parabola.*

The form the rope assumes under loading is called the chained curve or the chained linear arch. It can be described mathematically but is relatively complicated. We substitute the chain for a stiff bearing material and turn the form around; the same vertical load, uniformly distributed, results in compression forces only. But in order for it to stand, we must again neutralize both vertical and horizontal forces at the ends. If the tendency of the arch to deform is not resisted, the bearing mechanism will not be stable even if it has an arched form. This means that we have only an arched beam that bears when the beam bends. If it is to bear the same load as the arch, the dimension of the cross section will be larger.

If we now take a rope and load it with a vertical load, uniformly distributed along the length of the span, the rope will be parabola-shaped. We do not consider the weight of the rope itself, which we estimate to be a great deal less than the load it carries. The rope is bearing the load as tension forces, and in the same way the inverted shape will bear this load as compression force alone. For a uniformly distributed vertical load along the length of the span, the parabola will be a borderline case, bearing only under compression. The other extreme is the flat beam that bears the load as bending forces alone. Every intermediate shape will bear the load as a combination of compression and bending.

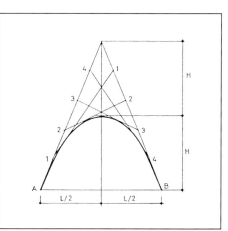

# 7.4 STRUCTURAL FUNCTION AS A CRITERION OF FORM

*Colegio Teresiano.*
*Architect:*
*Antoni Gaudi.*
*An arch with a*
*parabolic form.*

*St. Paul's Cathedral.*
*London, England.*
*Architect:*
*Christopher Wren.*
*The dome consists of*
*three parts with the*
*load bearing dome*
*in the middle. The*
*conical masonry*
*cupola has a section*
*that mainly follows*
*a catenary arch.*

*St. Peter's Cathedral.*
*Rome, Italy.*
*The cupola was*
*analyzed as a bearing*
*structure in 1748 by*
*engineer Giovanni*
*Poleni. At that time,*
*cracks had begun*
*to form.*

For every loading situation, there is an arched form that provides compression only in the cross section. This form is called the load's line of compression and can be found by hanging the actual load from a rope. The Catalan architect Antonio Gaudi (1852-1926) created his demanding structures in this manner.

The problem with seeking forms in this way is that the loading varies, especially when the load is significantly greater than the actual weight. We cannot change the form of the arch after the building is already standing. If one wishes to work with effective arches, the form of the arch can either be the form that maximizes compression forces and minimizes the bending forces for the changing load situations (that is, seek the line of compression for the dominant load, such as its own weight) or the form that minimizes the forces from tension bands at the support structures on each side of the arch.

The first documentation we have pertaining to the use of the chained line in a building

analysis is from 1748 when engineer Giovanni Poleni (1685-1761) was hired to explain and repair the cracking cupola of St. Peter's Cathedral in Rome. On a section drawing of the cupola he drew a chained line curve to trace the compression forces down through the structure. Likewise, Sir Christopher Wren must have had knowledge of the chained line when he designed the structural cupola of St. Paul's Cathedral in London around 1700.

We should point out that the chained line curve was a much more important design tool in earlier masonry building than it is today, mainly because the dead load of the structure itself was often the dominant load in a masonry building. In our times, material dimensions are thinner and the dead loads are reduced. Today, live loads like snow, wind, or the load of traffic on a bridge, increasingly dominate, and these loads vary in magnitude and direction over time. They cause bending forces in the arch in spite of the chained linear form. Modern materials, however, like steel and reinforced concrete, have greater resistance to bending forces.

Until now, we have looked at arches only as thin curves symbolizing their form. In prac-

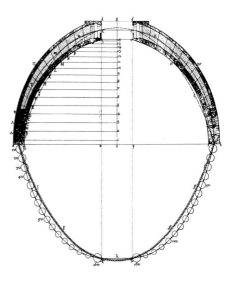

*If the arch follows the line of thrust, this line will also be the center line of the arch.*

*The line of thrust for a concentrated load will consist of straight lines. An arch in the shape of a semicircle will therefore be subjected to moments.*

tice, arches have thickness. If we look at a parabola-shaped arch that has only a vertical load uniformly distributed along the length of the span, the arch's line of compression will also be a parabola. The compression forces in the cross section are united at the center line of each arch. We have chosen to ignore the dead load of the arch itself. (If included, the compression line would be closer to the chained line.)

Even though the form of the arch changes, the compression line for this load will always be a parabola. With an arbitrary arch form different from the parabola, the position of the compression line will not be at the center line of the arch. Whether we still have compression forces in the cross section depends on how far the compression line (the parabola) is from the center line. This can be shown both mathematically and with simple models. As long as the compression line, which is also the resultant of the compression forces, falls within the inner third of the cross section, the cross section will only be under compression. This inner third is called the cross-sectional core (see chap. 5). If the compression line acts outside of the core, the arch will experience moments with tension in the cross section on the opposite side of the compression line.

If we have an arch built of a material, such as masonry, that has poor resistance to bending, we will experience fracturing of the material in the portion where the compression line lies outside the cross-sectional core. For materials with good tensile strength, we can dimension the arch for the bending forces.

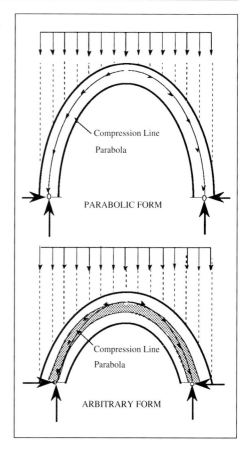

PARABOLIC FORM

Compression Line
Parabola

ARBITRARY FORM

Compression Line
Parabola

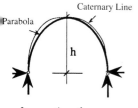

Parabola

Caternary Line

h

*In practice, the catenary curve and the parabola are nearly the same shape. We find it acceptable to treat the catenary curve as a parabola as long as the relationship between the height and width of the arch is less than 5.*

*For a uniformly distributed load, the parabola will always be the line of thrust. For arch shapes other than the parabola, bending moments will result if the line of thrust falls outside the middle third of the cross section.*

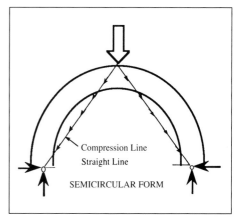

Compression Line
Straight Line

SEMICIRCULAR FORM

## 7.5 FORCE REACTIONS IN STATICALLY DETERMINATE THREE-HINGED ARCHES

Let's look closer at the theoretical analysis of an arch and the quantifying of the forces. We will work only with statically determinate arches. A so-called three-hinged arch is statically determinate. There are three unknown forces for each half of the arch. We know that there are three equations for equilibrium that must be fulfilled in order to have static equilibrium:

$$\Sigma M = 0 \quad \Sigma K_x = 0 \quad \Sigma K_y = 0$$

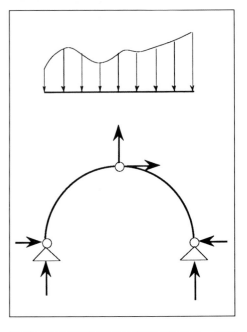

*The three-hinged arch is statically determinate. We have altogether six unknown reactions in the arch and we have 2 x 3 equations.*

A three-hinged arch consists of two symmetrical halves that must satisfy the conditions for equilibrium. Thus we have six equations. With six unknown force reactions, we have just as many unknowns as equations, and therefore the system is statically determinate.

We will now examine a three-hinged arch with a height h and a span L, which is loaded with a point load P at the top. The vertical reactions at the joints must be equal to P/2 on each side. So we must now find the horizontal reactions:

$\Sigma M = 0$, so that

$$H_1 \cdot h - P/2 \cdot L/2 = 0$$

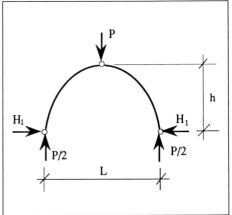

*Horizontal reactions $H_1$ from the arch with a height h.*

$$H_1 = P \cdot L/4h$$

For the sake of comparison, let's look at an arch with just half of the height but with the same span, we have:

$\Sigma M = 0$, so that

$$H_2 \cdot h/2 - P/2 \cdot L/2 = 0$$

$$H_2 = 2P \cdot L/4h = 2H_1$$

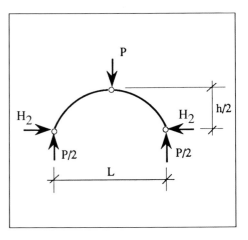

*For the arch with a height h/2 we have horizontal reactions $2H_1$.*

For an arch over the same span but with half of the height, the horizontal reaction force is doubled. Therefore, when the arch is flatter the horizontal supports will generally increase.

*Giovanni Battista*
*Piranesi (1704-1778).*
*Dark Prision. Etching.*

*Bridge. Zuoz, Switzerland. 1901. Engineer: Robert Maillart. The three-hinged arch is the point of departure in this structural system. The horizontal reactions will be resisted by the on-land foundations.*

*Ospedale degli Innocenti. Florence, Italy. 1421-1445. Architect: Filippo Brunelleschi. The horizontal reactions of arches or vaults are balanced by forces in the tension rods. They are made of iron and interconnect the supports of the arch.*

*Salginatobel Bridge. Switzerland. 1930. Engineer: Robert Maillart. Detail of the bridge's hinged joint.*

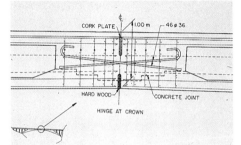

Reaction forces can also be found graphically. Let us look at an arch with a simple point load placed at an arbitrary point. We know that the resultant, which is supported on the half of the arch that is not loaded, must pass through the joint at the top; if it does not, it would have a moment arm and would result in a moment around the point at the top. But the arch is, by definition, free from moments. So we draw a line from the support joint that passes through the joint at the top of the arch to a point directly over the point load. The magnitudes of the resultant forces are found by creating a closed force triangle. The resultant can be decomposed into a horizontal and vertical reaction.

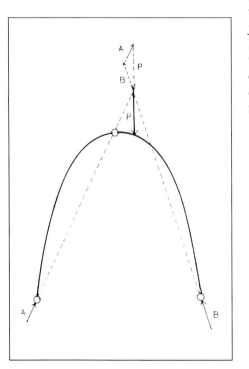

*Graphic method used to find the reaction forces in a three-hinged arch with a concentrated load.*

## 7.6 THE FOUNDATIONS OF THE ARCH

A building must find its architectonic and structural clarification. The arch and the vault, in contrast to vertical-standing, more static elements, have their innate dynamics. Solving the transition between the arch and its foundation is therefore especially challenging. We shall look at a few examples of how the arch "lands":

In the bridge at East 45th Street in New York, not far from Grand Central Station, the bearing arches are built in steel while the foundations are of granite blocks. The granite blocks, which transfer the force of

*East 45th Street Bridge. New York.*

the arches further down into the ground, are given a special design with an angled surface that meets the compression joint of the arch. This solution has many variations and represents a good structural tradition from the late nineteenth century.

In the Stortinget subway station in Oslo, Norway, the bearing plate ceiling is carried by arch systems of steel. The transition from the arch to the wall is made by large steel brackets.

Pier Luigi Nervi (1891-1979) built a series of hangars for the Italian air force at the end of the 1930s. The vaulted hangars are built with a diagonal rib system of prefabricated concrete. In order to accomodate the extremely large doors, the vault is carried by six poured-in-place concrete pillars. The angled pillars, with their sculptural form, transfer all the roof forces to the foundation in the ground.

In comparison to Nervi's hangars, it is interesting to examine the bridge in Barcelona by the Spanish architect and engineer Santiago Calatrava (born 1951). The bridge is carried by two steel parabola arches. The lower portions of the arches serve as side walls for the stairs coming up from the riverfront to the plane of the bridge.

In Norman Foster's 1983 competition project for a sports arena in Frankfurt, Germany, angled concrete foundations are also used. The hall and its foundations "sit" in the landscape without dominating the surrounds with its large volume.

Architects and engineers must go beyond their restricting professional limits and work together on cooperative solutions.

*Stortinget Metro Station.*
*Oslo, Norway. 1987.*
*Architects: Doxrud, Eggen & Mjøset.*
*Engineer: Ing. Bonde & Co.*

*Pier Luigi Nervi.*
*Hangar in prefabricated concrete elements.*
*Orrieto, Italy. 1939.*

*Santiago Calatrava.*
*Bridge Bach de*
*Roda-Felipe II.*
*Barcelona, Spain.*
*1987.*

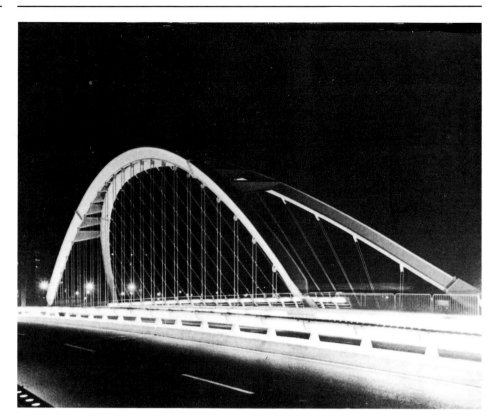

*Santiago Calatrava.*
*Bridge Bach de Roda-*
*Felipe II.*
*Barcelona, Spain.*
*1987.*
*Plan and elevation.*

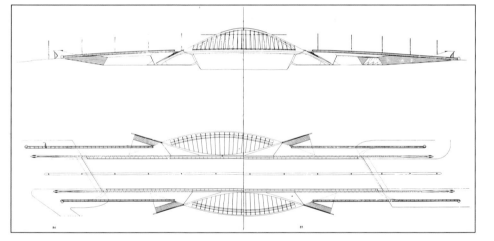

*Norman Foster.*
*Project for a*
*gymnasium.*
*Frankfurt, Germany.*
*1983.*

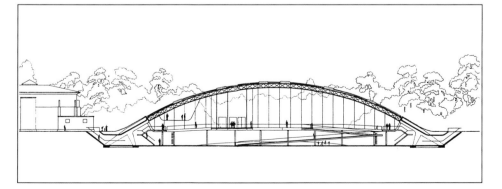

*Project for Palace of the Soviets. Moscow. 1931. Architect: Le Corbusier.*

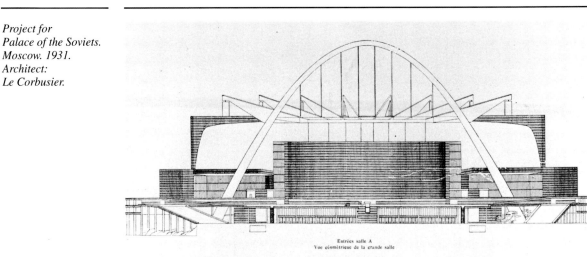

Entrées salle A
Vue géométrique de la grande salle

## 7.7 BENDING MOMENTS IN ARCHES

If an arch carrying a uniformly distributed vertical load is not parabola-shaped, it will experience bending. We will now look at how we generally find the moment at any point in an arch. But we shall use general static methods to actually show that the parabola under bending is moment-free.

As an example, we can use Le Corbusier's (1887-1965) project for the Palace of the Soviets in Moscow in 1931. The parabola-shaped arch has a uniformly distributed load along the entire width of the span.

In order to specify the mathematics of the parabola, we must establish a coordinate

*The parabola in an x-y coordinate system with load and force reactions.*

system so that every point along the parabola can be defined with an exact distance form both the x and y axis. The height of the arch (vector height) is h and the width of the span is L. We ignore the dead load of the arch. The general equation that specifies the parabola in an x-y coordinate system is:

$$y = a \cdot x^2$$

where the constant a is dependent on the relation between the height and the span. For this parabola we find:

$$y = h \quad \text{when} \quad x = \pm L/2$$

that is, we plot in the coordinates of the structure. Included in this general equation

$$h = a \cdot (\pm L/2)^2 = a \cdot L^2/4 \quad \text{or} \quad a = 4h/L^2$$

Thus we have:

$$y = x^2 \cdot 4h/L^2$$

The vertical reactions in the structure can be found by adding the external forces in the y direction.

*Loading on one half of the parabola.*

*Detail of the arch. In the section $(x_1, y_1)$, the moment $M_1$ is acting and must be in equilibrium with the external moments.*

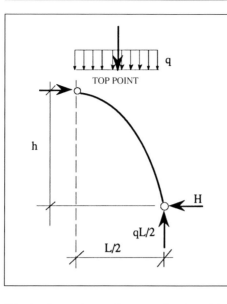

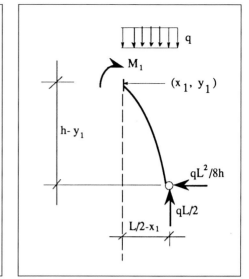

The horizontal reactions can be found by adding the moments about the top point:

$\Sigma M_{top} = 0$, which results in

$H \cdot h + q \cdot L/2 \cdot L/4 - q \cdot L/2 \cdot L/2 = 0$

$H \cdot h = qL^2/4 - q \cdot L^2/2 = q \cdot L^2/8$

$H = q \cdot L^2/8h$

To have equilibrium in the x direction for each half, the compression at the top of the arch must be equal to:

$qL^2/8h$

We examine the moment for an arbitrarily chosen point where:

$x = x_1$  and  $y = y_1 = x_1^2 \cdot 4h/L^2$

with the addition of the internal and external moments here:

$M_1$

$+(h-y_1) \cdot qL^2/8h + q \cdot (L/2-x_1) \cdot (L/2-x_1)$

$/2-q \cdot L/2 \cdot (L/2-x_1) = 0$

When we move over to the other side of the equal sign and multiply with the parenthesis, we get:

$M_1 = y_1 \cdot qL^2/8h - qx_1^2/2$

Now we can set in the equation for the parabola:

$y_1 = x_1^2 \cdot 4h/L^2$

and have

$M_1 = qx_1^2/2 - qx_1^2/2 = 0$

We see that the moment, arbitrarily chosen at point $(x_1, y_1)$, for all of the values of x and y, is equal to 0. Therefore, we have shown mathematically that the parabola under load is moment-free.

A semicircular arch with the same load can be analyzed in the same way. Here we will find that the bending moment will vary along the arch. The moment will, as before, be zero at the joints.

We have seen that some arches with varying loads and forms will experience bending. In fact, they will always produce a horizontal outward pressure that must be considered. Arches and vaults depend on having two symmetrical "halves" leaning against each other at their tops so that compression forces can be transferred. Now we shall look at how this structural requirement can be combined with the opening of the structure to admit the passage of light into a space.

*Aleppo in Syria.
17th century.*

*Aleppo in Syria.
17th century.*

## 7.8 THE VAULT AND LIGHT

> *No space, architecturally, is a space unless it has natural light.*
>
> —LOUIS KAHN

It is daylight that gives life to the vault. The variations in daylight tell us the time of day, which season it is, how the weather is, and so forth.

The light that enters a building through the openings in the facade dissipates as it reaches deeper into the room. A long skylight or ridge light gives evenly dispersed light throughout the entire room. The skylight gives us a direct view of the sky and therefore has a completely different light quality and character than lateral lighting, which is normally reflected from buildings and landscape outside.

It is therefore important to clearly understand that we need far less glass area with skylights than with lateral lighting in order to have the same light intensity. The direction of the light is also decisive in determining how we experience people and objects. The theme has many variations but we shall in this section look closer at three specific examples: The souk is a traditional street market in the Middle East and North Africa. Many of these streets are covered with various forms of masonry groin vaults as in Aleppo in Syria. Light from the sky seeps in through rectangular openings at the top of the vaults and contributes to the staging of daily life in the souk. In a masonry vault it is natural to have separate openings for light at the top, slits breaking the continuity of the vaults and making the transfer of forces impossible.

York Railway Station is the Victorian train station par excellence, designed by architects Thomas Prosser and William Packey in 1877. The train hall follows the curve of the tracks, and the skylight is constructed as

a continuous ridge light on the hall's secondary structure, the horizontal purlins, while the primary structure, the arches, pass uninterrupted through the space. The ridge light sitting at the top of the vault is very efficient in shedding water off the glass. The natural light washing over the curved track, the heavy masonry wall, and the perforated steel arches, contribute to giving the hall its elegant character.

Louis I. Kahn's Kimball Art Museum in Fort Worth, Texas, consists of a series of vault-shaped concrete shells. The profile of the shells is a so-called cycloid, a curve that is generated by a point on the circumference of a circle as it rolls along a straight line. Kahn himself describes the choice of the vault in this way: "My mind is full of Roman greatness and the vault so etched itself in my mind that, though I cannot employ it, it's there always ready. And the vault seems to be the best. And I realize that the light must come from a high point where the light is best in zenith. The vault, rising not high, not in an august manner, but somehow appropriate to the size of the individual. And its feeling of being home and safe came to mind."

Daylight seeps in through a horizontal slit cut in the top of the concrete vault. Cross ribs of concrete ensure connection between the two halves of the shell.

Light is controlled with the help of a perforated, polished aluminum reflector. The reflector lets most of the light directly down into the room, while the remainder is reflected on the interior surface of the vault. The surface of the vault is softly washed in light.

Design and modeling of natural light depends on the type of building and its orientation. Henning Larsen speaks about a half year of Nordic winter where one must literally "throw the light in," as in the glass-covered streets of his University Center in Trondheim, Norway. In his building for the Ministry of International Affairs in Riyadh, Saudi Arabia, he had to reduce the amount of daylight to just a few small streams.

*Louis I. Kahn:*
*Kimbell Art Museum.*
*Fort Worth, Texas.*
*1972.*

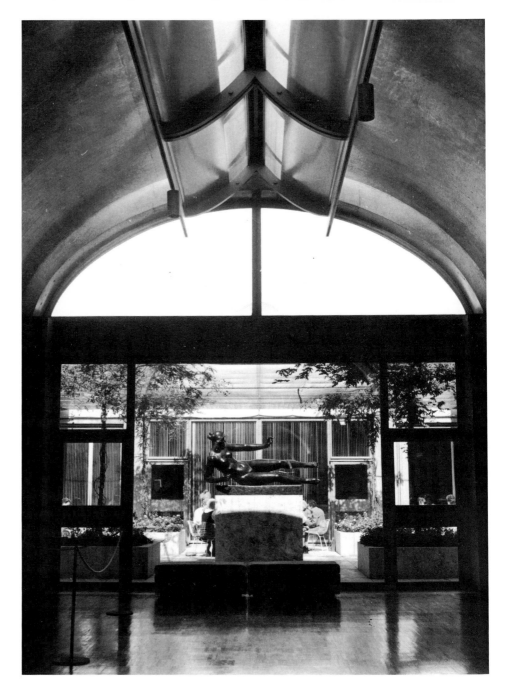

# Chapter 8

# THE CABLE AND THE MEMBRANE

*Ulvøy Bridge. Oslo, Norway. 1928. Designer and Engineer: Olaf Stang. Well-known landmark along the Oslo Fjord. The bridge has a span of 126.7 meters (415 feet) with 20.7-meter-high (68 foot) masts. The cables are anchored in the bedrock at each end. Originally it was constructed as a soft suspension bridge, but in 1981, the masts were strengthened and the concrete deck was replaced with a steel truss system.*

**8.1 Suspended Structures and Soft Shells**
**8.2 The Statics of Cables**
**8.3 Saarinen: Tension and Thrust**
**8.4 Networks of Cables and Fabric**
**8.5 Cable Structures in Paris and Tokyo**

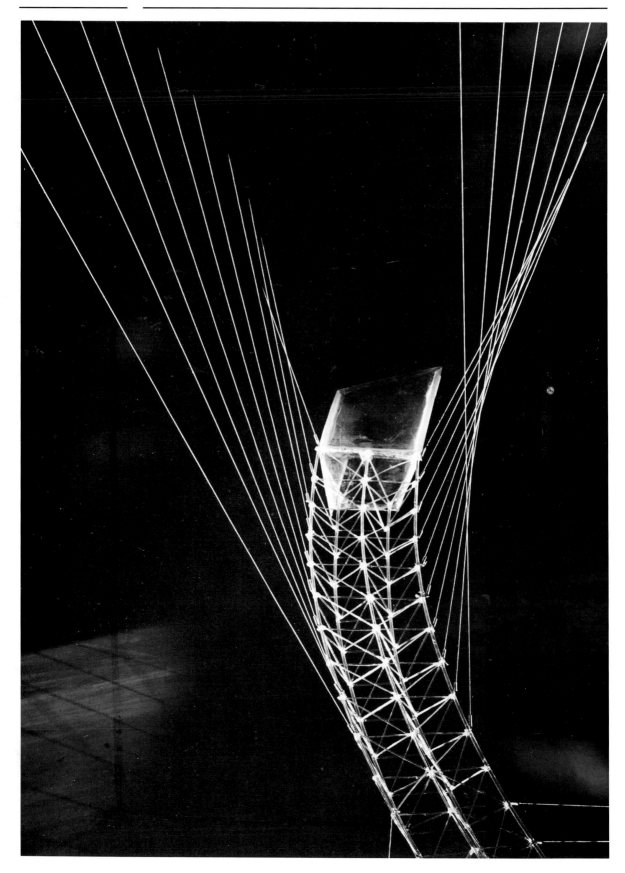

# 8.1 Suspended Structures and Soft Shells

*Ruck-a-Chucky Bridge. San Francisco. 1976. Architect: SOM, Chicago. Engineer: T. Y. Lin. Suspended structure with cables mounted from the walls of the mountains. Model by architecture students Edda Einarsdottir, Margrethe Friis, Geir Johnsen, and Vera Tesdal.*

The rope and the cable have long been used in one-dimensional suspension structures or in double-curve surfaces. In nature, such structures can be found in a spider's web or a fly's wing. A fishnet is also a membrane-like structure. Membranes made out of fabric, such as the sail, the tent, and the umbrella, employ the structural properties of rope and cloth.

The cable is ideal for lightweight bearing structures over long spans. The best-known works using cable structures in our times are suspension bridges. These elegant, almost floating, structures make full use of the tensile properties of steel cables and result in enormous spans. Humber Bridge in England and the Verrazano-Narrows Bridge in New York are examples of bridges having the greatest free span, about 1,300 to 1,400 meters (4,265 to 4,600 feet). In Sognefjorden, Norway, high-voltage power lines with a free span of 5.3 kilometers (3.3 miles) are a good example of steel cable's bearing capacity taken to the limit.

The steel used in cables can be made much stronger than the steel that is used in beams and columns. While ordinary steel in rolled sections has a strength of about 200 to 300 $N/mm^2$ (29,000 psi), steel cable can have a strength ranging from 1500 to 2000 $N/mm^2$ (2,000,000 to 3,000,000 psi). The strands of the cable are produced by cold stretching, a process that results in an enormous increase in the tensile strength of the steel. In addi-

tion, this type of steel has an increased hardness and is so difficult to saw or cut that its use is not practical in other than ropes and cables. Strands are made into steel ropes by spinning, and then the steel ropes are bundled to make larger cables.

Cable structures have properties that make them more difficult to use in buildings than in, for example, suspension bridges. The softness of the cable results in changes in form when there is a change in the load. Used in roof structures, the cable's movement would make it difficult to insure a watertight roof, and in addition, it could lead to vibration and oscillation of the roof surface.

Cable roof structures must be stabilized, that is, prevented from shifting whenever there is a change in the load's magnitude or direction. Changes may occur when the wind alternates from a compression to a suction force on the roof's surface. In addition, gusts of wind cause swinging motions or oscillations, which must be dampened. These changes require a special form of bracing. We can classify cable and membrane structures using formal and structural criteria. This classification also reflects the methods used in stabilizing the bearing systems:

• Simply suspended cable structures. The structures can be stabilized using several methods: by placing dead load on or sus-

*Olympic Stadium. Munich, Germany. 1972. Architects: Benisch and Partner with Frei Otto. Model by architecture students Trond Elverum, Kari Haselgård, Anne Margret Tomasdottir, and Merete Varøystrand.*

*Olympic Stadium. Detail of a cable joint.*

*Freely supported cable stabilized by its own weight plus the load of other structures.*

*Cable beam with the main cable and the underlying tension cable.*

*Cable beam with main cable and the overlying prestressed cable.*

*Simply supported cable stabilized by rigid elements.*

*Cable beam with main cable and partly overlying prestressed cable.*

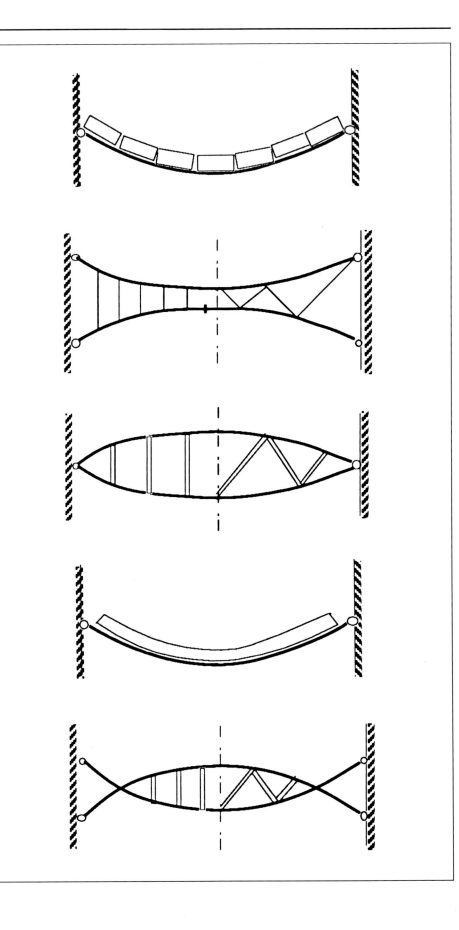

*Double curvature cable net.*

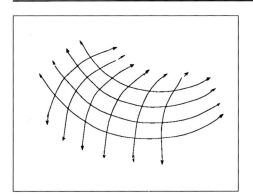

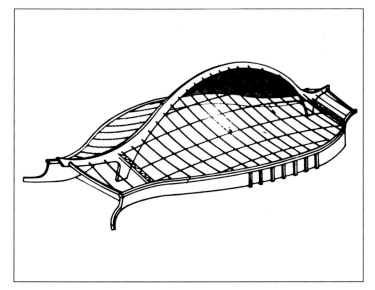

*Yale Hockey Rink. New Haven. 1959. Architect: Eero Saarinen. Double curvature cable net supported by a concrete arch along the middle axis.*

*Double curvature tent structure with a saddle form.*

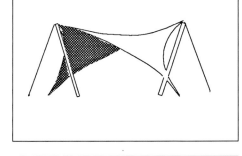

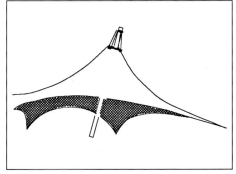

*Double curvature tent structure point supported by columns.*

pended from the cable roof—the permanent load must be a great deal larger than the asymmetrical live load to prevent asymmetrical deformation; by introducing rigid elements that act as beams or arches and supply the necessary stiffness; and by using rigid surfaces that act as vaults or shells—they can be prestressed by preloading the cables.

• Prestressed cable beams. The main cable (the suspension cable) is stiffened with the help of a secondary cable in the same plane that prestresses the main cable and keeps it permanently in tension. The secondary cable can be placed under the main cable and be connected to it by tension ties, or over the main cable where the prestressing forces are applied by stiff compression struts. This is also an effective bracing method for dynamic stress (vibration).

• Prestressed membrane tensile structures ("soft shells").

Here we can differentiate between two major types: a hyperboloid net of cables spanning between rigid frame structures—the main cables are rigid owing to the prestressing of the secondary cables that run perpendicular or diagonal, forming cable net that has a so-called anticlastic shape, that is, hyperboloid (for example, a saddle shape); and tent structures with flexible joints—the membrane can be a cable net or a cloth, and the form is anticlastic with respect to the bracing. Tensile structures can be designed into saddle shapes, fastened to the top end of a column, or a combination of both. The most flexible system is the cable net.

Before we study this building type and building elements more closely, we must understand how the cable works under loading.

# 8.2 THE STATICS OF CABLES

*Concentrated loads result in a broken line shape.*

UNIFORMLY DISTRIBUTED
LOAD ALONG THE SPAN
(2ND DEGREE PARABOLA)

THE DEAD LOAD OF THE CABLE
IS A CATERNARY LINE
(UNIFORMLY DISTRIBUTED
LOAD ALONG THE CABLE)

*The shape of the cables as a result of the distribution of the load.*

The problem with cables is the opposite of the problem with arches: The form of the arch is a compression line for a determinate load, and all other loads result in moments in the arch. The cable bears with tension forces, and therefore it changes form when the load changes in magnitude or direction.

We used the principles of the rope or the cable with arched structures in chapter 7, because the analogy between these structures is very clear. The method by which the cable works is most likely the easiest to understand intuitively: Everyone has experience with jump rope. We know that the rope required a "swing" force to maintain its form. The magnitude of the horizontal force varies with the slack in the rope or the vector height. The height of the vector has its greatest length from the line between the joint and the lowest point of the rope.

With a force polygon for the system, we see that the larger the vector height (f), the steeper the form of the cable and the smaller the horizontal force reaction. The horizontal force reaction will increase as the cable is tightened, that is, when the vector height diminishes. The vertical load will be constant. Likewise, with an increase in the span of the cable or the distance between the joints, the force reaction will also increase.

A tighter cable will result in a larger total tension force in the cable, since the horizontal component increases. If the diameter of the cable increases the vertical load, that is, the dead load of the cable, increases, and the tension force in the cable also increases.

Therefore, one must search for a reasonable balance between the slackness of the cable or the vector height and the span of the cable. For buildings, the optimal relationship between the vector height and the span lies in the zone:

$$1/10 < f/L < 1/20$$

For suspension bridges, the ratio is calculated to lie between 1/8 and 1/12. For very tight cables with a small f/L ratio, the tension force will be so large that the elastic deformation of the cable will be great. This pertains also to the search for a ratio between the slackness of the cable and the span that gives the best possible ratio for all of the building components that are affected.

Let's look at a rotation-free cable joint with a span L and the load q uniformly distributed over the length of the span: The joints have the same height, so that the cable is symmetrical at its midpoint. A simple suspended cable will be a statically determi-

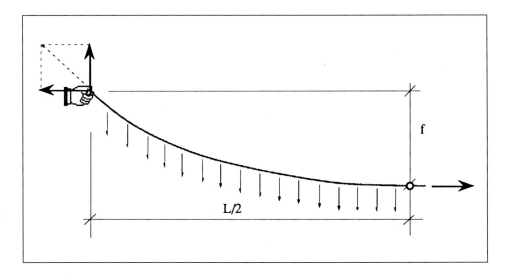

*The rope subjected to dead load and the tension that must be resisted.*

L/2

f

nate structure, and under load, the cable will take the form of a second-degree parabola. We are looking for the forces in the cable. The tension in the cable is comprised of a horizontal component $R_H$ and a vertical component $R_V$.

Horizontal equilibrium gives:

$$R_H = S$$

RADIAL LOAD GIVES
A CIRCULAR SEGMENT

Vertical equilibrium gives:

$$R_V = qL/2$$

TRIANGULAR LOAD GIVES
A 3RD DEGREE PARABOLA

*The shape of the cables as a result of the uniform distribution of the load.*

Moment equilibrium of the structure,

$$\Sigma M = 0, \quad \text{gives: } qL/2 \cdot L/4 - S \cdot f = 0$$

This equation gives us the tension at the center of the span:

$$S = qL^2/8f = R_H$$

The load $qL/2$ and the vertical reaction $R_V$ give the cable a moment of $qL^2/8$ that will be held in rotation equilibrium by the resisting moment that exists as a result of the force pair S and $R_H$. This is comparable to what occurs in a freely supported beam

with the difference that the curve of the rope creates the moment arm (f) for the resisting moment. This way, the moment contains two tension forces. For a linear beam, the moment arm must be established within the depth of the beam, with a large use of material required.

The tension in the cable is equal to R and will be:

$$R^2 = R_H{}^2 + R_V{}^2$$

$$R = \sqrt{S^2 + qL/2}$$

Since no external load acts horizontally on the cable, we can conclude that the horizontal component of the tension force in the cable is constant through the entire cable and is always in equilibrium with the horizontal reaction of the joints. This force is the cable's only component in the middle of the span. There is also a horizontal reaction equal to the total tension in the cable that therefore will be the tension force's negative value. The vertical component will thus vary and be largest at the joints. Therefore, we conclude that the total cable force is greatest at the joints and can be found by using the expression above.

*Cable forces and the support reactions in a simply supported cable with a uniformly distributed vertical load.*

If we wish to study the form of the cable, we can find the value for the height of the vector in the equation for tension at mid-point:

$$f = qL^2/8R_H = M_{max} \cdot 1/R_H$$

where $M_{max}$ = the maximum moment for a freely supported beam with the same load and span as the cable.

The greatest amount of slack and the vector height f are proportional to the maximum moment. This comparison is valid along the entire length of the cable so that:

$$y_x = M_x \cdot 1/R_H$$

Since $R_H$ is a constant, the cable has the same form as the moment diagram for a similar beam. The slackness in the cable, y, is found at each point and is equal to the moment at that point divided by the cable's horizontal reaction.

Drawing the parabola-shaped cable reactions can be useful in understanding the equation for its geometry. We assume that the joints are at the same height and the load is uniformly distributed. We take the lowest point of the cable as a starting point. Moment equilibrium at that point (x,y) for the detail of the cable gives:

$\Sigma M = 0$, so that

$$R_H \cdot y - qx \cdot x/2 = 0$$

$$y = qx^2/2R_H$$

Now $R_H = qL^2/8f$, so that

$$y = (qx^2/2) \cdot (8f/qL^2) = 4f\,(x/L)^2$$

This expression describes the parabola shape of the cable.

It is necessary to emphasize that the dynamic load on a suspended roof is as important as the static load. The wind load, which comes in gusts and with varying direction and intensity, will cause the suspended roof to swing. This type of roof movement must be controlled so that the swing time of the cables doesn't coincide with the loads.

Secondary cables are an effective dynamic bracing that prestresses the main cables, as in the prestressed cable beam. The use of the double cable system increases the bearing strength and stiffness in addition to reducing the swinging. Each cable is allowed to swing in a different way, but the cable joints determine that the movement in one cable works against the movement in the other.

The transmission of forces in such a system is very complex. The cable beam is statically indeterminate and cannot be considered

*The shape of the cable is compared to the moment diagram for a beam with the same load and support conditions.*

*Cable with a parabolic shape drawn in a x-y coordinate system.*

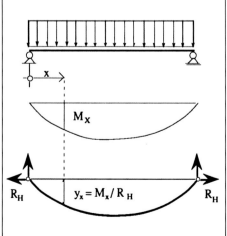

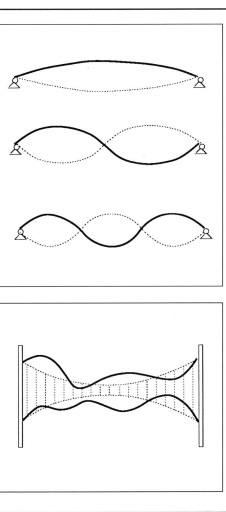

*Cable in oscillation. The period of oscillation is dependent on the sag in the cable and on the number of waves.*

*Dampening of a suspended cable with a prestressed cable.*

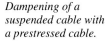

a stiff beam with linear and elastic behavior. In addition the effect of the large deformations must be resisted. Therefore, the distribution of forces between the two cables is incredibly difficult to determine with precision.

All of the loads are carried by the main cable, and the secondary cable's task is just to control the swinging. This would be a conservative assumption that will result in a main cable with a larger diameter than is necessary.

To gain an insight into what occurs in the system, we shall make a gross simplification. We assume a linear relationship in the cables' behavior and disregard the effect of deformation and dynamic loading. Thus, the first estimate of the cable's dimension can be made.

The first phase of the loading consists of tightening the prestressed cable beam. This is accomplished by tightening up the convex secondary cable so that the tension also affects the main cable. We assume that the vertical joints are placed often and tightly so that the main and secondary cables can

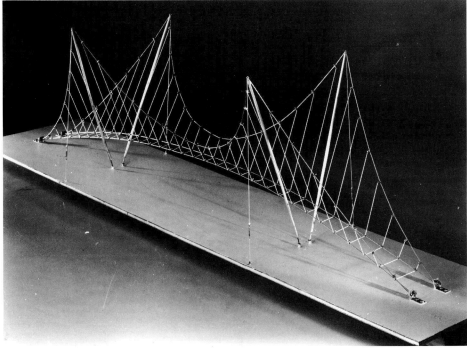

*Footbridge. Architect: David Boozer and William D. Olinger. Engineer: Frei Otto. Span approximately 40 meters (131 feet). Model by architecture student Gunnar Ridderström.*

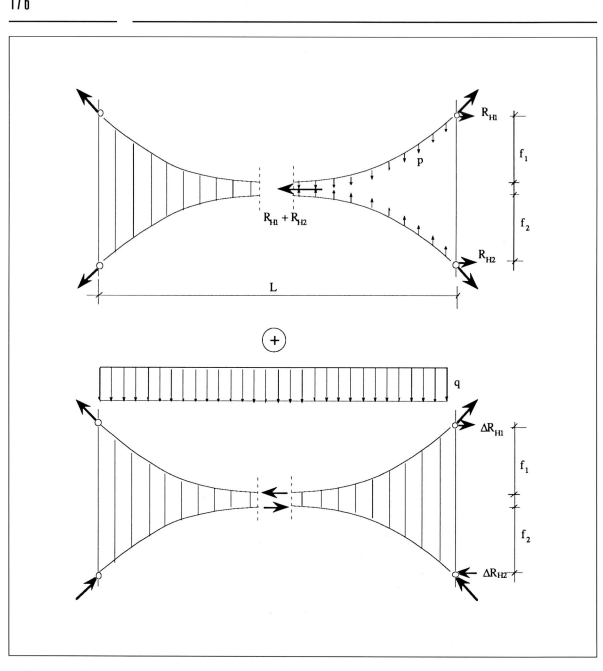

*Cable beam with a suspended cable and an arched cable. The forces in the system can be found by adding the forces from the prestressing load and the external vertical load.*

be assumed to be uniformly loaded, forming a parabola. The force of the prestressing must be greater than the compression force from the external roof loads and the dead load of the cables. If this is not the case, the cables will be slack.

If the vector height of the cables ($f_1$ and $f_2$) are different, the tension forces in the cables owed to prestressing will also be different. With that, the cables will not have the same natural swing time, and the swinging frequencies will have a tendency to work against each other.

By assuming the system to be stiff and linear, we can find the cable forces:

$$R_{H1} \cdot f_1 = pL^2/8 = R_{H2} \cdot f_2$$

where p = the force of the prestressing in the connector cables.

$$R_{H1} = pL^2/8f_1 \text{ and } R_{H2} = pL^2/8f_2$$

In the special situation where the cables have the same vector height ($f_1 = f_2 = f$) and the same dimension, the cables will have equal prestressing forces:

$$R_H = pL^2/8f$$

With the same geometry, we can estimate that the external roof load, q, is divided in half between the two cables. The external load will add to the tension force in the main cable, but the tension force in the secondary cable will decrease. Additional forces will be:

*Poul Kjaerholm. Chair of brushed stainless steel with seat and back of flag rope. Ca. 1956.*

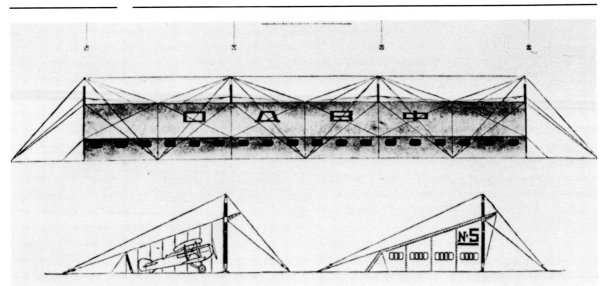

*Hangar project.*
*USSR. 1929.*
*Architects: Viktor,*
*Leonid, and*
*Alexander Vesnin.*
*Original drawings.*

*Hangar project. USSR*
*1929. Architects:*
*Viktor, Leonid, and*
*Alexander Vesnin.*
*Early example of the*
*use of steel masts and*
*cables. Model by*
*architecture student*
*Guri Tveito.*

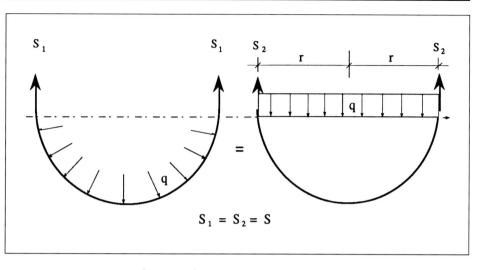

*Tension ring. The loads along the chord of the circle result in the same forces in the cable ring as radial load on the circle.*

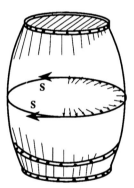

*Example of a tension ring: The ring of a barrel withstands the pressure of the liquid inside.*

$\Delta R_{H1} = \Delta R_{H2} = (q/2) \cdot L^2/8f = qL^2/16f = \Delta R_H$

where q = the sum of the dead load and vertical live load. The same result is obtained by taking the moment equilibrium between the force pair and the external moment:

$\Delta R_H \cdot 2f = qL^2/8$

$\Delta R_H = qL^2/16f$

Totally, the horizontal components of the cable tension in the two cables will be:

$R_{H1} + \Delta R_{H1} = qL^2/8f + qL^2/16f$ and

$R_{H2} - \Delta R_{H2} = qL^2/8f - qL^2/16f > 0$

The force in the prestressed cable must never be less than zero, so that it will not be slack. This means that $p > q/2$.

The circular form has pure axial forces if the load works radially in relation to the circle. A radial load that is directed outward from the center of the circle will result in circular compression. Examples of this are the steel band around a wooden barrel that holds the wood in place with tension force, and the circular-shaped concrete dam that holds the water back with compression force. Both of these examples have the type of load, that is, fluid pressure, that acts radially on a container of circular form.

We are interested in the magnitude of the tension force in a cable with a radially determinate load. This is easily found if we understand the following relationship: A radial load with a constant intensity, q, on a circular curve, is statically equivalent to q on the chord between the two ends of the semicircle (the diameter).

Statically equivalent means that the cable that forms the curve receives the same amount of force in the two different loading situations. Therefore, we use the load on the chord, because it is a straight line and naturally easier to calculate mathematically.

We draw the chord through the center of the circle and check for equilibrium between the tension reactions in the cable, S, and the load q uniformly distributed along the chord (the diameter):

$2 \cdot S - q \cdot 2r = 0$

$S = q \cdot r$

Thus, the magnitude of the tension force in the cable is found by multiplying the intensity of the load by the radius of the circle described by the cable. We will use this principle in section 8.4, where we investigate cable nets and tensile structures. But first we will study an example of the suspended roof.

*Dulles Airport.
Virginia. 1962.
Architect: Eero
Saarinen.*

## 8.3 SAARINEN: TENSION AND THRUST

The terminal building for Dulles Airport in Virginia (1958-1962), which serves Washington D.C., consists chiefly of one large space: a rectangular hall of 180 x 50 meters (590 x 164 feet). The passengers enter the building through one long facade and enter the planes via the other. Routine functions before departure, such as ticket control, baggage check-in, and waiting, take place in the large open space and for the most part on the same level, while baggage claim after arrival is on the lower level.

The space features 16 pairs of leaning concrete pillars along the long facades that bear the load of the curving suspended roof. We will take a closer look at the structural concept.

The concrete pillars lean outward, toward the exterior, and create the supports for the suspension cables that stretch over the width of the space. For every third meter in the longitudinal direction two cables are suspended. They are connected to a horizontal concrete beam, which spans between the top of the pillars over a distance of 12 meters (40 feet).

All of the cables are built inside concrete

ribs that have the same curvature as the suspension cables. Between these ribs, a distance of 3 meters (10 feet), there are prefabricated concrete elements. With that, the roof structure is complete; the steel cables carry the load, while the concrete structure provides the stiffness in the roof surface.

In the section, we see how the building is lifted on the side that functions as the entrance facade. With this gesture, the architect Eero Saarinen (1910-1961) lets the building welcome its visitors. The lifting of the entrance facade adds to the excitement of the project, but also provides a volumetric equilibrium in relation to the control tower on the opposite side.

Structurally, we are interested in the suspension cables where the supports are not at the same height. This extra difficulty will be resolved once we find the forces in the system. First we must determine the building dimensions and load data. We assume that:

L = the free span of the cables = 50 meters (164 feet)

h= the difference in height between the supports = 5.5 meters (18 feet)

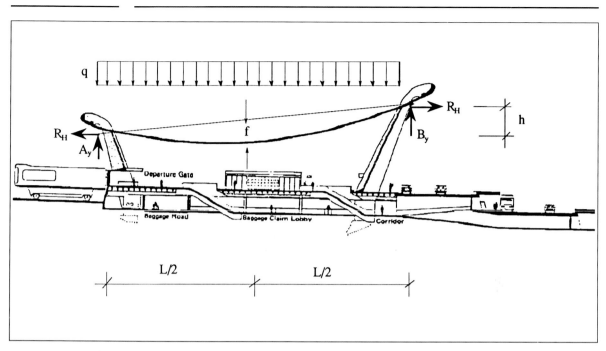

*Dulles Airport.
Typical section with
an indication of the
load, span, and cable
reaction forces.*

f = the vector height = 4.4 meters (14 feet)

q = 30 kN/m = dimension load

$f/L = 4.4m/50m \cong 1/11$

If the span, L is the horizontal projection between the columns, the cable will have its greatest slack at L/2, as if the cable were not leaning. The vector height, f, is also the same as it would be in the horizontally supported cable. The lowest point of the cable will be created with the leaning of the cable.

If no horizontal force is acting along the cable, we have:

$R_H = M_{max}/f = qL^2/8f =$

$(30kN/m \cdot 50^2m^2)/(8 \cdot 4.4m) = 2130$ kN

This force is also the horizontal reaction from the cable in the concrete pillars and the cable's minimum load at the lowest point where no vertical component is found. To find the largest load, we must look at the vertical reactions. Moment equilibrium around the left support results in:

$R_H \cdot h + q \cdot L \cdot L/2 - B_y \cdot L = 0$

$B_y = q \cdot L/2 + R_H \cdot h/L = 984$ kN

Moment equilibrium around the right support results in:

$A_y \cdot L + R_H \cdot h - q \cdot L \cdot L/2 = 0$

$A_y = q \cdot L/2 - R_H \cdot h/L = 516$ kN

The maximum force of the cable is also at the support B, that is, where the cable is the steepest. We find the force by using the Pythagorean theorem:

$S_{max} = \sqrt{B_y^2 + R_H^2} = 2346$ kN

This force is also divided between two cables. We assume that the modulus of elasticity of the cables $f_{sd} = 1500 \, N/mm^2$. Each cable must therefore have an area, A, so that:

$f_{sd} \cdot A > 1/2 \cdot 2346 \cdot 10^3$ N

$A > 782 \, mm^2$

If the cable consists of twisted steel strands, we can calculate that the effective area is $2/3 \cdot \pi \cdot d^2/4$, where d = the diameter of the cable. The thickness of the cable must therefore be:

*Twisted steel rod cable.*

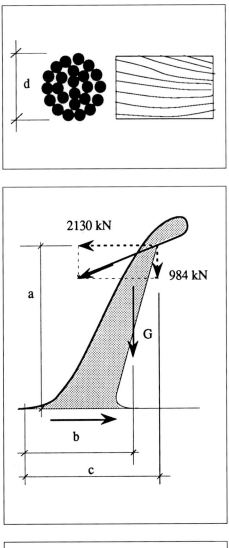

*The tension in the cables is resisted by bending stresses in the cantilevered pillar, which overturns and stabilizes forces.*

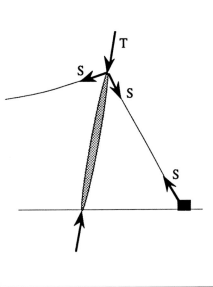

*The tension in the cable is resisted by compression and tension forces in a column and a guy.*

$$d^2 > 3 \cdot 782 \cdot 4/2\pi$$

$$d > 39 \text{ mm}$$

The cable, for now, is just one part of the structure. The support structure, which here consists of two concrete pillars, is of great importance both structurally and visually.

The structural task of the two concrete pillars is to hold back the tension forces in the cables. Their bending stiffness and strength withstand the moment from the tension cable. The leaning form reduces the bending moment, because a significant force results from the dead load of the pillars, the beams and the vertical component of the tension forces in the cables. These moments act in the opposite direction of the moment from the horizontal force of the cables and hinder the pillar from tipping. The design was made so that the weight of the overhanging roof places a load on the upper portion of the leaning pillar. Grooves are cut out of the overhanging roof so that the pillars pass uninterrupted through the roof until they meet the termination of the curved parapet. Thus, the effect of the moment arm increases, and the forces balance each other.

Even though the pillars are able to transfer the forces down to the ground, all of the problems are not solved: We have a significant horizontal force that attempts to pull the pillars inward. In order to reduce the foundations, the pillars are connected to each other by the poured concrete floor structure. The floor holds the pillars in place and acts as a stiff compression joint.

There are other methods of making a support structure. The moment load from the tension cable can be fastened in a compression and tension joint where, for example, a mast will be under compression stress and a guy under tension stress.

Another method is to let the horizontal beam take over the horizontal component. These forces can be transferred along the

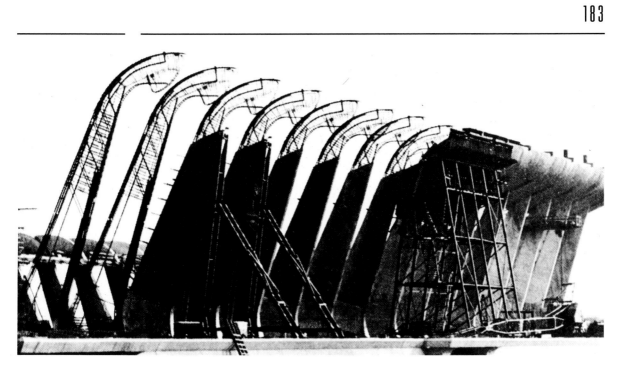

*Dulles Airport.
Concrete pillars under
construction.*

*Dulles Airport.
The cable roof with
concrete elements
under construction.*

*Principle for
transmission of cable
tension by use of a
beam in the horizontal
plane. The forces
are transferred to
stabilizing end walls.*

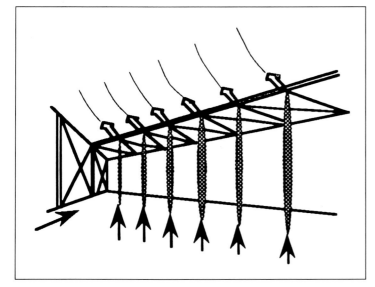

*Principle for anchoring in the ground. Friction and a V-form develop the resistance.*

*Gravity as a principle of resistance. The weight of the foundation and the earth are in balance with the tension load.*

*Foundations anchored by permanently mounted bolts in the bedrock.*

*Reinforced concrete slab or beams acting as compression struts between the foundations.*

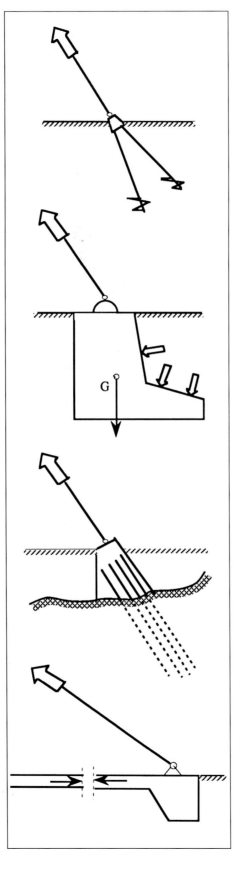

facade to the bracing, transverse gable walls. The vertical reaction from the tension cable goes down directly as compression in the columns. This principle is employed at Dulles Airport where the concrete pillars control several sets of cables that span between them. The horizontal beams, which transfer the forces over the 40-foot (12 m) span between the pillars, are also the concrete plates in the large overhanging roof.

As for the foundations for the tension forces, if the principle for the mast and guy is used, the guy wire must have a proper anchoring in the ground. The most common foundation types can be classified as:

• Anchoring in the ground, with the capacity that depends on the type of anchor and the firmness and friction of the ground. Such anchors can follow the wedge principle or be based on friction in the form of concrete tension piles.

• Gravitational anchors follow the ballast principle. The point is that the weight of the foundation itself or of the earthen mass on top of the foundation will outweigh the vertical lift. The horizontal force must counteract by passive earthen compression force due to its mass.

• Anchor bolts, where steel rods, for example, reinforcing steel, are cast in holes drilled into the bedrock. The capacity will be dependent on the hardness and the degree of fracturing in the bedrock.

• Tension rods or tension rings in situations where the guys have an acute angle in relation to the plane of the earth and the horizontal force reaction is especially large. Restraining guy wires can then be connected to a stiff compression element that nullifies the forces. The vertical reaction must be resolved by one or several of the other principles.

*Cable foundation for*
*a radio tower.*
*Tryvann, Oslo,*
*Norway. 1989.*
*Hinged steel detail*
*with bolts for*
*tightening of the guys.*

## 8.4 NETWORKS OF CABLES AND FABRIC

Now we shall look at the hyperbolic (doubly curved) surfaces that in this comparison are tensile membranes, that is, structures working in tension and shear on the surface plane. Since the structural material (cables, textiles) has neither bending or compression stiffness, the surface must curve in two directions and be prestressed. Only in this way can it be stable.

*An open umbrella is a prestressed fabric structure.*

A simple umbrella provides a good understanding of the behavior of such structures. By opening the umbrella, we press the hinged ribs against the cloth and set it in tension. The cloth of the umbrella is extended and tightened by the hinged ribs, which are under compression and bending stress.

A handkerchief held out the window of a car with one hand flaps wildly. The wind force causes vibration and continuous form change. If we hold the ends of the handkerchief and pull it tight, the vibrations will be significantly reduced. If we hold the handkerchief's four corners and tighten them, with two opposite corners pulled upward and the two others, downward, a stable and stiff saddle form will be created. Such a prestressed hyperbolic surface is optimal for soft-shell structures.

There is a tendency in modern architecture to minimize the structural elements by using tensile structures. Likewise, we see interesting projects where an outer skin is part of the structural system, whether in glass, textiles, or metal plates.

The combination of steel cables or wires and textile, as in tent structure, creates integrated and minimalistic structural forms. Distinguished by lightness and soft forms, a whole new aesthetic is required: Curves rather than straight lines are the driving force in spatial design.

*A piece of cloth has no bending stiffness or compression strength. To stabilize the form, a prestressed double curvature surface must be created.*

Let's look a little at some forms. Soft shells can be made with a cable net or with tex-

*Double curvature and anticlastic membrane forms. Left: a saddle form. Right: the point-supported tent.*

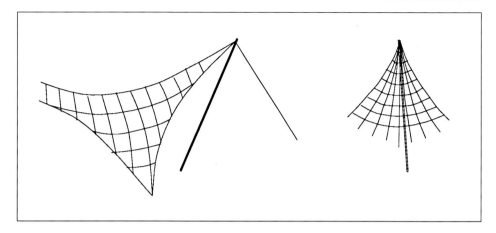

tiles, and the surface form is anticlastic. Saddle shapes are created by a cable net with a regular grid spacing, rectangular- or rhombus-shaped, or with a textile membrane. Point-supported surfaces use radial cable nets or membranes. They will have conical forms, and the radial net will be determined by the dispersion of the strain around the point load, which is radial and ring-shaped. Since all of the tension forces are concentrated at the top of the support and create a concentration of strain, it is necessary, when using textiles, to reinforce the membrane in that area. This can be done with radial cables or by transferring the forces to another element.

Prestressing stiffens and tightens the mem-

brane. The magnitude of the necessary tension in the membrane increases with the dimension of the construction. Therefore, natural fiber (cloth) is not well suited for large buildings, because the modulus of elasticity is poor. The fiberglass cloth, with a Teflon coating, is the most common material. The cloth has a modulus of elasticity in the area of 50 to 175 N/mm. In everyday terms that means that one square meter of fiberglass cloth can bear 17.5 metric tons of tension.

Fiberglass cloth can be produced with varying degrees of transparency, everything from almost full transparency to a translucent milky white. This means that the material can utilize the warmth of sunlight or

*With the use of fabric membranes point supported on columns, the fabric must be reinforced in order to reduce stress concentrations.*

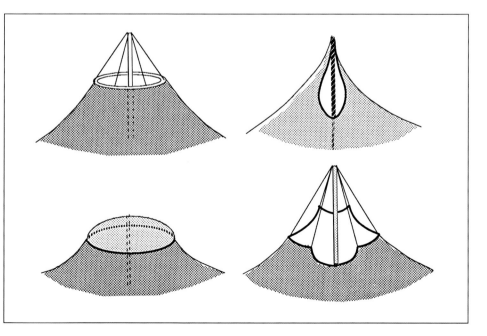

*Lord's Cricket Ground. London, England. 1987. Architect: Michael Hopkins and Partners. Engineer: Ove Arup with Peter Rice. Model by architecture students Ingunn Hafstad, Holmfridur Jonsdottir, and Ìystein Kaul Kartvedt.*

block it with the reflective Teflon coating. Teflon is, in addition, self cleaning, that is, dirt and air pollution do not cling to the surface of the fabric. This is an important feature in relation to the constancy of a building and its aesthetic longevity.

Let's take a look at a membrane structure with a quadratic plan, an anticlastic form with an inverse curvature in the two major axes. The suspended portion of the net is stabilized by the prestressing of the convex, arched portion.

This type of structure is statically indeterminate and not linear. This means that the forces in the membrane depend on the form of the supporting structure and its placement in space. Further, the geometry of the surface is directly dependent on the magnitude of the prestressing: The prestressing provides equilibrium in the surface under the different loading combinations. Calculations for a soft shell are a very complex assignment.

In estimating, we can assume the geometry from an original load assumption with constant, uniform surface tension. With this, the form is a function of the grid geometry of the supports.

Let's look at a situation under a prestress force. The tension in the two major axes will be proportional to the radii in the suspended and the arched directions. If they are equal, as here, the stresses will be:

$$T_{oy} = T_{ox} = T_o$$

Prestressing can be added directly to the tension cables or by tightening the boundary cables. The initial stress can also be established by adding an external load, p, which could, for example, consist of sandbags. It is important to consider prestressing as a predetermined external load, p.

The saddle form, which is a hyperbolic paraboloid, will have a uniform load where its surface has membrane forces (tension) per unit width along each of the two major axes, which results in:

$$T_{oy} = T_{ox} = T_o = pL^2/16f$$

A relatively large curvature radius is assumed here, so that the saddle form is correspondingly flat.

The vertical load q, dead load and live load, is carried by the soft shell in the same manner as the prestressing load. Equal amounts of curvature will give the structure equal tension force in the two major axes.

Under full vertical loading, with prestressing, the suspension cable or the cloth will

*Project for an open-air pavilion at Frogner Park in Oslo, Norway. Model, 1989. Architecture student Gina M. Nilsen*

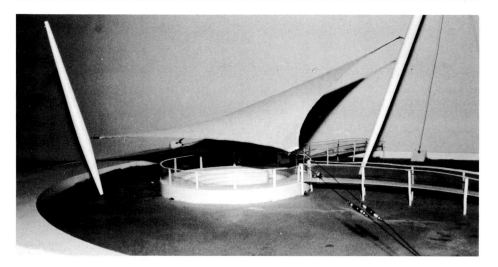

therefore have maximum tension force, while the prestressing cable or the corresponding convex portions of the textile membrane will have minimal force. For the latter, there must be just enough tension so that it will not be slack. The total of the tension forces in the two major axes will be:

$$T_{susp} = pL^2/16f + qL^2/16f$$

$$T_{prestr} = pL^2/16f - qL^2/16f > 0$$

Even ignoring the safety factors, the tension forces in the prestressing cable must never be less than zero. This means that:

$$pL^2/16f > qL^2/16f, \text{ or}$$

$$p > q$$

That is, the load that produces the prestressing must, at a minimum, be equal to the external vertical loads. If p = q the maxi-

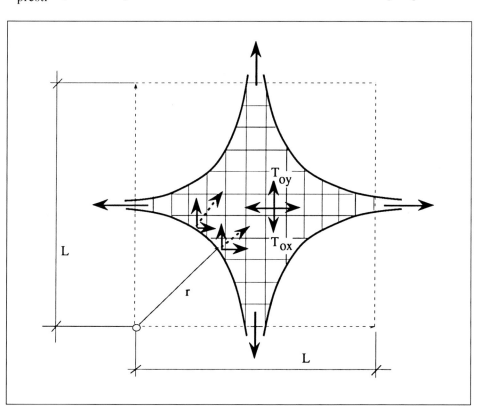

*Plan of a membrane construction. Force direction in the membrane and perimeter cables.*

*Three-Ring Circus (1930).*

mum tension force in the membrane per meter of width will be:

$$T_{max\ susp} = qL^2/16f + qL^2/16f$$

$$= qL^2/8f$$

We recognize this expression again from the horizontal force in the freely supported one-way cable. We can also conclude that the external loads on a flat membrane or a cable net will be carried by the suspension portion of the surface as in a one-way system, while the arched portion is only responsible for stability.

The load that produces the prestressing, p, is also, at a minimum, half of the total load in the system. Said in another way, this means that half of the tension capacity in the cables will be used up by the prestressing force. With full external vertical load on the suspension cables, the prestressing will therefore be equal to zero.

In most cases, to be on the safe side, the thickness of the prestressing cables is assumed to correspond to the thickness of the suspension cables. These are, in addition, dimensioned on the least desirable loading situation with maximum wind suction, which increases the prestressing forces. This also applies to textile structures where the thickness is the same throughout the entire membrane.

If we look at a structure with a prestressed cable net in a quadratic pattern, the resultant of the cable tension in the two axes will be radial in the boundary cables. Therefore, the size of the boundary cables will, with constant tension in the net, be determined by the circle segments principal. The force in the boundary cable will be:

$$S = T_0 \cdot r, \text{ where}$$

$T_0$ = the tension force in the membrane after prestressing, and

r = the radius of the curved boundary cable as described in plan.

When a suspension cable is under maximum load and prestressing is absent, the load on the boundary cables will be lopsided. Thus, this will change its form but it can be assumed to be a parabola.

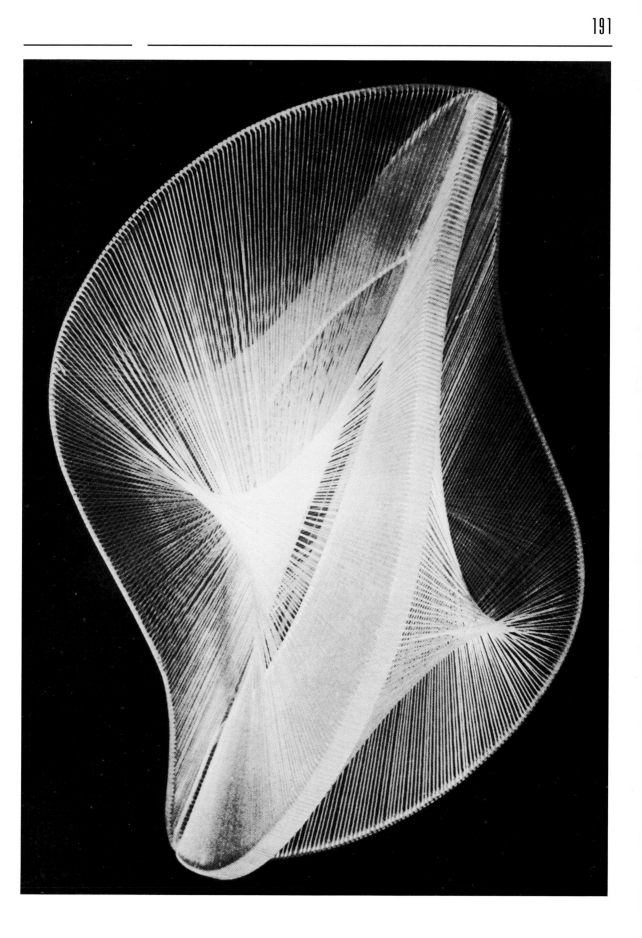

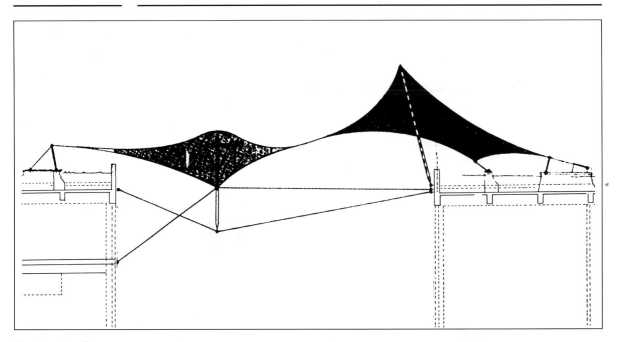

## 8.5 CABLE STRUCTURES IN PARIS AND TOKYO

We will illustrate the use of these structural possibilities by presenting two projects, one European and one Asian. In addition to the use of the hyperbolic paraboloid membrane, they both incorporate the structure's special formal and architectural characteristics in a meaningful way.

The most recent of these is the tensile structure for Schlumberger's in Paris from 1985 by architect Renzo Piano (born 1939). The project was part of the complete rehabilitation of this industrial complex from the turn of the century that began a gradual shift from heavy mechanical industry to light industry, computer technology, and research.

In the process, a series of red brick buildings received new interiors and exteriors, and simultaneously several of the industrial buildings in the complex were demolished. The demolition transformed the overbuilt complex into a garden or park system that became a meaningful and central element within the industrial complex.

The park forms a cover for the underground garages and an artificial ridge that houses

shared functions, such as lecture rooms, training rooms, cafeteria, bank, and travel agency. The entrance from the park to these facilities is from a "street" that penetrates the top of the ridge. This street is covered with a series of white translucent tents built of a Teflon-coated fiberglass cloth.

The choice of the partially buried building with a textile membrane cover came from the desire to place functions in a park system—"without having to build a building." To consider a building in a traditional way would have been a difficult formal problem in relation to the existing industrial architecture and the park. The solution was to build a form that represented a compromise between "nature" and "building"; the tensile structures become the boundary between the rigid network of office facades and the organic park.

The compression chords, together with the suspended cables, push the cloth up into a tent form. With that the structure is simultaneously formed and stabilized with the same method, prestressing. The transition between the compression chords and the cloth is accomplished with curved caps that

*Schlumberger's,
Paris.
"Street" covered
by a tent structure
of fiberglass fabric
with Teflon coating.*

*Schlumberger's,
Paris. A view of
the park and the
rehabilitated industry
buildings.*

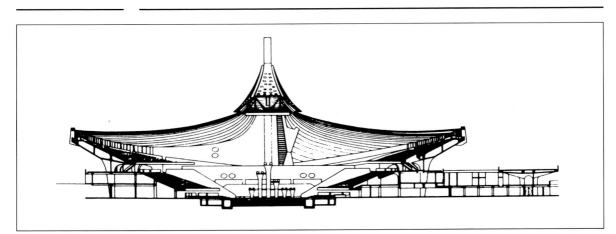

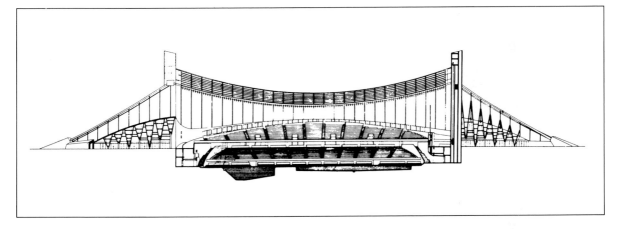

*Olympic Stadium
Tokyo.
1964.
Architect
Kenzo Tange.
Cross section of the
swimming pool.*

*Longitudinal section.*

*Christo.
The Running Fence.
Fabric and guys as
environmental art.*

reduce the concentrated stress loads. Some of the tents are conical and some are spherical forms, giving the tensile structures pointed or rounded tops.

Soft-shell structures originated in the 1950s when the cable net was used to form a soft membrane. The first truly large project that used this system and won world acclaim was Kenzo Tange's Olympic Stadium in Tokyo, which was completed for the Summer Olympics of 1964. There, the principle of the suspended and prestressed roof was the basis for the design of the whole building, both the large stadium and the smaller indoor arena.

In plan, the large stadium forms are oval-shaped, consisting of two curved halves that are separated from each other along the longitudinal axis. Thus, the entrances are between the curving long sides. Along the longitudinal axis, a cable spans between

two concrete towers at each end. The cable is the support for the cable net over the two halves of the arena and is anchored to the foundations with an angled cable extension along the exterior of the building. The concrete towers, the anchoring of the cable, and the openings between the two curved building halves create a beautiful structural motif for the entrances.

The tension of the membrane in the roof surface is, on the low side, anchored in the curved longsides. These are poured-in-place, reinforced concrete surfaces angling outward and creating the seating in the arena. The building curves in plan and section, which gives the roof surface the right double curves necessary for stiffness. At the same time, the curved concrete forms take the tension forces from the membrane and transfer them further down to the ground as compression forces in the curve. The building in section and plan, therefore,

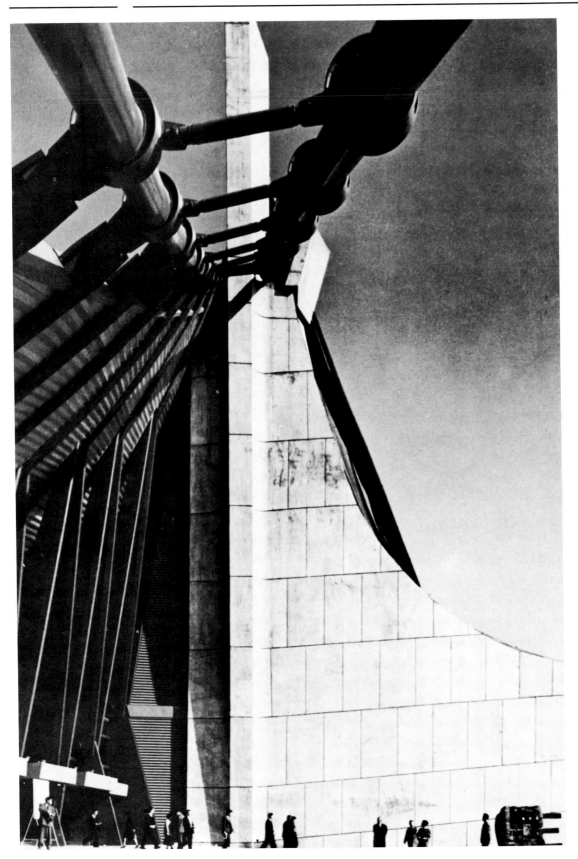

*Olympic Stadium Tokyo. 1964. Model by architecture students Pål Bjørnstad and Elise Christie.*

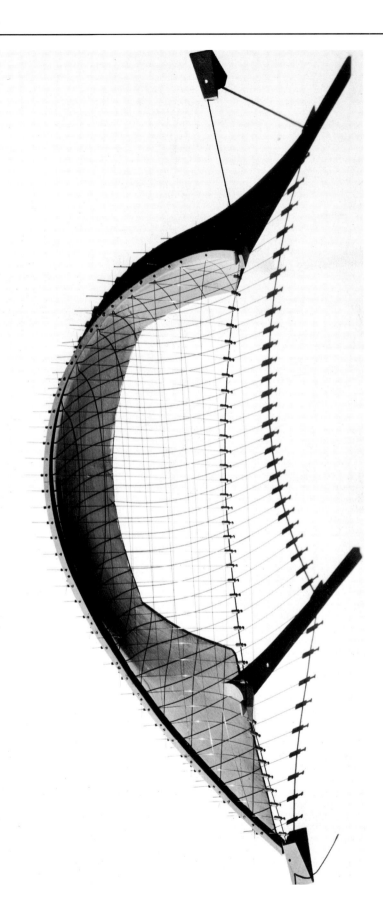

*(Opposite page.)*
*Olympic Stadium*
*Tokyo.*
*1964.*
*Detail from one*
*of the entrances.*

has a very close relationship with the properties of the roof structure.

The stadium is lit by daylight and by artificial lighting, which runs along the longitudinal axis. For the most part, the roof is sealed with painted steel plates that work as the connectors for the cable net.

All in all, it is a very estimable building with a strong, constructive expression and sculpture-like qualities.

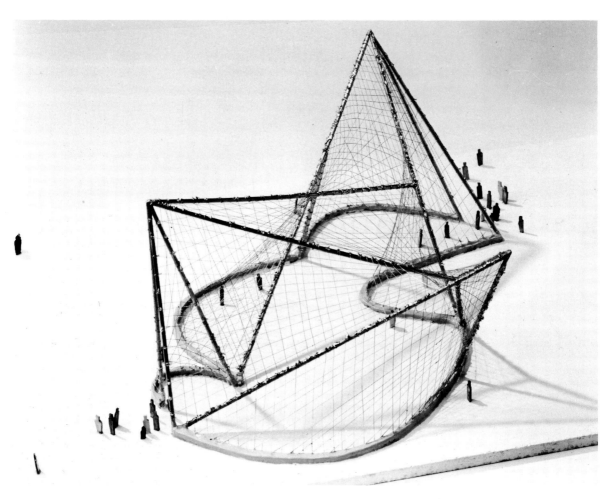

*Philips Pavilion, World Exposition. Brussels, Belgium. 1958. Architect: Le Corbusier. Model by architecture students Anita Hutcheson, Liv Kristine Ruud, and Kristin Øygarden. 1986.*

# Chapter 9

# STRUCTURAL DETAILS

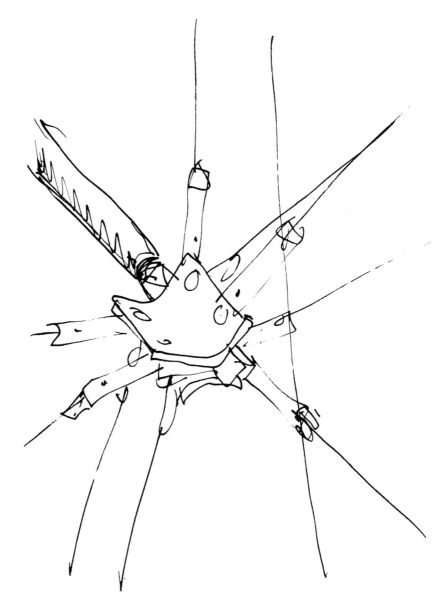

*I. M. Pei.*
*The pyramid at the*
*Louvre. Paris, France.*
*1989. Structural*
*detail: the intersection*
*point of the forces.*

# 9.1 A Detail

Two- and three-year-old children have the incredible ability to distinguish between types of cars and even the same models from different years. The details make the difference, the small changes around the lights or perhaps the form of the fenders.

Detailing gives a building its expressive character. If we place the window glass about an inch farther inward in the window frame, we see that the visual thickness of the wall increases accordingly. The relief in the facade will be deeper and the shadows more pronounced. The window details are very important to the character of the facade.

To design the roof overhang, we must know the thickness of the shingles and the profile of the gutter. The size and layout of the shingles are decisive in the general dimensioning of the building. In masonry, the type of bonding pattern gives us rules for the designing of window openings and pilasters.

The basis of an idea for large structures can lie in a few inspiring sketches by Nervi or

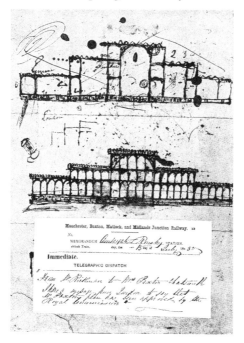

*Joseph Paxton.*
*Sketch of the Crystal*
*Palace.*
*Inlay: The telegram to*
*Paxton from June 15,*
*1850, with the*
*message saying that*
*the project was*
*accepted.*

Utzon, while the structural detailing can take months or even years. Peter Rice (born 1936), one of the engineers behind the Pompidou Center in Paris, points out the difference between what is drawn and what is built—the structural joints, "the pieces," must be formed through practical evaluation. "The pieces" give us the key, the genetic code to understanding the building.

Because the main structural components in a building are standard, such as the steel sections and concrete elements, the joints are also to some degree standardized. Naturally they require creative solutions and a creative understanding of the dominant system.

In the Victoria and Albert Museum in London, John Paxton's idea sketches for the Crystal Palace are exhibited—simple sheets of paper from a notepad. Thanks to a well-coordinated building system of cast iron components and glass, the 77,000 m$^2$ (825,000-square-foot) exhibition hall for the world exposition in London in 1851 was built in six short months. The produc-

*Joseph Paxton.*
*The Crystal Palace.*
*Erecting of a column*
*and beams.*

*Joseph Paxton.*
*The Crystal Palace.*
*Detailing of a column*
*and beams.*

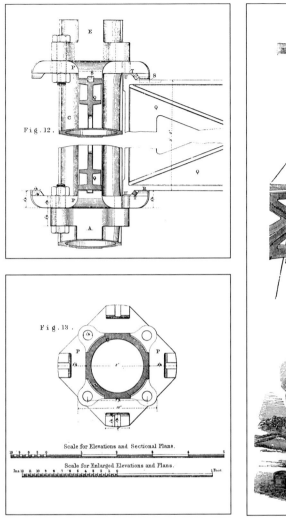

Fig. 12.

Fig. 13.

Scale for Elevations and Sectional Plans.

Scale for Enlarged Elevations and Plans.

tion drawings of Charles Fox, the engineer and producer of the cast iron, give us insight into the building system. The components and the structural details show their daring simplicity and consistency in production.

The main structure was a column/truss system in cast iron. The columns were hollow and divided into floor-height lengths where the joint was equal in height to the truss—joined with the help of bolted flanges. With mounting in mind, all of the columns had the same outer dimensions but varied in wall thickness according to the loads. Roof water ran down the hollow center of the

columns to an underground pipe system connected to the column foundations. The trusses had triple-chord crossing and were dimensioned for maximum load and therefore could be produced as 2,224 identical units.

England's highly developed industry and employment of the simplest and most rational production techniques in mass production were essential in the realization of the Crystal Palace. The driving force was the self-educated gardener and greenhouse builder Joseph Paxton, who had many years of experience experimenting with building elements.

*I. M. Pei.*
*The pyramid*
*at the Louvre.*
*Paris, France. 1989.*

*I. M. Pei.*
*The pyramid*
*at the Louvre.*
*Principles for the*
*bearing structures.*

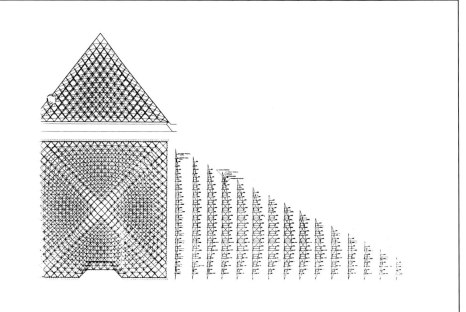

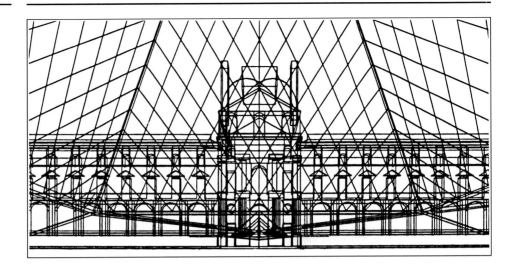

*I.M. Pei.*
*The pyramid*
*at the Louvre.*
*Interior perspective.*

## 9.2 THE GLASS PYRAMID

The glass pyramid at the Louvre Museum in Paris, designed by architect I. M. Pei (born 1917), represents the tip of a glacier emerging from within one of the greatest and most beautiful museums in the world.

In addition to being the main entrance and a source of natural light to the museum's new and spacious vestibule, the pyramid is the starting point of the axis: Louvre-Etoile-La Defence.

With a height of 21.5 meters (70 feet) and a length of 35 meters (115 feet), the glass pyramid is placed like a finely cut diamond in the Cour Napoleon surrounded by the museum's eighteenth-century stone buildings.

Let's look closer at what it takes to get a pyramid with 612 rhombus-shaped glass panels to stand.

Each surface of the pyramid consists of 2 x 16 intersecting trusses of different lengths, lying parallel to the edge of the surface. The trusses' compression numbers, primarily the top chord and the perpendicular chords, are built of hollow circular profiles, while the tension members, the bottom chord and the diagonal chords, are solid rods or cables. The glass panes are fastened at the intersecting points of the top chords by

extension bolts or nodes, so that they are connected to, but free from the bearing system.

From our study of trusses (see chap. 3), we know that trusses can bear wind loads from the surface of the pyramid. Suction on the glass surface is captured by another method. Sixteen tension cables, so-called counter cables, connect the joints along the bottom chord of the trusses and hold the entire structure together.

So far, the structure of the pyramid is in keeping with the French tradition that starts with Polonceau's achievements in the nineteenth century, incorporating subtle variations between compression and tension components in steel structures. The key to the pyramid's bearing system lies in the cast stainless steel joints. We recognize the turnbuckle and clevis (shackle) from the riggings of sailboats and yachts. This is a minimal structure designed exclusively to withstand tension in the same way that the rigging on a boat stiffens the mast with tension cables.

With the help of outstanding "seamanship," the successful rigging and stiffening of all the joints under the precise glass surfaces of the pyramid was possible.

Hans J. Wegner.
*The Peacock Chair.*

Hans J. Wegner.
*The Peacock Chair.*
*Corner detail.*

*(Opposite page.)*
I. M. Pei.
*The pyramid
at the Louvre.
The bearing
structure's complexity.*

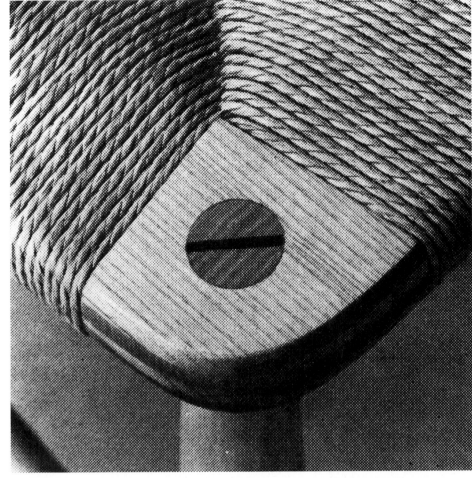

## 9.3 THE PEACOCK CHAIR

We do not know who built the first Windsor chair. Its simple useful form and light structure, however, has fascinated many. Siegfried Giedion mentions it in *Space, Time, and Architecture* and draws comparisons to the development of "balloon frames" (a light framework of wood). The chair exists in many variations on both sides of the Atlantic Ocean, from New England to Budalen in Trøndelag on the west coast of Norway.

In 1957, the Danish furniture designer Hans J. Wegner (born 1914) presented his version, the "Peacock Chair." With its high arched back and fine detailing, the chair stands as a landmark in Danish furniture design.

Let's take a closer look at how the two front legs are fastened to the seat. The natural termination of the caning exposes a rounded dovetail joint at front corners of the frame. The leg is pushed up into a hole and at the same time a wedge is pounded down into the leg from the top. This fine little construction detail is expressed by an ash circle and a teak diagonal. The wedge guarantees a solid bond between the leg and the seat.

In lightweight movable structures, such as wooden chairs, much of the challenge lies in solving the connection between the leg and the seat. While Alvar Aalto "bent around" the corners in his famous chairs from the 1930s, Wegner took on the problem and showed us his mastery at finding solutions for traditional joint details.

*Veritas I outside Oslo,*
*Norway. 1976.*
*Architects:*
*Lund & Slaato.*
*Engineer:*
*Multiconsult.*
*Coupling of the*
*column and the beam.*

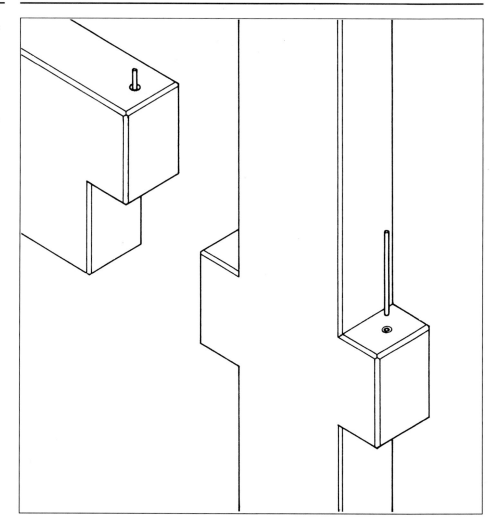

*Veritas I outside Oslo,*
*Norway.*
*1976.*
*Architects:*
*Lund & Slaato.*
*Engineer:*
*Multiconsult.*
*Mounting of the*
*prefabricated concrete*
*elements.*

*Bank of Norway,
home office.
1986.
Architects:
Lund & Slaato.
Engineer:
Multiconsult.
Coupling of the
column and the beam.*

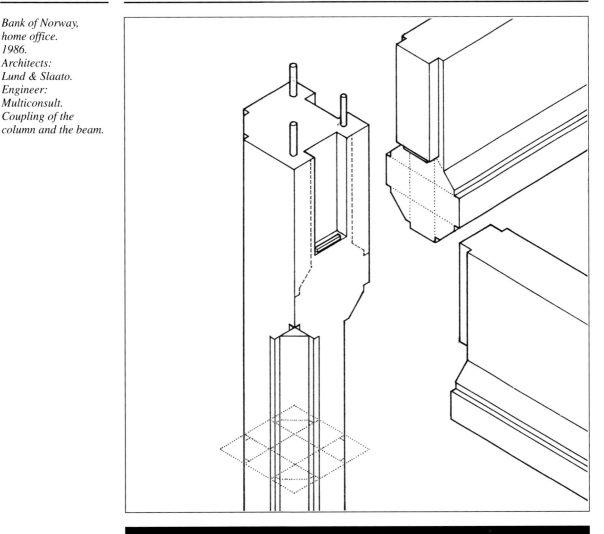

# 9.4 NORWEGIAN CONCRETE

With light shell structures of concrete elements, we face the same elementary challenge as with the use of wood or steel: How should the column meet the beam? Many requirements must be fulfilled. A good construction manager plans for the mounting of the elements at the building site. The secondary building components must also be incorporated in the bearing structure.

Three impressive projects by the architects Lund and Slaatto and the engineering company Multiconsult show an interesting development in the use of prefabricated concrete elements. Each project has its own individual architectural character, but all three share a clear structural principle that

creates the basis and reference for the design of all the other building components. The detail solutions are entirely the result of close cooperation between the architect, designer, engineer, and manufacturer. Starting with a simple column and beam system, the buildings show that there are many adequate variations and possible articulations of the same detail. The concrete surfaces and joints are beautiful and precise.

The original portion of the Veritas Center outside of Oslo, Norway, from 1976, consists of offices, laboratories, and computer systems for Det Norske Veritas, an institution that works with ship security and

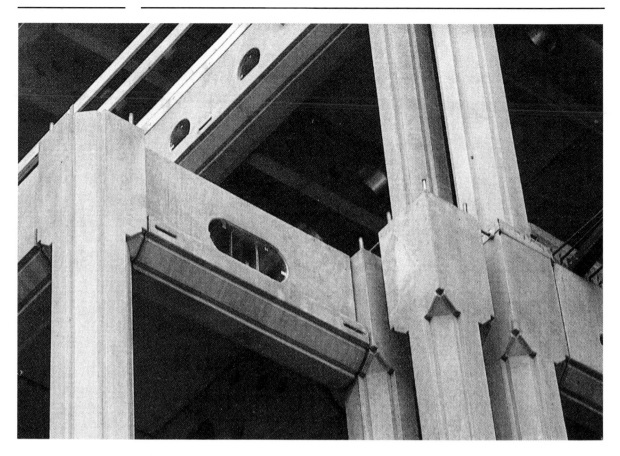

*Bank of Norway, home office. 1986. Architects: Lund & Slaato. Engineer: Multiconsult. Coupling of the columns and beams.*

installations on land and sea, insurance and material technology.

The plan follows a tartan grid with the major zones being 12 x 12 meters (40 x 40 feet). The bearing structure consists of pre-fabricated concrete elements where the columns, beams, and U-shaped deck elements are the main components. The elements are exposed smooth surfaces both on the interior and the exterior. The columns, with a rectangular cross section, are continuous up to the third floor. In order to limit the variations in the columns, there are uniform cross sections with varying degrees of reinforcement.

The columns are equipped with paired consoles to recieve the beams. Rectangular beams, with the same width as the columns, are prestressed and freely connected to the console and held in place by a center bolt. The console is the same height as the beam and doesn't interfere with the facade elements. The facades and knee walls are mounted as infill elements in the open concrete skeleton. The main structure, as well as the infill elements, are clearly defined.

After 13 years of intense planning, coordinating, and building, the fine-polished crown jewel in the Christian IV's district of Oslo, Norway, was completed in 1986.

The building, comprising 60,000 m$^2$ (650,000 square feet) and covering most of a city block, was planned using an axis system of 10.8 x 10.8 meters (35 x 35 feet). The structural system consists of an addition of independent, floor-high spatial units. Each spatial unit is defined by four columns, one in each corner, bound by four beams together with two types of deck elements, as a square table with four legs.

It is not the plan that controls the geometric order. The concrete elements also have their own geometry with precisely designed profiles.

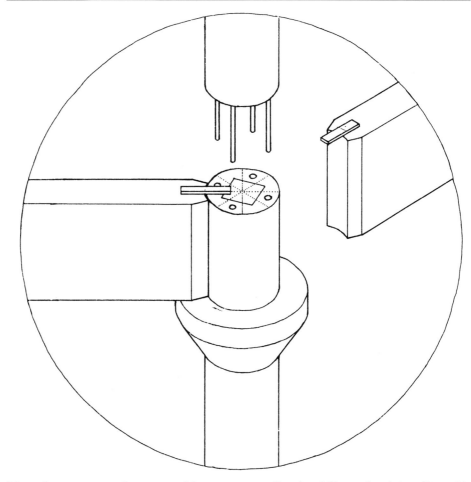

*Kreditkassen's new bank headquarters. Oslo, Norway. 1987. Architects: Lund & Slaato in cooperation with Østbye, Kleven, Almaas, Wike. Engineers: Multiconsult. Coupling of the columns and beams.*

The columns are nearly octagonal in cross section at the shaft, with niches at the head of the column to recieve the beam. The beams have a identical octagonal lower flange that corresponds to the form of the column. The beam consoles slide into the niches in the column.

In this connection between column and beam, there are no welded anchors; a simple steel bracket that functions almost like a bayonet lock secures the joint. After securing the joint, the inner details are not visible, and there is no gap between the column and the beam. The whole system is integrated, and there is a precise correspondence between the refined geometric form and the play of lines between the horizontal and vertical elements.

In Kreditkassen's headquarters (1987) at Majorstuen in Oslo, we find a third variation of the column/beam theme by archi-

tects Lund and Slaatto in a joint effort with Østebye, Kleven, Almaas & Wike. The central hall's open bridge structure takes into consideration the internal connections between the vertical circulation shaft and the office wings. The bearing system consists of prefabricated free-standing columns with circular cross sections. The columns, which are all one floor high, have conical-shaped consoles at their tops that create joints capable of accepting up to eight beams, all at 45° angles. On top of the beams rest the triangular deck elements. Thereby, we have the structural basis for the bridge's straight and diagonal course.

Theoretically, the conical console can accept beams from any angle. Compared to Veritas' and the Bank of Norway's right-angled one- and two-way planning patterns, this concept points toward possible new uses for concrete elements and a freer, more supple architectural form.

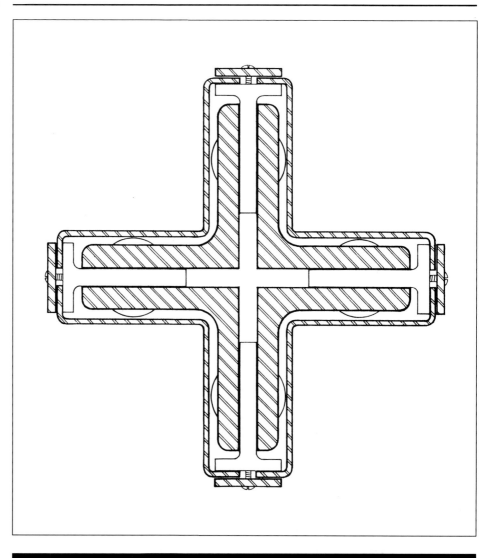

*Mies van der Rohe.
Barcelona Pavilion.
1929. Model of
the column by
architecture student
Ketill Berger. 1986.*

*Mies van der Rohe.
Barcelona Pavilion.
1929.
Column cross section.*

## 9.5 MIES VAN DER ROHE'S DETAILS

*Mies van der Rohe.
Barcelona Pavilion.
1929.*

Mies van der Rohe cultivated clear architectural ideas throughout his career. The choice of the correct method was always developed and mastered. This is clearly shown in the detailing of his buildings. Details had to contribute to clarifying a unity.

In all of his projects, the important details were developed in full scale. Of especial interest to us are his designs of the steel details. We shall focus on two projects, one from his European period and one from his American period.

Germany's Barcelona Pavilion was built for the 1929 World Exposition in

*Mies van der Rohe. Alumni Memorial Hall, Illinois Institute of Technology. Chicago. 1945. Building corner.*

*Mies van der Rohe. Alumni Memorial Hall. "The Miesian Corner."*

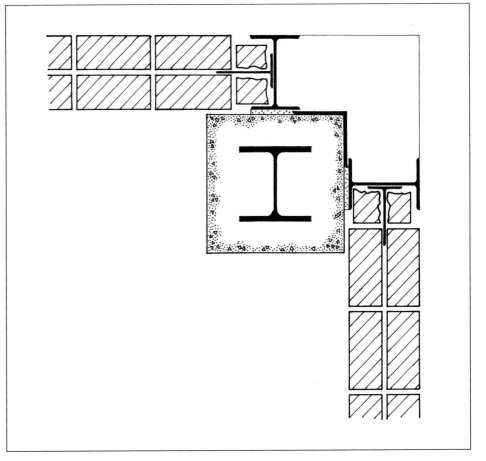

Barcelona. The pavilion, which was placed on a terrace of travertine marble, consisted of a horizontal roof lifted by eight free-standing steel columns. The spaces were defined by nonbearing partitions of glass and marble. The cruciform steel columns were built of four identical steel angles, jacketed in bent, chrome-plated steel plates.

The column's polished surface was well suited to the other materials used in the pavilion: polished honey-gold onyx, green tinos marble, and mirrored glass surfaces. The cruciform profile, which is spatially neutral in two directions, reinforces the free flow of space. After the exhibition, the pavilion was demolished, but it was later rebuilt on the same site in 1986. The observant guest will notice a nuance: the col-

umn's chrome plating is replaced with polished stainless steel.

At the Illinois Institute of Technology in Chicago, Mies's buildings are simple rectangular volumes comprised of a simple steel skeleton with facade infill panels of glass and sand-colored bricks. In the Alumni Memorial Hall from 1945, the detailing is especially beautiful and expressive.

In accordance with fire codes, the steel columns are cast in concrete, but the exposed exterior side of the corner columns is covered in plate steel to remind us that it is a steel building. The non-load-bearing exterior walls lie outside the columns. The steel in the exterior walls works as wind bracing and a stiffener.

John Hancock Center.
Chicago. 1969.
Architects:
Skidmore, Owings,
and Merrill.
Engineer:
Fazlur Khan.

John Hancock Center.
Chicago. 1969.
Architects:
Skidmore, Owings,
and Merrill.
Engineer:
Fazlur Khan.

"Take the beautiful tower made of bronze that was erected in New York. It is a bronze lady, incomparable in beauty, but you know she has corsets for 15 stories because the wind bracing is not seen. That which makes it an object against wind can be beautifully expressed, just like nature expresses the differences between the moss and the reed. The base of this building should be wider than the top," said Louis Kahn about the Seagram Building in 1960. He was showing that the wind loads in tall buildings are greater than the vertical loads. In spite of Mies van der Rohe's uncompromised structural clarity, the wind bracing in the Seagram Building lies hidden in the core walls.

As the tower becomes higher, the wind loads will be so great that they cannot be ignored. A 300-meter-high (985 foot) skyscraper in Chicago, the John Hancock Center (1969), uses the wind bracing as an expression of its architectural character.

With the cross bracing in the facades and the greatest width at its base, the building gradually tapers upward to a height of 100 floors. The John Hancock's conical silhouette and 18-story-high diagonal pairs combined to give the impression of absolute stability in one of the most beautiful and most elegant of all skyscrapers.

The most effective and resourceful use of materials to stiffen a frame is the diagonal. Diagonals run from one frame corner to the other. A pair of diagonals forms cross bracing. Under a lateral load, the forces follow the diagonals as pure axial forces. The tension force in the diagonals prevents the frame from moving laterally. Without cross bracing, the frame itself must be stiffened against moments, which is almost impossible (see chap. 6). Cross bracing in a steel skeleton has been used since the building of the Crystal Palace in 1851, and has often been used in bridge towers, but it was to be a long time before architects understood its possibilities. Ray and Charles Eames introduced cross bracing in a steel skeleton in their house in Santa Monica, California, in 1949. The house features white-painted steel cross bracing with the background of black-facade sandwich panels in a simple steel bearing skeleton.

An English example of cross bracing is the Electronics Factory at Swindon, designed in 1967 by the architects Norman and Wendy Foster and Richard Rogers. The design of the details in the building, which consist of exposed steel frames, demonstrates important aspects of form and statics. In the cross bracing, the detailing of the connections consists of welded steel plates. The chords act as turnbuckles with small clevises at each end so that the steel structure can be set in tension and be stabilized at the time of construction. The diagonals should ideally lie in the same plane.

Back in the United States, in the United Airlines Terminal at the world's busiest airport, Chicago's O'Hare, we find architect Helmut Jahn's 300-meter-long (985 foot) building, a lesson in steel architecture. The wind bracing is 7 x 7 meters (23 x 23 feet) with a cruciform steel plate at its center—similar diagonals as those in the factory at Swindon with a turnbuckle for tension setting.

The cross bracing doesn't necessarily have to be fastened to a steel building. It can also be incorporated with brackets that can be used in wood structures. An example of this is found at the Haltdalen Savings Bank in Norway (1985), by architect Arne Petter Eggen from Eggen & Mjøset and structural engineer Per Nøklebye from A. L. Høyer AS. The building is constructed using a laminated-wood structure with specially designed brackets. The diagonal chords of the wind bracing meet at a double ring of plate steel. Tension in the diagonal is achieved by a system of nuts located inside the ring. One of the advantages with this solution is that the rings can be fastened to a chord at any angle within the plane of the rings.

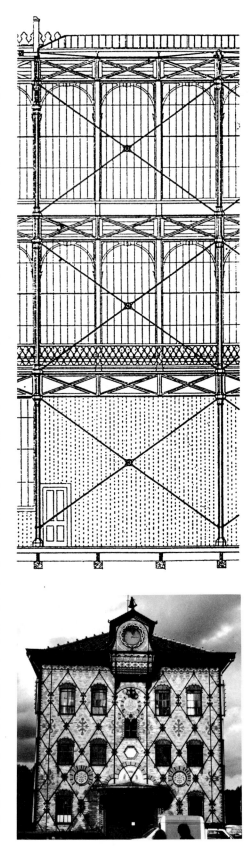

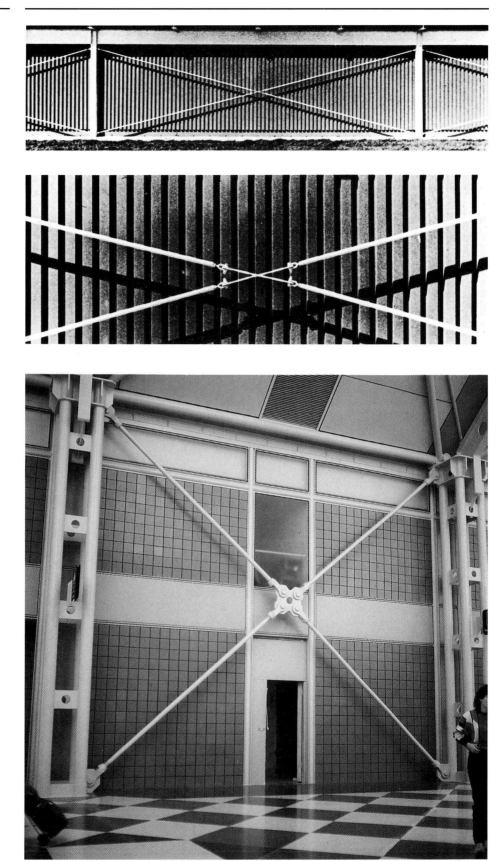

*Foster and Rogers.*
*Electronics Factory.*
*Swindon, England.*
*1967.*

*Helmut Jahn.*
*United Airline*
*Terminal.*
*O'Hare Airport,*
*Chicago.*
*1988.*

*Santiago Calatrava.*
*Wohlen Highschool.*
*Auditorium.*
*Argau, Switzerland.*
*1988*

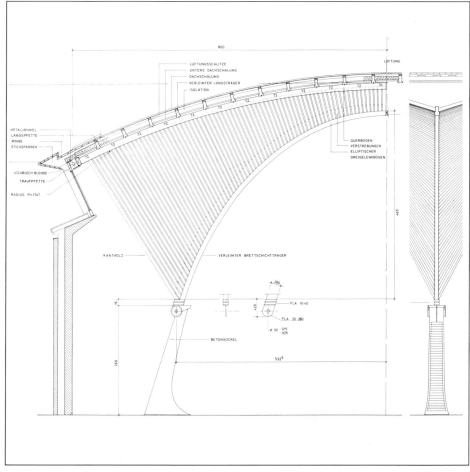

*Santiago Calatrava.*
*Wohlen Highschool.*
*Auditorium.*
*Bearing structure.*

*Haltdalen Savings*
*Bank. 1985.*
*Horizontal cross*
*bracing in the roof*
*structure.*
*Architects: Eggen and*
*Mjøseth with Arne*
*Petter Eggen.*
*Engineer: Ing. A. L.*
*Høyer with Per*
*Nøkleby.*

## 9.7 SANTIAGO CALATRAVA

The eminent architect and engineer, Santiago Calatrava, was born in Valencia, Spain, in 1951. In his projects, the influences of magnificent characters such as Antonio Gaudi and Robert Maillart are united. A skeleton of a dog in his office in Ilgenstrasse in Zurich is proof of his interest in organic forms.

Wohlen Highschool in Argau (1988) was drawn by local architects, while Calatrava was responsible for the cover of four rooms, including an auditorium. A light, vaulted roof is supported by fan-shaped ribs that rest on parabolic arches, all in wood. The arches land on angled concrete piers.

Typical for several Calatrava projects is the dialogue among several materials; in this example, wood and concrete. The angled piers, which climax with angled capitals, receive the arches. The forces in an arch cause the capital's only volute to swell before they progress further down to the foundations.

The result is an exciting space where daylight from the high skylights trickles down through the fanning ribs.

*Santiago Calatrava. Wohlen Highschool. Coupling between the angled pier and the arch.*

*Midtstubakken ski jump. Oslo, Norway. 1965 (later additions were made). Consulting engineers: Multiconcult.*

## 9.8 THE MIDTSTUBAKKEN SKI JUMP

Below the ski jump, everyone is interested in the person setting off at the top of the scaffolding—his concentration at the take-off, his daring in flight, and his landing in the transition zone. The basis for the ski jumper's performance has much to do with the design of the profile of the hill. The modern jumping hill is the result of one hundred years of development.

Most of the larger ski jumps are now built in concrete, while in Midtstubakken in Oslo, tarred, round wooden timbers still stand. The scaffolding, with an impressive height of 36 meters (120 feet), is among the tallest wooden structures in Scandinavia. With its characteristic profile, the scaffolding stands beautifully in its forest setting with the city and the Oslo Fjord in the background.

The scaffolding structure follows clear principles of order. The timber connections are simple, systematic, and designed to accept timbers of varying diameters. On the drawing board, it is easy to forget that the base and the top of a timber do not have the same diameter.

A series of A-formed frames with heights corresponding to the terrain and the profile of the slope are raised with blocks and tackles. The leg frames are connected to each other by double horizontal chords in so-called half clovers, placed on the outside of the frame, one at each end and fastened together by through bolts, dowels, and

washers. The angled leg frames withstand the wind loads perpendicular to the slope of the hill, and parallel with the hill, the structure is secured by a system of angled piers. The joining of the 18-meter-long (60 foot) angled timber piers occurs at the simplest place: in the middle.

The foundations are also worth noting. Triangular concrete pylons follow the contours of the slope and receive the masts with flat steel brackets that are cast in the concrete. The timber is held free from the concrete in order to avoid rotting.

*Midstubakken
ski jump.
Oslo, Norway.
Consulting engineers:
Multiconsult.
Working drawings.*

The construction documents from Multiconsult show that all apparently simple and obvious details are drawn. The timber is specified and calculated to the minimum cross section required, and just a single bolt cross section, cut to length, is used for all of the connections. The terrain under the scaffolding has been maintained in its natural state.

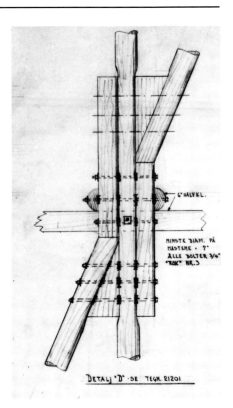

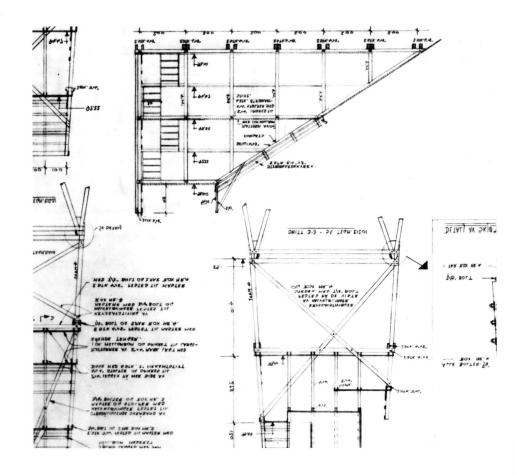

# Illustration Credits

Page 11-Arne Petter Eggen; 11-Franco Borsi/Gemo Pampaloni, *Le Piazze,* Istituto Geografico de Agostici, Novara, 1975; 12-GA Document no. 16, Tokyo; 12-Architectural Review 1986; 13-Riccardo Bofill. *Taller de Arquitectura.* Rizzoli, New York, 1985; 13-Riccardo Bofill. *Taller de Arquitectura.* Rizzoli, New York, 1985; 15-Museum of Contemporary Art, Chicago; 15-Museum of Contemporary Art, Chicago; 18-Jonathan Lipman, *Frank Lloyd Wright and the Johnson Wax Building,* Rizzoli, New York, 1986; 18-N. J. Wiig, *Bygningsprosjektering.* Tapir, Trondheim, 1972; 18-N. J. Wiig, *Bygningsprosjektering.* Tapir, Trondheim, 1972; 19-Aldo Rossi, *Opere recenti,* Edizioni Panini, Perugia, 1983; 23-Guirgola & Mehta, *Louis I. Kahn,* Verlag für Architektur, Zurich, 1975; 24-Galileo Galilei, *Two New Sciences,* Dover Publications, New York, 1954; 25-Osborn and Mook, 1921; 26-Myron Goldsmith/Jim Ferris; 26-Teigen; 26-Arne Petter Eggen; 27-Arne Petter Eggen; 28-Le Corbusier, *Oeuvre Complète: 1946-52,* Verlag für Architectur, Zurich, 1965; 29-Erik Lundberg, *Arkitekturens Formspråk,* vol. 4, Nordisk Rotogravur, Stockholm, 1950; 30-Guirgola & Metha, *Louis I. Kahn,* Verlag für Architektur, Zurich, 1975; 30-Teigen; 33-Statoil; 34-Arne Petter Eggen; 34-Arne Petter Eggen; 35-British Museum; 37-The Art Institute of Chicago; 37-Bjørn N. Sandaker; 37-Bjørn N. Sandaker; 38-Whitney Museum of American Art; 39-Coop Himmelblau, Philip Johnson, and Mark Wigley, *Deconstructivist Architecture,* MoMa, New York, 1988; 42-Rowland Mainstone, *Developments in Structural Form,* Allen Lane, London, 1975; 42-Rowland Mainstone, *Developments in Structural Form,* Allen Lane, London, 1975; 45-Håkon Christie, *Nes stavkirke,* Fabritius Forlagshus, Oslo, 1979; 46-Teigen; 47-*Alvar Aalto,* vol.

1, Verlag für Architektur, Zurich, 1963; 48-Arne Petter Eggen; 48-Strüwing; 49-Arne Petter Eggen; 50-Andrea Palladio, "I quattro libri dell' architettura 1570"; 51-Bjørn N. Sandaker; 51-Siegfried Giedion, *Space, Time, and Architecture,* Harvard University Press, Cambridge, Mass., 1962; 52-Arne Petter Eggen; 52-Henry J. Cowan, *The Master Builders,* John Wiley & Sons, New York, 1977; 53-Chemetov and Marrey, *Architecture à Paris,* Dunod, Paris, 1980; 61-ADAGP, Paris, 1987; 62-Teigen; 63-R. Mainstone, *Developments in Structural Form,* Allen Lane, London, 1975; 64-65-Teigen; 66-Derek Walker, *Great Engineers,* Academy Editions, London, 1987; 71-*Architectural Review,* May 1977; 76-Massimo Dini, *Renzo Piano: Projects and Buildings: 1964-1988,* Rizzoli, New York, 1984; 77-Konrad Wachsmann, *The Turning Point of Building,* Reynold Publishing Company, New York, 1961; 78-Konrad Wachsmann, *The Turning Point of Building,* Reynold Publishing Company, New York, 1961; 78-Konrad Wachsmann, *The Turning Point of Building,* Reynold Publishing Company, New York, 1961; 79-Arne Petter Eggen; 89-English Heritage; 81-Annales du Service des antiquités de l'Egypte, vol. 23-2; 81-Arne Petter Eggen; 83-Bert Heinrich, *Brucken,* Deutsches Museum 1983; 87-Musèe National Fernand Lèger, Biot; 89-*Newcomer Society Transactions,* vol. 30; 90-*Architectural Library,* London, A. J. Taylor, 1817; 93-*Zodiak* 14, 1965; 94-*Architecten* (Copenhagen) no. 9, 1959; 94-*Architecten* (Copenhagen) no. 9, 1959; 94-*Architecten* (Copenhagen) no. 4, 1960; 95-*Architecten* (Copenhagen) no. 4, 1960; 95-*Architecten* (Copenhagen) no. 4, 1960; 97-Ruedi Vogler; 99-Selmer-Furuholmen; 101-*AA [L'architecture d'aujourd hui]* no. 105; 101-*AA* no. 105; 102-Frank Lloyd Wright, *A Testament,* Architectural Press,

London, 1957; 103-Arne Petter Eggen; 105-Henry Cowan, *Science and Building,* John Wiley & Sons, New York, 1978; 106-Henry Cowan, *Science and Building,* John Wiley & Sons, New York, 1978; 107-Mario Salvadori, *Why Buildings Stand Up,* W. W. Norton, New York, 1980; 107-Arne Petter Eggen; 108-*Architectural Journal* 4, Nov. 1987; 108-Le Corbusier and Pierre Jeanneret, *Oeuvre Complète: 1910-1929,* Verlag für Architektur, Zurich, 1937; 109-Arne Petter Eggen; 110-Arne Petter Eggen; 111-Werner Blaser, *Myron Goldsmith: Bauten med Projekt,* Birkhäuser Verlag, Basel, 1986; 112-Arne Petter Eggen; 112-Arne Petter Eggen; 112-Arne Petter Eggen; 112-*Byggekunst* (The Norwegian review of architecture); 112-D. Sudjic, *New Architecture: Foster, Rogers, Stirling,* Royal Academy of Arts, London, 1986; 112-Anders Bugge, *Norske stavkirker,* Dreyers Forlag, Oslo, 1933; 116-Arne Petter Eggen; 120-Gustave Dore, "Bibelen i bilder"; 123-Anders Kirkhus; 124-Arne Petter Eggen; 126-Werner Blaser, *Santiago Calatrava,* Birkhäuser Verlag, Basel, 1988; 126-Bjørn N. Sandaker; 127-*Alvar Aalto,* vol. 1, Verlag für Architektur, Zurich, 1963; 128-*Dansk Arkitektur* (Copenhagen) no. 23, 1984; 129-Arne Petter Eggen; 130-*Dansk Arkitektur* no. 23, 1984; 131-Arne Petter Eggen; 134-Mario Salvadori, *Why Buildings Stand Up,* W. W. Norton, New York, 1980; 134-Rowland Mainstone, *Developments in Structural Form,* Allen Lane, London, 1975; 135-Bjørn N. Sandaker; 136-Goran Schildt, *Moderna tider,* Wahlström & Widstrand, Stockholm, 1985; 137-*Alvar Aalto,* vol. 3, Verlag für Architektur, Zurich, 1978; 137-*Alvar Aalto,* vol. 3, Verlag für Architektur, Zurich, 1978; 141-Reikjsmuseum, Kroller-Muller; 142-Bjørn N. Sandaker; 144-Siegfried Giedion, *Space, Time, and Architecture,* Harvard

University Press, Cambridge, Mass., 1962; 145-Curt Siegel, *Strukturformen der Modernen Architektur,* Callwey, Munich, 1960; 145-Curt Siegel, *Strukturformen der Modernen Architektur,* Callwey, Munich, 1960; 146-Anders Kirkhus; 146-Dunnet and Stamp, *Ernö Goldfinger,* Architectural Association, London, 1983; 147-Arne Petter Eggen; 147-Arne Petter Eggen; 148-*Quaderns,* October 1986; 149-Arne Petter Eggen; 150-*Scientific American,* July 1987; 151-*National Geographic Magazine*; 151-Karl Friedrich Schinkel, *Spreeufer bei Stralau,* Staatliche Museum, Preussischer Kulturbesitz; 152-British Museum; 154-Rainer Zerbst, *Antoni Gaudi,* Benedikt Taschen Verlag, Cologne, 1988; 154-Elias Cornell, *Byggnadstekniken,* Byggförlaget, Sweden, 1979; 154-Robert Mark, "The Architecture of Christopher Wren," *Scientific American,* July 1981; 157-Miranda Harvey, *Piranesi: The Imaginary Views,* Academy Editions, London, 1979; 158-David Billington, *Robert Maillart's Bridges,* Princeton University Press, Princeton, 1979; 158-Bjørn N. Sandaker; 158-Bjørn N. Sandaker; 159-Arne Petter Eggen; 160-Teigen; 160-Pier Luigi Nervi, *Construire Correttamente,* Ulrico Hoepli, Milan, 1955; 161-Werner Blaser, *Santiago Calatrava,* Birkhäuser Verlag, Basel, 1988; 161-Werner Blaser, *Santiago Calatrava,* Birkhäuser Verlag, Basel, 1988; 161-Chastin, Herver, and Lavalou, *Norman Foster,* Electa Moniteur, Paris, 1986; 162-Le

Corbusier, *Oeuvre Complète: 1929-1934,* 6th ed., Verlag für Architektur, Zurich, 1957; 164-Mohamed Scharabi, *Der Bazar,* Verlag Ernst Wasmuth, Tübingen, 1984; 165-Marcus Binney. *Great Railway Stations of Europe,* Thames & Hudson, New York, 1984; 166-Arne Petter Eggen; 167-Arne Petter Eggen; 168-Teigen; 169-Steinar Eriksrud; 169-Oskar Büttner, Erhard Hampe. *Bauwerk-Tragwerk: Tragstruktur,* vol. 1, Verlag Gerd Hatje, Stuttgart; 169-Oskar Büttner, Erhard Hampe, *Bauwerk-Tragwerk: Tragstruktur,* vol. 1, Verlag Gerd Hatje, Stuttgart; 171-Wolfgang Schüeller, *Horizontal Span Building Structures,* John Wiley & Son, New York, 1983; 175-Teigen; 177-Fritz Hansen; 178-Selim O. Chan Magomedow, *Alexander Vesnin,* Verlag Gerd Hatje, Stuttgart, 1987; 178-Teigen; 180-*A + U* 1984, no. 4; 183-Allan Temko, *Eero Saarinen,* G. Braziller, New York, 1962; 183-Allan Temko, *Eero Saarinen,* G. Braziller, New York, 1962; 185-Arne Petter Eggen; 188-Steinar Eriksrud; 189-Gina M. Nielsen; 190-Jean Lipman & Nancy Foote, *Calder's Circus,* Whitney Museum of American Art, 1972; 191-Steven A. Nash and Jöm Merkert, *Naum Gabo: 60 Years of Constructivism,"* Prestel Verlag, Munich, 1985; 192-*GA Documents,* no. 14, Tokyo; 193-*GA Documents,* no. 14, Tokyo; 193-Bjørn N. Sandaker; 194-Werner Spies and Wolfgang Votz,* The Running Fence, Harry N. Abrams Inc., New York, 1977; 195-Udo Kultermann, *Kenzo

Tange 1946-1969,* Verlag fur Architektur, Zurich, 1970; 196-Udo Kultermann, *Kenzo Tange 1946-1969,* Verlag für Architektur, Zurich, 1970; 197-Teigen; 198-Teigen; 199-Arne Petter Eggen; 200-*Illustrated London News,* 1851; 200-*Illustrated London News,* 1851; 201-*Illustrated London News,* 1851; 201-*Illustrated London News,* 1851; 201-*Illustrated London News,* 1851; 202-Arne Petter Eggen; 202-*Techniques & Architecture,* Sept. 1988; 203-Musée Louvre; 204-Alfred Wolf, "La Pyramide du grand Louvre," *Explorer*; 205-Johan Møller Nielsen, *Wegner, en dansk møbelkunstner,* Gyldendal, Copenhagen, 1976; 205-Johan Møller Nielsen, *Wegner, en dansk møbelkunstner,* Gyldendal, Copenhagen, 1976; 206-Anders Kirkhus; 206-Jon Haug; 207-Anders Kirkhus; 208-Martin Roubik/Jiri Havran; 209-Anders Kirkhus; 210-Teigen; 211-Anders Kirkhus; 211-Werner Blaser, *Mies van der Rohe,* Verlag für Architektur, Zurich, 1965; 212-Werner Blaser, *Mies van der Rohe,* Verlag für Architektur, Zurich, 1965; 212-Anders Kirkhus; 215-Arne Petter Eggen; 214-*Illustrated London News,* 1851; 214-Akkelies van Nes; 215-*Architectural Review,* July 1967; 215-Arne Petter Eggen; 216-Teigen; 217-Werner Blaser, *Santiago Calatrava,* Birkhäuser Verlag, Basel, 1988; 217-Arne Petter Eggen; 218-Arne Petter Eggen; 219-Arne Petter Eggen; 220-Ingeniørfirmaet Multiconsult.

# Bibliography

*Aalto, Alvar.* Vols. 1, 3. Zurich: Verlag far Architektur, 1963, 1978.

*Architectural Journal* 4 (Nov. 1987).

Aldo Rossi. *Opere recenti.* Perugia: Edizioni Panini, 1983.

*Annales du Service des antiquités de l'Egypte* 23-1.

Apeland, Kristoffer. "Fragmenter av konstruksjonslaren." *Architectural Review* (May 1977).

*Architectural Library.* London: A. J. Taylor, 1817.

*Architectural Review* (July 1967).

*Architectural Review* (1986).

*A + U* 4 (1984).

Bach, Ira J. *Chicago's Famous Buildings.* Chicago: University of Chicago Press, 1980.

Billington, David P. *The Tower and the Bridge.* Princeton: Princeton University Press, 1983.

—. *Robert Maillart's Bridges.* Princeton: Princeton University Press, 1979.

Binney, Marcus. *Great Railway Stations of Europe.* New York: Thames & Hudson, 1984.

Blake, Peter. *Mies van der Rohe: Architecture and Structure.* London: Pelican Books, 1960.

Blaser, Werner. *Mies van der Rohe.* Zurich: Verlag für Architektur, 1965.

—. *Myron Goldsmith: Bauten und Projekte.* Basel: Birkhäuser Verlag, 1986.

—. *Santiago Calatrava.* Basel: Birkhäuser Verlag, 1988.

Bofill, Riccardo. *Taller de Arquitectura.* New York: Rizzoli, 1985.

Borsi, Franco, and Gemo Pampaloni. *Le Piazze.* Novara: Istituto Geografico de Agostici, 1975.

Bugge, Anders. *Norske stavkirker.* Oslo: Dreyers Forlag, 1933.

Büttner, Oskar/Hampe, Erhard. *Bauwerk-Tragwerk: Tragstruktur.* Vol. 1. Stuttgart: Verlag Gerd Hatje, 1977.

Chan Magomedow, Selim O. *Alexander Vesnin.* Stuttgart: Verlag Gerd Hatje, 1987.

Chastin, Herver, and Lavalou. *Norman Foster.* Paris: Electa Moniteur, 1986.

Chemetov and Marrey. *Architecture a Paris.* Paris: Dunod, 1980.

Christie, Håkon. *Nes stavkirke.* Oslo: Fabritius Forlagshus, 1979.

Cornell, Elias. *Byggnadstekniken.* Sweden: Byggforlaget, 1979.

Cowan, Henry J. *Architectural Structures.* Amsterdam: Elsevier Scientific Publishing Company, 1976.

—. *Science and Building.* New York: John Wiley & Sons, 1978.

—. *The Master Builders.* New York: John Wiley & Sons, 1977.

*Dansk Arkitektur* 23 (1984).

Dini, Massimo. *Renzo Piano: Projects and Buildings: 1964-1983.* New York: Rizzoli, 1984.

Dunnet and Stamp. *Ernö Coldfinger.* London: Architectural Association, 1983.

*Emnebiblioteket.* Gyldendal Norsk Forlag, 1970.

Galilei, Galileo. *Two New Sciences.* New York: Dover Publications, 1954.

GA Document no. 14. Tokyo.

GA Document no. 16. Tokyo.

Giedion, Siegfried. *Space, Time, and Architecture.* Cambridge, Mass.: Harvard University Press, 1962.

Guirgola & Metha. *Louis I. Kahn.* Zurich: Verlag für Architektur, 1975.

Heinrich, Bert. *Brucken.* Munich: Deutsches Museum, 1983.

Hellan, Kare. *Mekanikk.* Trondheim: Tapir forlag, 1970.

Irgens, Fridtjof. *Statikk.* Trondheim: Tapir forlag, 1985.

Johnson, Philip, and Mark Wigley. *Deconstructivist Architecture.* New York: MoMa.

Kultermann, Udo. *Kenzo Tange: 1946-1969,* Zurich: Verlag für Architektur, 1970.

Le Corbusier. *Oeuvre Complète: 1940-1952,* Zurich: Verlag für Architektur, 1965.

—. *Oeuvre Complète: 1929-1934.* 6th ed. Zurich: Verlag für Architektur, 1957.

Le Corbusier and Pierre Jeanneret. *Oeuvre Complète: 1910-1929,* Zurich: Verlag für Architektur, 1937.

Lipman, Jean, and Nancy Foote. *Calder's Circus.* New York: Whitney Museum of American Art, 1972.

Lipman, Jonathan. *Frank Lloyd Wright and the Johnson Wax Building.* New York: Rizzoli, 1986.

L'Orange, H. P. *Centrum and Periphery.* Oslo: Dreyers Forlag, 1973.

Lundberg, Erik. *Arkitekturens Formspråk.* Vol. 4. Stockholm: Nordisk Rotogravur, 1950.

Mainstone, Rowland. *Developments in Structural Form.* London: Allen Lane, 1975.

Mark, Robert, "The Architecture of Christopher Wren," *Scientific American* (July 1981).

Nervi, Pier Luigi. *Construire Correttamente.* Milan: Ulrico Hoepli, 1955.

*Newcomer Society Transactions* 30.

Nielsen, Johan Möller. *Wegner, en dansk møbelkunstner.* Copenhagen: Gyldendal, 1976.

Norberg-Schulz, Christian. *Meaning in Western Architecture.* London: Studio Vista, 1986.

Palladio, Andrea, I *quattro libri dell'architettura 150*

Pevsner, Nikolaus. *An Outline of European Architecture.* London: Pelican Books, 1963.

Reitzel Erik. *Fra Brud til Form.* Copenhagen: Polyteknisk Forlag, 1979.

Salvadori, Mario. *Why Buildings Stand Up.* New York: W. W. Norton, 1980.

Scharabi, Mohamed. *Der Bazar.* Tübingen: Verlag Emst Wasmuth, 1984.

Schildt, Goran. *Moderna tider.* Stockholm: Wahlström & Widstrand, 1985.

Schueller, Wolfgang. *Horizontal Span Building Structures.* New York: John Wiley & Sons, 1983.

*Scientific American.* July 1987.

Siegel, Curt. *Strukturformen der Modernen Architekur.* Munich: Verlag Georg D. W. Callwey, 1960.

Spies, Wemer, and Wolfgang Vorz. *The Running Fence.* New York: Harry N. Abrams Inc., 1977.

Sudjic, D. *New Architecture: Foster, Rogers, Stirling.* London: Royal Academy of Arts, 1986.

*Techniques & Architecture* (Sept. 1988).

Ternko, Allan. *Eero Saarinen.* New York: G. Braziller, 1962.

Thiis-Evensen, Thomas. *Arkitekurens uttrykksformer.* Oslo: Universitetsforlaget, 1982.

Wachsmann, Konrad. *The Turning Point of Building.* New York: Reynold Publishing Company, 1961.

Walker, Derek. *Great Engineers.* London: Academy Editions, 1987.

Wiig, N. J. *Bygningsprosjekering.* Trondheim: Tapir, 1972.

Wright, Frank Lloyd. *A Testament.* London: Architectural Press, 1957.

Zannos, Alex. *Form and Structure in Architecture.* New York: Van Nostrand Reinhold, 1987.

Zerbst, Rainer. *Antoni Gaudi.* Cologne: Benedikt Taschen Verlag, 1988.

# Index